THE COLOR OF THE ELEPHANT

Memoir of a Muzungu

CHRISTINE HERBERT

The Future of Publishing

eBook ISBN: 978-1-952919-75-6
eBook PCN: 1-952919-76-2
Paperback ISBN: 978-1-952919-76-3
Paperback PCN: 1-952919-75-4

GenZPublishing.org
Aberdeen, NJ

🌼 Created with Vellum

For Clemente, Kabu Kabu, Christobel, and Cared. Your love, guidance, and companionship meant the world to me. May we meet again in the next life.

INTRODUCTION

What follows is a true account of my Peace Corps service in the African nation of Zambia from 2004-2006. This is not presented as a retrospective—no moments presented in the twenty-twenty rearview mirror of hindsight—the reader gets to be in the front seat with me taking the bumps on the journey as they come. All names but my own have been changed to protect the identities of those in the tales. In some cases, when someone in the narrative also goes by the name Christine—and I felt it important to mention it as part of the story—I have changed or omitted her surname.

Everything that follows is depicted in as true a manner as I could describe, though some situations or characters may be a composite, mostly for the sake of brevity. All opinions are my own. Any misrepresentation of the Zambian people, place, language, and culture are unintentional, and failures of my own understanding or storytelling abilities. I am all too aware of my knack for miscomprehension or misinterpretation, which is why the narrative leans more heavily on my transgressions than on my successes. In fact, this is more of a confessional than anything—picking apart every embarrassing misstep in such unflinching detail that it becomes laughable. Writing this book has been a life-changing journey —equal in its measure of grief and joy—much like my Peace Corps service. In both cases, I had absolutely no idea what kind of a ride I was in for.

When I received my acceptance letter to serve in the Peace Corps, I was told by a former volunteer, "This is it. You are about to have the experience that will change and define your life. Your entire life will be thought of in terms of *before* Peace Corps and *after* Peace Corps. There will be no going back." I suppose the same could be said for any life-changing event, such as parenthood, and navigating one's way through such a defining event is all part of the human experience. But serving in the Peace Corps is an endeavor very few people get to experience, and one that is difficult to explain. It's like asking someone who has returned from a space mission, "Wow, what was that like?" Words are feeble, and the experience too personal to divulge, even if one is keen to do so.

You can't possibly describe all the ways in which the experience has broken you and remade you into someone new. You can't talk about the things you held on to in the night. The scraps of dreams you would cling to that would get you through to the next day, and the next, and the next. Ideas that were utterly precious, yet if described to someone, held in the light of day, they would dissolve or seem foolish, childish, impossible to ascribe power to.

I will tell you this—and brace yourself for some full-on melodrama here. There is one thing that brings me back to that tender, emotional place of my volunteer years every time. One thing that makes me remember what it felt like—the true, deep inner landscape of my heart during those years of living in a mud hut, knowing one day I would have to return to my life in America. Watching a war movie. Why? Because there is always a scene with a soldier huddled in the trenches, caked in filth. The fight is far enough away that his platoon has been ordered to get some shuteye, rest up for what lies ahead. Maybe gunfire is heard in the background. Snipers picking off soldiers one by one, keeping the smell of fear alive in the trenches. There is always a soldier who is clinging to a small tattered photograph of his girl. His thumb strokes the photograph along the curve of her cheek, imagines the comfort she would bring him, if only he could get home to her. But the pain in his eyes tells you that there is no going home, not like that, not really. Because he's seen too much. Done too many things that he cannot take back, things that the old him had no idea he was capable of. When I see that, the soldier holding the picture, I crumble. *That is me,* I think. *Someone knows. They have been like me.*

This is not about a voyage of self-discovery, of becoming more "woke" in the world, or learning how to survive a Peace Corps term of service, though I have experienced those things as a matter of course. This is about my experience of being broken and reforged, again and again. These are the snapshots of my life that would not rest, the little vignettes that would roll around in my head over and over in the dead of night when sleep would not come. Putting them on the page was a way of exorcising them from my mind. A way of putting them to sleep. And through the process of writing my experiences, the lense with which I view the world—and my human experience within it—has become ... not more refined, exactly, but more encompassing, the scope widened. Rather than gaining a more firm ground on which to build my belief systems, what I've gained is a suppleness to how I view the world. I am more ready than ever to open my heart and mind to new ways of being, ready to break down and reemerge once again, able to embrace a new and interesting idea of who I am and what my purpose in the world is and may yet be.

My hope is that in reading about my experiences, your own curiosity will be awakened and lead you on your own journey of discovery. I briefly mention or allude to weighty topics that are difficult to "unpack" in a way that would do them justice here, such as colonialism, apartheid, and Africa's complicated history with mission work and non-government aid agencies. I encourage further exploration of these and other important topics that deeply affect the lives of Africans —past, present, and future.

Thank you, dear reader, for undertaking this journey with me. I would caution you that now is the time to buckle up for the adventure ahead, but the fasten seatbelt sign has just been turned off. The plane has landed. Adventure awaits. Let's begin.

Houston, We Have Landed

The Zambian flight attendant searches my tear-stained face, her brow wrinkling with worry.

"You are too sick, madam. Shall I call a doctor for you?"

"No. That's all right," I assure her. She's been my guardian angel, bringing me water to sip and extra blankets during the flight. She's right to be worried. I have been dry heaving for seven hours straight and feel as if every ounce of energy and bodily fluid has been forcibly sucked out of me. An adverse reaction to one of the vaccines administered by the Peace Corps medical staff before takeoff has forced me to sit apart from the rest of the volunteers. I've been reduced to a shivering, convulsing, huddled mass of blankets and bile-filled airsick bags in the rear of the aircraft—no one's idea of a good time.

It wasn't until the airplane began its slow descent that my

spirits lifted. Like a tonic, the sight of land coming into view stilled my quivering stomach. Tapping some hidden reserve of water in my exhausted body, my eyes brim with tears at the mere sight of it. Africa.

"I'm actually feeling much better now," I say. "It's just that I can't believe I'm really here. I've dreamed of coming to Africa for so long that I can't believe it's finally happened. I'm just so," a sob catches in my throat, "... happy!"

"Oh," she replies, looking rather confused. "That's good, madam." She backs away uncertainly, leaving me to weep quietly as I gaze out the tiny oblong airplane window.

My hand presses against the cool glass and I lean forward to drink in my first vista of Zambia. Swaying gently in the breeze, a field of shoulder-high emerald grass stretches into the horizon, extending far beyond my line of sight. Not a single building, roadway or telephone pole in view. Hardly what I had expected to find at Lusaka International Airport —the beating heart of the capital city's transportation and logistics system. Holding any expectations of this place, I realize, would be futile. I am a stranger in a strange land now.

I feel like my whole life up to this moment has merely been a prologue; now it's time for scene one, take one. The slate has clapped down, the director has called for action, and I'm standing center stage with my mouth agape, trying to improvise my opening line.

I can't imagine what is going to happen to me now. All I know is that what lies ahead is going to change me forever. I'm not afraid of that. I've come here to change. To feel *alive*.

I have no illusions that my being here will somehow "save the world," but I do feel that I can bring about some small but positive change in the world if I set my mind to it. I want to see what one individual can do to improve the quality of life for those who truly need it. I am a bodyworker by trade— a profession I got into because I wanted to help people—but

I've become increasingly disenchanted with my work over the years. The health spa industry caters to those who have it all —not those in need.

But I can't pretend that I'm here for purely noble reasons, either. Sure, I've come to volunteer, to dedicate the next twenty-seven months of my life to the needs of others, but I've come here for myself too. I've come for an adventure. I've come to learn a new language, experience a totally different culture, explore new ways of being, live a never-before-dreamed-of life.

In short, be a different me.

I've lived such a quiet life—a safe life—until this point. I'm the girl who doesn't date, doesn't go out and paint the town red, doesn't speed on the highway; the girl who is consistently elected as the designated driver when she goes to a party with her friends: that's me. I'm the house-sitter, the baby-sitter, the pet-sitter. So when Miss Responsible decides to do something a little crazy, like join the Peace Corps, her family and friends can't believe their ears.

Convinced I am having some kind of early mid-life crisis, suffering some single-woman-on-the-edge syndrome, they have begged and pleaded for me to "see reason." Resistance from my parents has been particularly troubling and surprising, especially from my father, who's lived practically his whole life in service to others (Boy Scouts, ROTC, Army, service clubs, Sunday school teacher—you name it). But the more adamant that my family has become about this being "absolutely not the right time for Americans to be overseas," the more resolved I have become to do it.

It has been two years since the terrorist attacks of 9/11, but we are still at war. Our country would like us to believe that our troops are merely keeping the peace, acting the part of the big brother with their guns pointing—not at *people*— but at terrorism. But it's not "terrorism" getting blown to bits by the suicide bombers I read about in the papers. It's human beings. Just regular people doing regular things: going to work, enjoying a dinner out with their families, praying at their mosque, or temple, or church. I don't think that going abroad is insanity, as everyone feels compelled to tell me. What could be more important than developing an under-standing of people different from ourselves? It's fear of the unknown that drives men to hate and kill one another. I will not hide in my own country until the War on Terror blows over. I refuse.

I want to feel bolstered by the strength of that conviction now, but I can't seem to stop crying. I blame the wistful melody that's been piping through the airplane's speakers since we landed. A breathy, ethereal woman's voice sings in a language I can't understand, but tugs firmly at my heart-strings all the same. She makes me feel homesick for a place I've never known. A place that I know I'll soon call home. Each time I think I might get a grip on myself, the voice lulls me back into a sobbing sentimental stupor.

I sit and try to master my emotions while I watch the other passengers descend the rickety metal staircase to the tarmac. One by one, they file out of the open hatch into the sweltering afternoon sun and wend their way towards the baggage claim area.

My fellow volunteers are easy to pick out. They're a bubbly bunch of young people, most of them white, fresh out of college, and have no idea what they are going to do with their lives beyond this stint in the Peace Corps. Not that their hearts aren't in it. I'm sure they are very sincere in their desire to do volunteer work. It's just that for most of the people I've talked to, this is a way to delay getting a "real" job, acquire a great résumé boost, and avoid living with their parents for a while. They're all out there now, under the "Wel-come to Zambia" sign hanging from the eaves of the airport, posing arm in arm for the first photographs of their service. Each of them sports some bit of newly-purchased volunteer garb: stiff hiking boots, white t-shirts, crisp bandannas, brand-new backpacks with pristine Nalgene containers clipped to them by carabineers. They look more like an ad for a sporting goods store than a group of people heading to the remote African bush to live in mud huts.

I look down and study my plain-Jane, Peace Corps recommended clothing: sturdy sandals, below-the-knee skirt, and cotton button-up top with sleeves. My sensible, wide-brimmed straw sunhat is occupying the seat next to me. I feel —and certainly look—every bit of my thirty-something years. I feel annoyed that I stand out from the other female volunteers so starkly, with their spaghetti strap tank tops and hip-hugging shorts. Annoyed that I seem to be the only one who actually read the clothing guide we were given, yes, but mostly annoyed that I felt compelled to follow it to the letter. Why am I such a goody-goody?

The beautiful singing on the loudspeakers suddenly comes to a halt as the plane powers down. I look around to discover I'm the only passenger left on the plane. Only my flight attendant has remained behind to see that I make it off safely. She's been sitting quietly in the jump seat behind me for who knows how long.

I realize with a start that I need to re-join my group before I'm missed, or worse yet, forgotten and left behind. I hastily mop my face with a soggy wad of tissues and toss them in my purse. *Pull yourself together, Christine.* I take a few deep breaths with my eyes closed, the cabin's stale, recirculated air now thick and humid with the door open and fans off. I stand, bid my flight attendant farewell with thanks, don my sunhat, and step out into the sunshine.

2

The Price is Right

How many goats am I worth? I'm certainly worth more than my weight in goats, but by how much in the standard of this culture? Pound for pound, am I twice as valuable? Five times? Ten? It's hard to say. I've never thought of myself in these terms before. In my culture, a human being is considered priceless—especially the human being you choose as a spouse. But in Zambia, a man purchases a woman from her father or guardian, like a dowry in reverse. This is meant as an "appreciation fee" for raising the daughter well. In this way, a girl is not a financial burden to the family. A girl child will one day be a source of her father's wealth when a trade is made for her hand.

A young man has been visiting this house each day and asking one of my fellow Peace Corps trainees how much her father is asking for her. Pretending to be writing in my journal under a thicket of mango trees at the edge of the yard, I spy the drama out of the corner of my eye as the man pleads with her.

"He must see reason, madam. The price is just too much. Fifty goats!?" He shakes his head with disbelief and leaves the yard muttering to himself. She has also informed him that her father requires thirty head of cattle and seventy-five chickens, but somehow it's the goats that have pushed him over the edge of reason.

Realizing that this seems to be an excellent way to rid oneself of unwanted suitors, I decide that my father is also asking for fifty goats. And possibly a motorcar—a rare and precious commodity here. When our Land Rover pulled into the village of Chimpungu—where we are to keep in the company of a current volunteer for a week—children ran alongside the vehicle screaming with delight, "Moto-kaa! Moto-kaa!" An equal number of kids were yelling, "*Muzungu! Muzungu!*" I soon learned that meant me. A *muzungu* is an "English speaker," a white person, a foreigner.

I've been a *muzungu* for four days now, and so far, it suits me.

I haven't documented a single word of my experiences since I've landed in county. I told myself I was "too busy" soaking it all in, but "too lazy" is closer to the truth. I've seen my fellow volunteers take the time to write in their journals and compose multiple letters to their families. Guilt has been gnawing at my insides all morning. No more procrastinating.

I grab my airmail stationery, settle back against the trunk of the mango tree, and chew on the end of my pencil, wondering where to begin. My tissue-thin paper flutters in the breeze as I adjust it to fit over the lined sheet provided in the stationery book so handwriting doesn't go all slanted and waste precious space. I figure I should just record as much of my goings-on as possible, then send these journals to my family back in the States and let them share it amongst themselves.

Having settled on a plan of attack, I begin pouring out every detail I can remember onto the tiny sheets of paper. I'm just picking out the weird little things like how you can find cold bottles of Coke for sale in the middle of nowhere in places that obviously have no access to electricity. How you have to pay someone to pee in a hole in the ground by the roadside. How you see people walking on endless stretches of roadway wearing only one shoe. How it's perfectly acceptable to pick your nose in public. Turns out it's like scratching your ear here. No big deal.

This was made evident to us during our first day in a village. We'd been split into groups of fours and fives and sent to live in the bush for a week with a current volunteer to receive a crash course in mud hut living, presumably to weed out the cowards early on. We've been holding meetings with the rural health centers for discussions about the Zambian health care system and how we, as Peace Corps volunteers, can best assist them. During our first meeting, the chairman of the Neighborhood Health Committee stood up to intro- duce himself, beaming ear to ear with pride, pleased as punch to be speaking with, what he believes, is an extremely powerful and important group of muzungus from the United States.

"Welcome, Peace Corps!" He pronounced corps as *corpse*, which appears to be standard in the African nations familiar with our group. "I am the chairman of the health committee. My name is Radio," he said, and deftly plunged his index finger into his left nostril. While rooting out the offending crusty bit obstructing his breathing, he politely introduced the rest of the group. There was a Beauty, a Bornface, a Lekeya, a Martin, a Bwalya, and another Bornface. What a great name. I'm sure there's a story there. Perhaps when the child was to be named, his face had that "just-born" look to it?

We've spent several days discussing the health care structure: the Ministry of Health, the Central Board of Health, the Provincial Health Offices, the District Health Offices, the Rural Health Centers, and the Neighborhood Health Committees. It's the bottom rung of this chain of command that we will be working with the most. Grassroots development it's called. Our job is to live in the most rural and depressed areas of the country in order to form and train groups of volunteers to go door-to-door—or mud hut to mud hut, as the case may be—and assess the state of health in their community. These groups will perform village inspections and create detailed reports and maps indicating the different resources and health problems of the area. These get submitted to the District Health Office, and in turn, the rest of the political machine. Ideally, the information about who needs a new well or latrine or bridge gets to the people who have the money to do something about it.

I readjust my tightly wrapped legs to kneel to the other side as I flip my sheet of stationery over. My hip is starting to get pins and needles. I didn't count on having nothing to sit on for two years.

What a cushy life I've led. Really cushy. With cushions.

There's nothing here but crunchy, split bamboo mats or tiny wooden stools no more than a foot high. I tried one once and my butt was asleep within five minutes. It's just as well that I prefer the ground because that's a woman's place anyway. Stools are for men. The *citenge* is for women. This traditional garment, a two-meter length of colorful fabric, is worn around the waist over the clothes. I've become quite fond of my *citenge*. It's helpful in keeping your clothes clean because, as a woman, not only are you relegated to sit on the ground, but you spend a fair amount of time walking around on your knees when you are in the presence of a man.

What an embarrassing lesson to learn. My pencil scribbles furiously at the page as I document the humiliation of my faux pas at yesterday's supper. The volunteer we are visiting invited both the village and regional headmen of the area to meet us and join us for a meal. I thought it would be a nice gesture to help the women serve the food, though I realized almost at once this was a mistake. I am also considered a guest of honor, and the women seemed mortified that I offered my assistance. After some small bit of arguing in broken English, I just grabbed one of the serving plates and set it down gently at the feet of the headmen, smiled at them, stood up and walked back to the kitchen. The whole place burst into hysterics. My attempt at graciousness proved to be the most ham-handed and pitiable excuse for deference they'd ever seen in their lives. Apparently, proper protocol requires that I kneel several paces away, walk on my knees toward them without raising my eyes to meet theirs, place the food down with a gracious gesture of a slight bow and hand clap, and then back away on my knees before rising to take my leave. Jeez, I have a lot to learn.

That was actually only the preamble to the day of humiliation. In an effort to redeem myself, I foolishly decided to help the women draw water afterwards for washing dishes. I lugged a fifteen-liter plastic jug to the nearby borehole and pumped the metal lever until water gurgled out of the mouth of the container. I secured the screw top and asked another woman to help me lift the heavy container onto my head so I could carry it back to the house. I was immediately sorry I did this the moment its full weight rested on my head. I seriously thought my neck would break. I hadn't thought to fill the container only half full or to bring a cushion for my head. My skull felt like someone cracked me over the head with a club. The wobbly container held in a death grip with both hands, I attempted to walk down the dirt path without falling over. My eyes strained toward the ground to navigate the uneven road. There was no way I could move my head or everything would topple. I quickened my pace as fast as I could without losing my balance.

And then I felt it. My *citenge* was falling off. There was no way to rescue it; I hadn't a hand to spare. My skirt-like garment dropped to the ground. Fortunately, I had enough sense to wear something under it, but the tiny bike shorts I had on barely covered more than my rear end. Women never show their thighs here. They are considered private parts and are taboo. If I thought that I had been the object of ridicule earlier, that was nothing compared to how I felt with my rear end on full display in spandex. The group of children that had been shadowing me suddenly dropped to the ground in hysterical fits of laughter.

I figure, on the bright side, at least everyone is enjoying my visit and will doubtless have entertaining stories to tell about me after I've gone.

It's beginning to get dark, so I pack up my letter, straighten my *citenge*, and join the other trainees. Jana has told us that we're going to a neighbor's house for dinner tonight. Jana, our host, has been at this site for a year now. She dresses, acts and speaks like she has been here for ten. She fascinates me. I watch her every move, study her mannerisms, listen to the inflection of her voice as she speaks in the local language. I wonder if this is what I will be like a year from now: someone so transformed as to be unrecognizable even to myself.

Nightfall drops like a curtain. The lot of us flick on our flashlights and stand around dumbly in the yard waiting to be led to dinner. I can hear people walking by us on nearby paths. They obviously have no use for flashlights. They must know the terrain by heart and have much better night vision than I have. Jana walks into view.

"Does your neighbor have lights?" I ask. "I mean, we're not just going to sit out in the pitch dark and eat food, are we?"

"Yes, that's exactly what we are going to do," she replies.

I suddenly feel snobby and foolish. Of course we are going to eat in the dark; that's what people without electric lights do.

"Don't worry, there's a bit of a moon tonight, so you'll be able to see the plates. I'll just tell you what's in them. You get used to it. I know it's a little strange at first, but you get used to living without electricity pretty fast," she says sympathetically. "Okay, so I want everyone to follow behind me closely. I'll go ahead first with a walking stick and I'll be checking for snakes on the path, but don't worry so much about them coming up from the rear or the sides. They're not generally aggressive. It's really just a matter of making sure we don't step on one. Any noise we make should drive them off anyway. Okay? Let's go."

There's nothing she could say that would make us less likely to wander off. We stick to her like glue, sure to make lots of noise with stomping and shuffling steps. After about half a mile, we detour down a tiny path leading to a minuscule mud hut, about ten feet square. In the yard, a small charcoal fire glows warmly in a blackened metal brazier, and several covered plates lay in the center of a tattered bamboo mat. A weathered, middle-aged woman wrapped in layers of *citenge* looks up at us from the fire, her features distorted from the light below like a child telling a ghost story at night with a flashlight under their chin. She beams a slightly ghoulish smile at us and she rises to take each of us warmly by the hand. The woman speaks no English, but her intentions are clear and her joy genuine.

She is a widow, this woman. Someone who's lost all family due to hardship and circumstance and now has only herself to rely on and take care of. She and Jana are alike in this respect. They often eat together to stave off loneliness. The fact that the woman doesn't speak English hasn't been a problem; it's actually helped Jana learn the local language that much faster. She's proven to be a patient and loving tutor.

The woman presents us with a single bowl of water. We've been here long enough to understand its intended purpose. One by one, we dip our hands into the bowl, gently rub them together, let the excess drip off the ends of our fingers, and pass it along to the next person. I'm sure I'm not the only one who feels that my hands were cleaner before this process, but this hand washing ritual is an important part of the culture that we must observe. The idea of it certainly has merit, it's just the means that I have issues with. Being the first in line is fine, but after that, forget it.

Once we have all washed up, the plates are uncovered and Jana tells us we will be eating pumpkin leaves for dinner. These must be the plates with the dark lumps of what looks like seaweed. The other plates are piled with lumps of something whitish we know must be the *nshima*. This is the staple food of Zambia. Every meal is *nshima*. The word is synonymous with "food."

I guess I never really understood what a staple food was until now. It is something that you eat every day, every meal, for the entirety of your life. You can't imagine not eating it, because that is all you have ever known. Any other food that is presented with the staple food is merely "relish." The *nshima* is almost always made from maize meal, but can be made from things like sorghum, millet, or cassava roots. It depends where you are in Zambia and what traditionally might be grown in that region.

The thing about *nshima* is it can actually hurt you if you

are not used to eating it. It is hot. And I mean Chernobyl meltdown hot. I have seriously had to use mind over matter to fight the impulse to throw the food out of my hand and scream. The outside seems relatively cool, but once you break off a piece, live steam escapes into your hand. You have to quickly knead it over and over until it becomes a tolerable temperature, then you fashion a spoon in the lump of dough by depressing your thumb into it. This is used to scoop up your relish. This is a one handed, and interestingly enough, a right-handed operation. (Unless you don't have a right hand, then I guess it would be okay to switch.) Every time I eat, I'm convinced my hand will be blistered from the steam, but it only looks mildly red afterwards. I'm told that my hand will get harder after a while and the heat won't bother me so much. I'm definitely looking forward to that day.

I try making some light conversation with our hostess, having Jana serve as translator. I am amazed at how well she is able to converse in local language after living here for only one year. I hope to be as good as she is, but I'd settle for even half as good. I've never been able to master a foreign language before. I barely managed to scrape passing grades in all the years I studied Spanish at school. And compared to the Bantu languages spoken here, Spanish is not all that different from English. I'm hoping that total immersion will be the magical key to opening this recalcitrant part of my brain.

The stars are majestic tonight. No clouds, no air pollution, no city lights to dim their glory. Even back home in the California wine country, the night skies are never this clear. As I scan the heavens, there doesn't appear to be a single familiar landmark in the sky. What strange constellations are these? It has just occurred to me that I am in the southern hemisphere now and these stars are not my own. Then I see him. His belt caught my eye, and I had to do a double take to make sure it was him. Sure enough, there is Orion, stoic and battle-ready as ever, but in a whimsical twist he appears standing on his head. I ask our hostess if there are any local legends about figures they might see in the stars, any mythological or astrological figures she can point out to us. Jana has a hard time getting the woman to understand what I mean by that. After a good ten minutes of strained discussion, repetition of the question, and bewildered looks in my direction, the answer comes: "No."

Drums have been booming in the distance for the last hour or so. Nice dinner music, actually. I ask Jana if that is normal, just to hear drumming all the time. This is Africa, after all. She says no, that there must be some dancing going on tonight. We all decide that this would be really interesting to watch. We thank our hostess, wash our hands in the single bowl again and head off towards the direction of the drumming.

Fear of snakes forgotten, we forge new paths through the bush, making a beeline for the music. We soon break into a clearing lit by several large fires. The effect is like walking into a bar as a record screeches to a halt. Everyone stops what they are doing, turns, and stares. Not quite what we were hoping for. Jana greets them and asks them to resume dancing. Something to the effect of, "Don't mind us." We kneel down at the edge of the yard and try to look as inconspicuous as possible.

Once the drumming starts back up, we get a real treat. Young dancers are practicing something called *nyau*. In this type of ritual, the dancer is supposed to be in a trance state and will channel the energy of an animal. We watch a child practice a rooster dance as he spins around flapping his arms, cocking his neck back and forth and pawing the ground with his feet. His identity is concealed with layers of dried grass tied around his head, torso, and waist. They remind me of little hula skirts. Mid-dance, one of the hula skirts falls off and everyone laughs. I am briefly reminded of myself and feel sorry for the kid. He takes it in good stride, though, ties the skirt back on and picks up where he left off. Jana tells us that this is only play; the real dance would be performed by adults.

I feel a light touch on the back of my head and turn to see a group of young children running away, laughing and squealing wildly. I comb my hands through my hair to check if something has been thrown on it, but it is clean. The kids had simply been daring each other to touch my long, blonde hair.

A group of men approach us, a strong, sour smell of alcohol in their wake, and ask Josh, our sole male trainee, to partake in their homemade brew. Being a brave sort, and not wanting to be rude, he accepts a swig from a tiny plastic cup. The crowd grows silent again as they await his verdict. With utmost sincerity, as if proclaiming the highest praise, he raises his cup.

"Horrible," he declares.

A cheer rises up and everyone dances with pure elation as the drums begin booming out a new rhythm. The pronouncement, utterly lost in translation, has made the moment perfect.

3

For the Love of All that is Oily

I'm in trouble. Not the dangerous, adventurous or naughty kind of trouble that makes your blood race with jolts of adrenaline. No, this is more like the what-in-the-hell-have-I-got-myself-into kind. The kind of trouble you asked for, and now that you have it you wonder why you wanted it so badly. I don't regret coming here, but I am having serious doubts about my work.

The key speaker of the afternoon has been droning on for hours about the decentralized healthcare structure in Zambia. I'm trying to look politely interested, but inside, I'm screaming. This system is awful. And I'm here to perpetuate it. Crap.

I glance around at the other trainees, hoping to make eye contact with one and have a mutual eye-rolling moment. Everyone seems to be genuinely interested, though. Pens briskly sail along pages of British-standard double-hole punch notebooks, hands dart in the air when the time comes for us to ask questions. I think I've been out of school for too long. I seem to remember being able to write down notes and listen to a lecture and formulate intelligent questions at the same time, but this pat-your-head-and-rub-your-tummy routine must have died with my twenties. I've been listening carefully but only have about two sentences jotted down in my notebook.

"Anyone else have questions?" The lecturer scans the rows of split log benches set for us in a semi-circle around his flip chart presentation.

My hand shoots up from my usual spot on the ground. "Yeah, um, I've got a question about the saladi," I say. The lecturer strolls over to the spreadsheet on the flip chart and directs a fluorescent ruler to the field I've indicated, tapping it with significance. "I mean, I understand what a budget sheet is and how it's constructed and everything. I see that you've got these make-believe health committee people buying pens and notebooks and stuff for their training and we've allotted money to hire people to cook for them to drive to town for them to buy supplies and so forth. But you've written 'saladi' with the food items." The lecturer looks at me blankly. I can't tell if I'm giving him too much information or not enough. I decide to go for broke. This wouldn't be the first time I've looked like a moron. "I don't know what saladi is," I admit bluntly.

He shakes his head incredulously. Saladi is, apparently, the stuff of life in Zambia. It's cooking oil. This is a brand name that has, over time, replaced the actual product name. Kind of like the way we use the word Kleenex in America. The name may have been derived from "salad oil," but who can say for sure? One thing is certain, though, and that's that anything tasty to eat is prepared with the help of saladi. Whether the meal includes meat, chicken, fish, vegetables or insects, I haven't seen a single relish prepared without copious amounts of salt and cooking oil. *Nshima*, on the other hand, is just a water and flour concoction, which ranks it just slightly above zero on the flavor scale. So I guess it all evens out in the end.

Now that I clearly understood what everything was in the budget, it still left the lingering question why all of these things were necessary. The office supplies and food and hired help seemed obvious, but what about bars of soap, rolls of toilet tissue, tubes of toothpaste, jars of Vaseline? Where did these come into play during a three-day HIV/AIDS workshop in a remote village? After some thought, I realize this is a bonus, an incentive for villagers to participate in the program. Not only would they eat well, but they would have access to all the toiletries that they would like to own, but can't afford. For three whole days they get to live like rich people. Rich for them, anyway.

So, this is what it boils down to? I'll be bribing villagers to take part in volunteer groups "for their own good?" This is how I am going to be saving the world: one bottle of saladi at a time? I'm not sure I had any thought about what my job here would entail besides health education, but this just seems off. Then again, this whole country seems a bit off.

Bribery is common currency here. We were told that Zambia ranks third on the list of most corrupt countries. I can't imagine what the top two countries are. The corruption is so rampant and pervasive that even Zambians joke about it. During a taxi ride in the capitol city of Lusaka last week, the driver pointed out a rusted skeleton of an unfinished building, vines crawling through the gaping concrete window holes, saplings poking through the floor beams. He turned and gave me a wacky, but not entirely disagreeable smile with the dozen or so teeth he had left in his mouth.

"You see this building here, madam," he said, jabbing his

finger towards the ruins. "This is the building site for an important branch of the Ministry. But, you see, there was some bad dealings going on. Some bad dealings with money. So now the money is finished, but the building, it is not finished."

"That's too bad," I said. "What branch of the ministry was that?"

"The Anti-Corruption Commission," he replied. Wheezy laughter whistled through his jack-o'-lantern grin. He raised his eyebrows in a conspiratorial way to indicate that he was only pulling my leg. At least I think he was trying to tell me he was only pulling my leg. I'm about 85% certain on that.

Later that day, as we traveled across the country to reach our training site in Kitwe, and I became more familiar with how the wheels of society are greased, I wasn't so sure this was such a far-fetched story after all. Roadblock after road-block presented themselves across the highway. Some were official police roadblocks, checking to make sure that we were driving a properly registered vehicle with all the required up-to-date, stamped, certified, receipt-attached paperwork on board. Then they checked to make sure we were up-to-date, registered, stamped, certified, receipt-attached passengers. This was an eye-opening experience for me. I actually had to prove that I had a right to exist in a certain place at a certain time in the company of certain people, and on top of that, I had to show a receipt of sale for my documents to prove that I was the purchaser of that right. The most basic human right that I had always taken for granted, the right to exist, had been called into question. A vague sense of something akin to violation has stuck with me since then, especially because after the document check, the police would still ask for money, or magazines, or our sunglasses for going through the trouble of lifting the roadblock for us.

Then there are the unofficial roadblock guys. These entrepreneurs take up residence at old roadblocks and demand payment for whatever reason they can come up with. One guy had hand painted a sign that read "tsetse fly checkpoint." He actually poked his head inside the vehicle on the pretense of checking for flies, which of course gave him the opportunity to case the joint so that he could ask for "that man's shoes" or "that small novel under the seat" when the inspection was over.

Eventually our group falls silent, the query for more questions about the lecture gone unanswered. We are dismissed for a tea break, which will no doubt consist not of actual tea, but our regular fare of watered down Mazoe, a syrupy orange drink, and biscuits. Biscuits, no matter what the British say, are not to be confused with cookies. Cookies are crispy, sweet, and mouthwateringly delicious. They are considered a guilty pleasure, an indulgence of too much fat, too much sugar, and way too many calories, but worth it all the same. A biscuit is none of these things.

The group packs up its books and unhurriedly saunters over to the tables spread with battered plastic pitchers of bright orange liquid and plates of chalky discs sandwiched together with something white and pasty. I stand in line with the others, awaiting my ration of snacks. I find that I am becoming addicted to these tea breaks. Not that I long for the food, but cramming things into my mouth makes a nice break from cramming things into my mind.

We've been going non-stop for weeks. Every day is hours upon hours of new information regarding Zambian culture, language, geography, statistics, history, and politics. We are asked to assimilate this information as it's presented and then make informed decisions. For example, we learned about the seventy-two tribal languages in this country, their current locations, populations, history and culture. Then we were asked to pick one. Basically just pick one out of the air and say, "that's the tribe I want to live with for the next two years." Gee, this is only the most important decision of our entire lives, so sure, five minutes is ample time to decide. No pressure.

I asked which language was the easiest to learn. Bemba? Great. Send me to Bemba-land. I've always wanted to be a Bemba, I just didn't know it until now. If I'm not going to have sufficient time to mull over a decision as big as this, I'm not going to give myself any time to regret or second-guess the decision. I figure the best way to go about it is to jump in with both feet and not look back. I've decided to trust myself like never before, to walk into each situation with an open mind and an open heart and let my intuition guide me. Too bad my intuition is currently telling me that my job is a sham.

I am hoping that the more I understand my job and the culture that I'm operating in, the more sense this will all make. And even if it doesn't, well, that doesn't mean that I can't live and work in a community in a way that is meaningful and important. I'll have to make my own meaning. It's my life to create, after all, isn't it?

This is one point that Peace Corps is really great about. As long as you're doing the job required of you, you are free to explore any other venture you choose. If you've ever been curious about what it's like to be a beekeeper, or a livestock owner, or a farmer, you can go ahead and do it. If you want to tear down your house and build a new one, then go for it. It's all about learning and having new experiences. As long as it entails you being at your post, working within your budget, and operating within reasonable behavioral guidelines, there are no limits as to what you can do during your service.

So I figure, what's to stop me from creating my own groups? If my job isn't creating the kind of satisfaction that I had hoped for, then I'll just do something else on the side. Of course, I have no idea what that could be since I'm not at my site yet, hanging out with the Bembas, doing whatever it is Bembas do.

I ponder this for a while, imagining the life I'll soon lead: pounding maize into meal, washing clothes on a riverbank, collecting firewood from the forest to cook with. What will be important to me then? What will motivate me and create a sense of job satisfaction when I am living that kind of life?

I slowly suck at the sugary orange drink from my cup, savoring the sweetness in my mouth, lost in the romantic daydream of what will soon be my everyday existence where even the mundane is exotic. I snap back into my present as someone lays a gentle hand on my shoulder and leans in conspiratorially. It's my friend Josh, the male trainee who spent his site visit with me at Jana's. Thankfully, the home-brew he consumed at the *nyau* dance did not make him go blind. He appears no worse for wear.

"Thanks for that," he whispers.

"For what?" I ask. I can't imagine why anyone would thank me for standing around with a glazed expression, holding up the progress in a line for biscuits.

"The saladi," he says, and reaches around me to grab a handful of biscuits. I stare at him blankly while he tosses one in his mouth and crunches away. "Dude," he says, his voice thick with half chewed biscuit. He takes a swig of the orange drink. "I didn't know what the hell he was talking about either."

I grin and nudge his shoulder as I edge past him to take my snack out to the courtyard. I perch on the bumper of one of the Land Rovers in the lot. One of the volunteer leaders ambles up and leans against the car next to me.

"You have that look," he says without preamble.

"I have a look?"

"Yup. It's the look I had when I first came here. Man, I thought I knew everything. And what I *knew*, above all, was that this job was a load of bullcrap. Once I got outfitted with my bicycle, it felt like my golden ticket out of here. I figured the minute this job started going sideways—and trust me on this, it will—I was just going to hop on the bike and take off." He draws his arm out in front of him, shoots a finger into the distance. "Never to be seen again. That was my big plan." He chokes out a self-conscious laugh.

"Some plan. What happened then? What changed your mind?"

"A lot of things. The people, mostly. It didn't take long to make friends and there was no way I was going to give up and let my village down. And honestly, after a while I realized America could learn a thing or two about decentralized healthcare."

"Really?" My voice strains up a good octave. "Why do you say that?"

"Well think about it. How much influence do you, as a regular American citizen, have in regard to deciding what health services should be available in your hometown?"

I think about it. Healthcare in America—a baffling snarl of privatized networks, pharmaceutical companies, and government agencies—can make even the savviest consumers throw their hands up in disgust when trying to suss out in-network coverage, out-of-pocket costs, deductibles, co-pays and so on. And insurance premiums? It's the albatross around the neck of every working man and woman I know.

"Little to none," I reply.

"Exactly. At least here, people have an opportunity to say how they think the government funds should be spent in their community."

"Yeah, you're right about that. The American system is ..." Incomprehensible? Embarrassing? A bureaucratic quagmire that even red tape has nightmares about? I settle on, "broken."

"There you have it. Keep that in mind when you start thinking about the system here. Not perfect, not even close, but it does have its merits."

I nod and finish my drink. I stare at the bottom of the cup, swirling around the last bright orange drop. *Around and around and around she goes, where she stops nobody knows.*

"Find any answers in there?" He nods at my cup.

"Not yet." I squint up at him. "I may need to practice my brooding skills along with everything else."

"Well, you've got nothing but time out here. Years of it. Pretty soon you'll be able to brood with the best of them. Like, Batman-level brooding."

"Hmmm." I pretend to consider this seriously. "That might be too dark. That's like the French Roast of broods. Maybe something a little lighter, like an Austen character. Mr. Darcy, perhaps? Enigmatic. Misunderstood. I can see myself going there. And—bonus—I could help bring the cravat back into style."

"Sure. Though, it might be a little much in this heat—"

"Hey, the hallmark of any truly great brood is a tortured look, as everyone knows."

"Everyone knows this, yes." He nods encouragingly.

"So, a cravat could help me in the suffering department, in the unlikely event I need assistance to get me started. And if not, well, it should at least lend me some gravitas."

"Mad gravitas," he agrees. He sizes me up with a crooked smile. "You're funny."

I shrug off the compliment.

"Hey, that's not nothing," he says. "A good sense of humor is going to serve you well out here. It's a critical survival skill, and you'll need it more than anything you're going to learn in that lecture hall."

As if on cue, a call goes out to reel us back in to the classroom. Break time is over. I sigh dramatically.

"C'mon." He offers me a hand. "They're playing our song."

I let him pull me from my seat on the car bumper and saunter by his side toward the lecture hall.

"So, what language did you choose?" he asks.

"Bemba."

"Awesome. That means you'll be in my district. There's a couple of really nice sites available this year. Of course, only the very coolest of the cool people will be considered for those posts."

"You don't say. And—just asking for a friend, here—is being funny considered cool?"

"Definitely."

"This bodes well. For my friend, that is. So, exactly whose palm needs to be greased to be considered for one of these primo sites?"

"Consider it already greased." He pantomimes comically slicked palms, tossing his empty cup hand to hand, chucking it higher the harder I laugh.

※ 4 ※

Hut Sweet Hut

I t's odd how sometimes when you are introduced to someone, the moment your eyes meet you feel a kinship with them. It's as if you knew all along that you were supposed to be friends, but you had forgotten until this moment that this is how you first meet.

"My mother! My mother!" I exclaim. I exit the Land Rover and rush into the open arms of a tiny *citenge*-clad woman. For some reason I begin weeping tears of joy. She is laughing and grabbing onto me too, and as I release her, I see she is also fighting back happy tears.

I stand back, feeling a little embarrassed now, hastily wipe my face and straighten out my clothes, ironing them with my hands while the rest of my new family gathers around me. I am introduced to my three new little sisters: Charity, Faith, and Betty standing in front of me in their Sunday best. Aged twelve, ten, and eight, they are like a little descending staircase of frilly lace and satin bows. Each face is a cookie-cutter image of her mother, every one of them hiding an embarrassed grin behind a hand or pressing their lips together in an attempt to bottle up nervous laughter.

My host father makes a slow appearance from the larger of the two mud huts on the property. He saunters over with an easy grace, a wide smile framed by a thick mustache. This surprises me because I haven't met many Zambians who go in for bold facial hair (which seems a shame, really, since arm and leg hair is nearly non-existent). This unusual trait gives my father such a jaunty and avuncular air that I take to him immediately. He strides forward in slow motion, arms raised in welcome, his gait slightly lopsided due to the fact that he is wearing one dress shoe and one flip-flop. His dress slacks are nearly worn through at the knees and cuffs but are clean and pressed, his short-sleeved dress shirt wildly adorned with amateur silk-screened drawings of Sylvester Stallone with the caption "Rambo: First Blood" emblazoned on it.

Now, I would have thought that this was an odd shirt to wear in order to make a good first impression, but I've noticed that this type of thing is considered high fashion around here. Whether it's Beyoncé or 50 Cent or Madonna, prints of modern American icons are just about the coolest thing you can buy at a clothes market. These men's shirts are commonly referred to as "amaguy" shirts. This is following in the great Zambian tradition of changing English words into Bantu words by simply adding the "ama" prefix to make them sound more authentic. The Americans here have taken to calling it Zamlish. I'm a fan. It makes some things just sound funnier. Especially when you mix up real "ama" words with made up ones. Like, "Hey, that amaguy over there has been checking out your amabutt for the last ten minutes. He's not bad if you don't mind goiters. I'm sure if you want any amakids he'd be happy to help you out." An appropriate response to this might be, "amaeff you, man."

The driver climbs up into the vehicle to loose my two enormous suitcases from the roof rack while I awkwardly introduce myself to my host father with the half-curtsy-hand-shake-no-direct-eye-contact thing that women are supposed to do. I can't help but look at him in the eye eventually, though. This is a hard cultural habit to break. Plus, I'm curious. I want to see how he is reacting to me, to see if he is as pleased to meet me as I am to meet him. As my eyes meet his, I'm relieved to see curiosity and amusement in his gaze. I wonder when the last time was that a woman looked at him— really looked at him—in the eye like an equal. I'm sure it's disconcerting for some of the men who host the American women. What a bold group we are; brazen women of independent means, used to having an equal say, an equal share, and equal influence. How threatening we must seem to these men who are not used to having their authority questioned.

My suitcases hit the ground with a resounding thud and a puff of dust as they hit the hard-packed earth of the yard. Before I can protest, my host mother descends upon the oversized luggage and, with the help of the driver, hauls one of the bags onto her head. I feel almost certain it will crush her. I've got my whole life packed into those two bags: two years' worth of clothes, shoes, books, tools, and toiletries. I'm pretty sure I've got more things packed in those two bags than this family has in their entire house. Gales of laughter and swirls of dust trail behind the three girls as they half-drag, half-carry the other suitcase towards the smaller, white-washed mud hut on the property.

As I make a move to help them, I receive a gentle admonishment from my host father as he shakes his head and says something I can't understand. His meaning is clear enough. I am their honored guest and I am not to carry my bags onto the property. They are greeting me and making me welcome by taking my things for me. I appreciate the gesture, but it burns me a little to see the women killing themselves lugging my insanely heavy bags while the man makes no effort to assist them.

I've been told that my host parents speak a fair amount of English, but they have been instructed to speak only in Bemba during my three-month stay with them. This will help me learn the language faster and keep me totally immersed in a state of learning twenty-four hours a day. During the day, I'll be in various training sessions to learn language and job skills, then I'll come home to a household where I'll have no opportunity to relax and shut my mind off for a while. My main task will be to simply act as a Bemba sponge.

We have the day to settle into our new homes and get to know our families before reporting in for language training tomorrow. We were given only one directive: do not hide inside your house. This seemed like obvious advice, but now that I'm here and I'm exhausted from traveling, I'd like nothing better than to unpack my belongings and curl into a ball on my bed surrounded by the comfort of familiar things.

My host father escorts me to my new home in a slow easy pace. I have to actually pause between each step so I can keep in time with him. This is the escorting pace. While excruciatingly slow for an American, it is the height of Zambian courtesy. I've been introduced to this concept during my Zambian culture training, but this is my first time experiencing it firsthand. Anytime someone comes to visit you should escort them onto your property and escort them on the first leg of their journey back home. It could be twenty steps, it could be a mile. It's up you to decide when the escort is over and say your farewells. This is all part of the visit and considered an important aspect of social etiquette. To not offer an escort to a guest would be as good as saying "you're not welcome, don't show your face around here again."

Step, pause. Step, pause. The absurdity of the pace reminds me of a father walking his daughter down the aisle at her wedding, except instead of a groom waiting at the end of the line for me, it's a toolshed-sized hut of mud and straw. As we draw closer, it becomes clear that this little hut was constructed shortly before my arrival. The freshly lime-slathered walls gleam in the afternoon sun, the reflected rays creating that kind of white that makes you squint your eyes against its brilliance. The rectangular structure stands about ten by twenty feet upon a six-inch platform of red mud, the roof dipping in the middle like an old swayback horse.

I poke my head under the low overhang of grass to peer at the inside. The stark contrast of the bright outer walls to the dim interior leaves me temporarily blinded. An eight-inch square hole covered with wire mesh punctures the dark. This appears to be the only source of light and ventilation other than the front door. As my eyes adjust, the rest of the room comes slowly into focus: A bamboo mat topped with a bare twin-size mattress and pillow, simple shelves of woven dry grass, a small chair and a table constructed of old two-by-fours adorned by a red cloth edged with amateur crewel-work flowers of bright yellow and green. On top of the table sits a Peace Corps standard-issue kerosene hurricane lantern, its gleaming steel and glass dome looking out of place in the humble surroundings.

I glance up at the ceiling and cringe. A canopy of black plastic held up by a network of raw wooden support beams spans the entire roof. Although it's an eyesore, I know that this is probably the most important aspect of the whole building since we're smack in the middle of rainy season.

I look back to the family who are nervously awaiting my verdict, then smile and nod my approval. My host mother places my bags just inside the door and motions that I should enter so I can unpack. Grateful for the opportunity to take a break from all the standing around and smiling at each other, I almost hug her again.

I allow myself a good solid hour to set out my belongings and decompress. I make up the bed, hang my mosquito net, assemble my water filter, and stack clothes on the grass shelves. There's a long strand of pliable bark hanging down from the ceiling near the front door where the support beams are lashed together. I pick up the loose end, roll it into a skinny tube and shove it through the tiny hole punch in my calendar. I grab a ballpoint pen out of my bag and tick off all the days since leaving home. The few meager rows of hatch marks swing tauntingly, pendulously, as I release the calendar. So few lines. I have yet to complete one month out of twenty-seven, but my life in America already seems like a hazy half-remembered dream. A mantra rolls around my brain: it's only two years, you're going to make it, two years, you're going to make it , two years, you're going to make it ...

... *Kambushi kalilalila* ...

... two years, you're going to make it ...

... *Ndefwaya umunandi* ...

A childlike melody mixed with giggles and the beat of tiny hands clapping along in time drifts in through the open door. It's clear that the girls are trying to coax me out of my little hut to come and join them.

... *mee mee* ...

I am charmed by them, enchanted by the sweet tune that reminds me of my own youth, of singing rhymes and skipping rope and clapping hands with girlfriends in the schoolyard. I dig through my bag for my spiral bound notepad and drift towards the girls like a child towards the pied piper. I am scribbling away at the little notepad, hoping to get at least some of the lyrics down although I have no idea what they are saying or what the proper way would be to spell it out.

The girls stand in a circle, wiggling their hips and shooting nervous glances in my direction. Though their complexions are a deep shade of brown, I can tell without a doubt that they are blushing furiously. Our mother smiles over at us from her place by the fire, her face also glowing, a sheen of sweat on her brow as she prepares *nshima* in the heat of mid-day. Handfuls of maize meal slowly sift through her fingers into a large pot of steaming water, her other hand swirling a long, flat wooden spoon slowly through the thin porridge.

Part of me wants to join the girls at the dancing circle, but I am feeling too self-conscious to let everyone have a laugh at me just yet. Wrapping my *citenge* more comfortably around my waist, I take a seat on a half-shredded bamboo mat set on the raised mud platform surrounding the home. I admire the structure of the shaded porch: a row of medium-sized peeled tree trunks lines the perimeter like Greek columns several feet from the outer walls, creating the look and feel of a grand, Victorian-era, wrap-around porch to the humble earthen abode. I resist an insane urge to chat up my host mother with insipid niceties like, "Gee, I love what you've done with the place." The fact that I can't even make small talk makes me feel utterly powerless. I feel a bit like an illiterate attendee at a book club meeting, hoping to God that no one will ask me any questions so my ignorance can go unnoticed.

I glance down at the scribbles on my notepad. *Ooo, moo, naan, dee.* Okay, cute, but this is getting me nowhere. What does it mean? Maybe it doesn't mean anything. This could be the Bemba version of "fa la la" for all I know. As I listen to the girls chant on, a sense of humbleness washes over me, because whether I understand what they are saying or not, I realize that these blushing darlings are my first tutors.

All three giggling girls cover their faces in embarrassment as I hoot and clap my appreciation at the end of their recital. I motion them over with my hand and offer them a place on the bamboo mat next to me. With shy and awkward steps, the girls approach the porch, slide off their flip-flops, and enter on hands and tip toes, careful not to drag the hem of their best gowns in the dirt. I scan the yard for everyday objects: a hen with a group of chicks in her wake, a dog dozing under a mango tree, a clothesline strewn with drying laundry, the rope and bucket at the side of the well. I decide that the mango tree looks the easiest to draw, so I start with that. Line, line, squiggly thing on top. I'm not much of an artist, so I point to the tree in illustration since my rendering looks more like a nuclear explosion than a mango tree. The girls are still giving me blank looks, so I write in big block letters TREE.

"Tree," I say. The oldest of the girls catches on.

"Mango," she says.

Okay, not quite what I was going for, but it is a start. I write down MANGO under the word TREE. I go for the chicken next. I entertain the girls by making little "bak, bak, bak" sounds under my breath as I draw something resembling a mop with a triangular beak and stick legs.

"Chicken," I declare, writing the letters in a bold block script.

"*Nkoko*," the girls say together.

A thrill runs through me. Communication! I can't even figure out exactly what their mouths are doing or how to begin writing it down but I'm elated all the same. I make the girls repeat it over and over until my mind makes sense of the word. I decide that phonetic spelling seems like my best game plan until I learn the rules of writing in Bemba, so I jot down IN COCOA. Chicken is about that last thing I'd want in my cocoa, but the disgusting mental image is a strong mnemonic device.

Slowly, carefully, I say my new vocabulary word out loud for the first time to my tutors. They howl with laughter and drop down on the bamboo mat, rolling around with their hands over their embarrassed faces. There is laughter behind me too, and I turn to see my host mother beaming in my direction, her arms poised in mid stroke above the pot of thickening *nshima*, each foot wrapped in a rag and braced against the base of the pot for leverage. I'm not sure where my father has gone, but since I don't hear the deep rumble of masculine chuckling, I can only assume he's well out of earshot.

I am laughing too, laughing at myself for being so self-conscious, and laughing for the pure joy of it. I am learning an entirely new way of communicating, something I was afraid I would fail at because I thought maybe my mind didn't work that way, that I lacked the discipline, or the skill, or the mental capacity to succeed at it. Now that I've got one solid Bemba word under my belt—one word—my ghosts of doubt have been chased away. I realize I have been telling a story about myself, a story based in fear and not in truth, and that I believed in this story without ever putting it to the test. I feel liberated, relieved.

My pen goes back to work, scratching out my best approximation of each object and I look to the girls to tell me what each one is. One by one, exciting new words begin to fill the page: *nganda* (house), *icishima* (well), *imbwa* (dog), *panshi* (ground), *makumbi* (sky), *ifyakufwala* (clothes). My mouth savors each word like an exotic and indescribable flavor, my tongue twisting on each combination of syllables, trying to make sense of what it is experiencing, but coming up with no basis for comparison. This sense of wonder, fun, and accomplishment is intoxicating. I wonder if I felt this way as a toddler, learning to communicate with words for the first time.

Our mother calls over to us, and the girls obediently spring into action. One begins to draw water from the well, one trots off into the fields, presumably to fetch her father, and one enters the house carrying a large metal platter piled with hot lumps of *nshima*, an upside-down bowl resting over the top like a hat to hold in the steam. My host mother walks towards me on her knees, bows, claps her hands together lightly and addresses me with an entreating tone of voice. She motions towards the open front door where pairs of tattered flip flops in various sizes line the side of a multi-colored welcome mat of woven rags. I rise, kick my shoes off and place them neatly at the end of the line before entering. My host mother holds me back with a gentle grip around my wrist. Her other hand grabs my shoes and plops them back in front of me on the rag mat.

It seems that as a guest, I am not to trouble myself with such niceties. I try to protest but the more fuss I make about not needing my shoes in the house, the more she insists I wear them. I decide that this must be another custom that I'm not familiar with, that it shall be the good pleasure of the host to allow a guest to wear their shoes in the house. This must be a sign of respect and deference. Not wishing to dishonor the custom or my host family, I wiggle each foot back into its shoe and bow to my mother, thanking her for her generosity.

I step onto the spotless floor inside, the cement gleaming with countless layers of hand applied wax polish in a deep crimson stain. The space inside is surprisingly large, about five times that of my private little bungalow, even with the section portioned off by hanging *citenge* cloth for the sleeping quarters. The grassy ceiling soars high above our heads in rafters of unpeeled saplings, the central support beam shooting up from the middle of the floor and nesting in the roof peak like a tree growing inside the house. The walls have not been smeared with lime to brighten the interior as mine has, but remain the dull hue of sunbaked mud, the hand-molded blocks stacked in rows with mortar spilling out in uneven blobs through the cracks. The mottled grayish-brown of the mud has that unmistakable look of a once rich, moist, and living thing gone dead from exposure, like old, fossilized dog turds you might find on a sidewalk. I raise a hand to the wall and let my fingers brush along its chalky surface as I step farther into the room.

A low-lying, threadbare couch and chair overlaid with crocheted doilies crowd around a coffee table crammed with metal bowls of chipped enamel. Each sporting an upside-down plate or bowl to protect the food within, they look like a colony of giant, tattered, metallic clamshells competing for space to exist on the same small rock. A single panel of a lace curtain has been tacked up like wallpaper on the left-hand wall, the adjoining far wall adorned by a torn poster advertising a beer I've never heard of, a two-year out-of-date calendar, and a cheapie glass and composite wood wall clock, the words "High-Class Quartz Clock" emblazoned in gold script along the bottom edge. This is it. This is all of their prized possessions, the sum total of their wealth.

My host mother soundlessly brushes past me as she enters with the bowl of hand-washing water. The rest of the family respectfully follows behind her in perfect silence. Smiling to myself, I compare this dignified procession to a meal at my family's house in America: an earsplitting scream of "DINNER!" from me (the perennial table-setter) followed by the pounding of feet on stairs as my sister breaks from homework up in her room and my brother emerges from his dungeon-like video gaming nest in the basement.

My host father takes a seat in the low chair with enormously overstuffed arms and offers me a seat on the couch. I lower myself onto one of the perfectly pressed cloths with the crocheted edge covering the seat and back of every couch cushion. I know my mother has put a lot of work into setting those doilies up just right and I feel a little guilty for crushing one underneath me, but I know that it would be the wrong thing to do to peel one off the seat before plunking myself down. Besides, now that I'm getting a whiff of the moldering seat cushion, I'm kind of glad that there is something clean between me and the foam slab of mildew. The girls and my mother gather around and sit on the floor around the little coffee table. I want to insist that someone sit with me on the couch since it could easily fit two or three other bodies, but I stop myself before I make another faux pas like I did with the shoes.

No thought of an argument or polite protest is raised from me, however, as my mother offers me first dibs on the bowl of water for hand washing. Once the bowl has gone around, my father offers a lengthy prayer to bless the food. I keep opening my eyes and peeking around at the girls' faces, checking to make sure their eyes are closed and we are still in prayer mode. I'm not sure how many minutes have passed, but my washed hands are completely dry by the time "amen" rolls around. The lids are removed from the dishes and passed to each of us to serve as our eating plate. Lid by lid, the table reveals its bounty: pumpkin leaves, vegetables in peanut sauce, *nshima*, and a roast chicken. My heart lifts and I smile up at my host father, pointing to the main course dish.

"Oh!" I exclaim, and point to my icebreaker. "In cocoa!"

Losing It

Panting and trembling, I stand up in my seat and force the bicycle pedals down by the sheer weight of each leg. The bike weaves side to side, swerving in slow motion as I ascend the muddy incline in low gear. I swear if I were moving any slower, I'd be going backwards.

The worst part of all of this is not the exhaustion or the embarrassment of being the oldest, most out-of-shape, slowest moving volunteer of the group, although that's bad enough, it's the fact that the group of children that has been trotting along side of me is now skipping around me in lazy laps. Witnessing their youthful energy is infuriating.

"How are you? How are you? How are you?"

The children's chant has become a taunt in my mind. How am I? I'm lousy. I want to give up. I want to lay down right here in the mud and never get up, thanks for asking.

Fourteen kilometers a day shouldn't be this exhausting.

Seven to class, seven back home. It should be a cinch. For some volunteers it is. A twenty-minute jaunt and there they are. For me it can take anywhere from forty-five minutes to an hour and a half depending on the weather and how tired I am.

"How are you? How are you? How are you?"

The bare feet of the children pad effortlessly atop the mud while my tires grind deep grooves under my weight. They spin down and down until the mud shoots up like Play-Doh spaghetti from the rear of the tires. Stuck again. I stand astride the bike and catch my breath, cursing silently while I shift my helmet around in a maddening attempt to scratch my head. The mixture of trickling sweat, rainwater, and heat trapped under my bicycle helmet itches like hell.

I fantasize about a hot shower at the end of the ride, my fingers massaging my scalp and shampooing my hair into a rich lather, the steaming water pounding my shoulders. But there won't be any hot shower at the end of the line. There won't even be a radiator to lean against, or a hairdryer to cook my head until my ears burn, or a simple cup of tea to take the chill off. I'll be coming home to a drafty mud hut, dry my body and hair with a towel chilly and damp from this morning's bucket bath, and put on a fresh set of clean, but damp, clothes. Nothing dries well in the rainy season. The perpetual rain permeates everything with moisture. The bed and pillow are musty sponges. The bath towel—more of a terry cloth petri dish than anything—smells like the absolute last thing you'd want to rub on your body after you bathe.

In slow motion, I swing my right leg over the seat and haul the bicycle out of the mud. Every tread, spoke, and gear is clogged with gunk. The thing weighs at least twice what it should. I drag it over to the nearest tree, the frozen wheels sliding rather than turning, and search the ground for a small stick to clear the globs of mud off. As I poke and brush away the worst of the mud around the moving parts, the kids crowd around me to watch the proceedings.

I'm losing my temper. I want to tell the kids to buzz off, that I'm sick of them following me around and watching my every move. I've been told that being a Peace Corps volunteer feels like living in a fish bowl, but I feel more like Shamu in a stadium-sized aquarium with a line of kids pressing their sticky hands and snotty faces up to the glass in anticipation of my next trick. I know that the children are curious and fascinated by me. It's just disconcerting to constantly have a flock of twenty or so kids flanking you at all times. For kids with no TV, real-life is where the entertainment's at. The most interesting thing they have to watch is the "all-*muzungu*, all-the-time network" of which I'm the star.

I rip up a handful of dry grass, fashion a broom, and brush more mud off the gears. My host mother will do a better job of this when I get back. She actually washes the bicycle every day, scrubs every nook and cranny with soap and water, even the treads of the tires, dries it raised on bricks under the eaves of the house and carries it into my hut so the tires won't track any dirt inside. I have—on numerous occasions—gotten the piccolo trumpet solo from The Beatles' "Penny Lane" stuck in my head when I look at it because it's such a clean machine. Cleaner than me at the end of the day, for sure.

Once the tires are reasonably unglued, I straighten up, take off my backpack and loop the straps around the handlebars to give my shoulders a rest. The pack has a line of mud straight up the middle, and I know without even checking a mirror that my butt and the back of my neck are sporting the continuation of that line. Some fashion statement. I grab the handlebars and ease the bike forward, trudging through the soggy grass at the edge of the road. The mere thought of putting my sore rear end onto that tiny seat again makes walking for the next hour sound like a great idea.

Some of the kids lay their hands on the bicycle and help me push it along. I must look pretty pathetic by now because no one is asking me how I am anymore. I am utterly destroyed. I'd cry but I have no more tears to shed. Today was my breakdown day. I finally lost it.

I don't know how it happened. I was feeling perfectly fine this morning. Maybe a bit nervous for my first oral examination in local language, but pretty confident that I was doing okay since I seem to be doing the best in my class so far. My accent is better, my vocabulary is better, my grammar is better. Everyone says so. But the moment I walked into the first examination room and faced an unfamiliar teacher, I panicked. My mind became a complete blank. I don't know why, she seemed very non-threatening and the objective of this part of the exam was clear and simple. Before her were piles of food: a sack of maize meal, a pile of fritters, bunches of vegetables, dishes filled with beans, rice, peanuts, dried fish and the like.

Of the four different stations in today's exam, this should have been the easiest. If there's one thing I know how to ask for in local language, it's food. I do this with my host mother every day. Each meal begins with the unveiling of the dishes, which I have to name before I can begin eating. She's a real disciplinarian about it too, which I appreciate. I have to repeat it over and over until I pronounce it to her satisfaction.

It was all there, familiar objects, everyday vocabulary that I have practiced time and again, and nothing was registering. Panic flooded my body as my gaze fell on a bowl of peanuts. Now, my host father is a peanut farmer and we eat peanuts in some form or another almost every day. This is a word I know. But as I searched the familiar dusty and pitted surface of the shells, nothing came. Not even the English word of "peanut." Curiously, the only thing that came to mind was a vision of the animated Mr. Peanut figure in a top hat, cane, and monocle tap dancing across the table in a jaunty side step. My heart felt like a lightning rod as bolts of electric fear struck again and again. My throat constricted tighter with each passing second, an invisible fist of terror wrenching my vocal cords into petrified silence.

This short circuit was so unexpected, so maddening, that it pushed me over the edge of reason. I hadn't known I was teetering on the brink, until I started plummeting. I kept going down and down and down ... the tears wouldn't stop coming. I now understand what the term "hysterical" means. There was no control and no end in sight. And, oh, that poor instructor. Talk about mortified. Here I come, walking into the examination room, take one look at her and start bawling like a child lost in a mall. How embarrassing for both of us.

It took about ten minutes of tears and mute apologies, my mouth gaping like a fish out of water, before I regained my voice. The sobbing didn't cease, but at least I was able to string words together and make myself understood.

"I'm so sorry," I said. "I don't know what's wrong with me."

"It's just stress," she said. "This happens sometimes. You're just pushing yourself too hard. This is not that important. We are only trying to assess your language abilities at this stage of training. No one is getting kicked out for not knowing enough vocabulary. Let's just see where you're at, okay? Let's start with something easy." She uncovered a plate of white doughy lumps and looked at me expectantly.

"*Nshima*," I choked out, then began laughing through the tears. One by one, the names started to come back, although some things, like the peanut, remained obstinately behind the locked doors of my mind.

The other three stations had similar situations, a one-on-one with an unfamiliar teacher to name objects in the classroom, greet each other and make small talk, and to describe someone of mutual acquaintance so that the other person could hazard a guess at their identity. The quizzes could have been fun had I been able to stanch the constant flow of tears. I cried through each exam. I cried in between each exam. I cried when it was all over. I cried for three and a half hours straight. Each teacher tried to insist that I calm myself down before I came into the room, that they would be happy to have me come later once I stopped crying. But I told them that it was no use, that it wasn't letting up and we should just go ahead anyway. Ignore the crying, I said, let's just get on with it and get it over.

"Madam, how are you?" The boy pushing the other handle bar asks me for the umpteenth time. His head is covered with a plastic Shoprite bag, two knots on the sides cinching it to his head and sticking out like horns above his ears.

"I'm stressed," I reply. "Apparently, I'm so stressed that I can lose my mind at any moment. My world can come crashing down at any second, without warning, and leave me a senseless, blithering idiot. I'm a freak show waiting to happen. I may look like a normal human being, but don't be fooled. I'm a lunatic, kid. They're probably coming to ship me out of here any second. And good riddance, too. Who needs a basket case like me around, falling apart at the slightest thing?

"Oh, and you know what else? This is fun. I've got a worm living in my leg. Yeah, so that's great. Just when I think my day is over and done and I can have a good night's sleep, this stupid hookworm starts wiggling around under my skin and keeps me up all night." I stop walking for a second and lift my right trouser leg to show him the snaky red line looping up and down the inside of my calf.

"Pretty sick, huh? Have you ever had one of these?" I study his blank face, clearly not understanding a word I've said. "You look unsurprised, so I'm going to go with yes."

The PCMO (Peace Corps Medical Officer) has informed me I'm experiencing what is known as a 'creeping eruption' and they don't have any medicine for it right now. They can't get it out either. I'm just supposed to wait until it dies and then my body will absorb it, whenever that will be. That's a nice thought—worm guts living in my leg forever. This will be my souvenir from Africa. Not everybody gets to have one of these, so heck, guess I'm just lucky.

I'm on a roll, now. Every pent-up frustration and upset over the past couple of months has bubbled to the surface and is fighting to come pouring out of my mouth first. I blather on about my exhaustion, how lonely I feel here, how none of my friends have bothered to write or send me a care package, how I can't study at night because the kerosene lantern is too dim, how I have a toad living in my bed that I have to evict each night, how I can't make or receive phone calls from my family, how the internet is so painfully slow here that even when I can go into town to use it, it can take an hour for one e-mail to open up, and how when I actually did open an e-mail the other day it was to tell me—by a third party—that the man I have been having a long-distance romance with has dumped me to get back together with his ex-girlfriend—the one he swore up, down, and sideways he was over—and he's been deployed to Iraq to boot, which is fine by me because I just decided I won't shed so much as a single tear if he gets himself blown to bits, that two-faced, fibber-McGee, liar-liar-pants-on-fire.

My confessor in the shopping bag hat simply looks up at me blankly through all of this. He is waiting for the response to his question. He asked me how I was, and there is only one response to that. I stop walking the bike, take a deep breath, and look at the boy.

"I'm fine," I say.

"I'm fine! I'm fine! How are you, madam? I'm fine," he replies enthusiastically. This is about the extent of conversational English that children know, unless they are raised in a city where it is used more frequently. The other kids trailing behind us join in. Soon, I'm bombarded with the chant of "how are you" all over again. I grab my backpack and plop myself down on the bicycle seat. There is a long downhill stretch in front of me and, if I'm lucky, I'll be able to outrun all these kids before my temper flares up again.

My legs pump furiously as I descend the hill. The kids start off at a run, holding on to the bicycle with one hand and squealing with delight. Eventually they fall back as I outpace them, the chant petering out as they give up the chase. I push myself harder and faster. What a jerk I am. Why would I take my anger out on these kids? What have they done to deserve my wrath? I let the leaves of a low hanging branch whip me across the cheek as I pass by. The sting feels like penance; it hurts so good I almost feel like turning around and doing it over again. Instead, I attack the next incline with brutal speed. Each stroke of the pedal is met with a primal shout. It's like it's not even me making the noise. It's coming from somewhere deep inside. The nameless, changeless part, that spark of life that knows no language but communicates in pure emotion, that's who is yelling.

Every muscle fires as I crank the wheel one last turn to summit the crest, and as I do, something in me breaks. My feet touch the ground and I stand fixed, aware of nothing at all but my breath. My lungs burn with the force of it, each inhale is as painful and urgent as the exhale. Humility washes over me, wave after merciful wave. I have limits. I am human. I'm going to try my best to do everything right, but I'm going to make mistakes sometimes. Mistakes are lessons, and if I choose to learn from them, then I'll have gained something more valuable than any easy victory could afford. That's life. And I'm living it, really living it like I never have before. That's worth something.

I lift my eyes to the horizon and am greeted by the familiar sight of marketplace shanties that line the entrance to my village. Home, at last. Ten minutes, tops, and I'll be able to kick off these filthy clothes, wash my face, and crawl into my musty bed with my shortwave radio until my mother calls me to dinner. If I'm lucky I might get an hour of "Special English" on the Voice of America. I'll get the news in extremely slow, clear phrases designed to be understood by people who don't speak English as a first language. It's like being read a soothing bedtime story, except it's all about politics and world news, with occasional pop culture tidbits thrown in for kicks.

I take the last warm swig of water from my sport bottle I've been saving for the end of the trip and begin pedaling down into the village. I am determined to ride all the way back to the house without stopping. If I get off and walk now, I'll just be accosted by all the vendors and marketplace drunks who know my name, and I'll be forced to greet them and sit with them. Some days it's a welcome diversion, but I just don't have it in me to be social right now.

As if on cue, I am greeted with shouts of welcome as I enter the market. I feel like Norm on *Cheers* every time I come through here.

"Ba Chri! *Muli Shani*?" The adults here know I'm learning Bemba, so they give me the whole "how are you" routine in local language. I like my new pet name they've given me. "Ba Christine" is kind of long. Zambians give the Ba prefix to names to indicate respect, and with their accent, my name comes out like "Ba Cheereesteenee." So now I'm Ba Chri.

"*Ndifye bwino*," I reply. *I'm just fine.* I'm tempted to be honest and say "*panono*" instead. This means I'm only a "little bit" fine, or not so great. But then you are supposed to launch into your myriad reasons about why life is only a little bit fine, so that you can gain some sympathy. You can't just drop the bomb of "my life sucks" and walk away. Besides I'm too young for that excuse. Unless you've just suffered a loss in your family or something equally tragic, "*panono*" is usually reserved for old people. You are supposed to sit with them and listen about their failing eyesight and aching joints and children that don't come visiting often enough.

I weave through the puddles and pedestrians of the market and tackle the last steep incline up to my family's farm. Faith and Betty, the younger two of my three sisters, see me inching up the hill and run to escort me on the last leg home. As I turn onto the path leading to our home, my relief gives way to exhaustion. Slowing my pace to dismount, I begin to lose balance. My handlebars swerve wildly to one side and I fly off to the other, crashing right into the maize field. My mother cries out in alarm and rushes over to help me up.

Slowly, I extricate myself from the bicycle and stalks of maize. Nope, nothing bruised but my pride. I'm fine, I assure her. I fear I've hurt the girls, but thankfully, they missed being caught up in the wreck. My mother gently unclips my bike helmet, slips the heavy backpack from my shoulders, and instructs the girls to push the bicycle back to the house. I linger behind for a moment to inspect the damage. Four stalks of maize lie broken on the ground. That's a meal or two for this family. And I've as good as stolen it right out of their mouths. Brilliant.

My legs feel strangely light as I walk up the path. It's almost as if they've fallen asleep, like the blood in my veins has been replaced by ginger ale. My feet don't even feel like they are touching the ground beneath me, but I can hear the heavy footfall of my mud-caked hiking boots keeping time with my step. I am amazed that they are keeping me aloft, moving me forward.

The path opens up to the wide expanse of swept earth that our mud huts occupy. I used to think the dirt lot was pathetic, a poor man's lawn. Now I see that it's practical, necessary even. There are fewer places for bugs to live or snakes to hide. At night, the bare ground reflects the moonlight so you can navigate through the yard and down the path to the pit latrine without a lantern. I watch the ground pass beneath my buzzing legs and admire the pattern of the meticulously swept surface. My mother is up every morning just before sunrise to draw water, make a fire, and sweep the yard. The *shick, shick, shick* is the first sound I hear in the morning, even before the cock crows. I think of it as my snooze button. It wakes me, but not enough to actually get up out of bed. I fade in and out, dozing on the edge of consciousness as the twig broom makes its rounds up and down the yard. It's almost a shame to walk on it when she's finished; the dirt resembles a freshly mowed lawn or vacuumed rug, alternating rows of directionality patterning the lot.

I hear a man's voice greeting me as I near the hut, a timbre much deeper than my father's. Great. A visitor. Just what I need. The swooshing rows of dirt vanish from my sight as I squeeze my eyes shut and do a mental head slap. Whoever it is just saw me make the face-plant of the century in the maize field. The hits just keep coming today, don't they? After a deep inhale, I look up and return the greeting to the man waiting on the porch.

It's Ba Lubasi, the head director of Peace Corps Zambia's training program. So they are chucking me out after all. The head honcho himself has come in person to give me the news. I can hear what he is going to say already. *Sorry, Ba Christine, we can't afford to have someone like you in our program. We've got our reputation to consider, you understand. No hard feelings. Let's get you packed up and I'll drive you out to Lusaka International. We've got you booked on the first flight back home ...*

You can't argue with a man like Ba Lubasi. You just have to suck it up and say "yes, sir." He has a kind of warrior magic about him. He is a Lozi, you see. The Lozi people from Western Province remain detached, mysterious, even in the face of modern tribal integration. They are practically a separatist movement. They have their own language, their own mode of dress, their own cultural traditions and festivals. They remind me of modern-day U.S. southerners who proudly fly the confederate flag and still use the word Yankee. The Peace Corps doesn't even go out to Lozi land. The language is too difficult, the land too wild. And the people, well, they don't seem to want or need our help the way I hear it. They have their own way of doing things. I've only met a handful of Lozis, and they are all in powerful, government appointed positions. A Lozi is always taken seriously; no one wipes his boots on him.

Ba Lubasi shoots me a disarming smile, the one that makes all the female volunteers go weak in the knees, his slightly-too-long teeth gleaming in contrast to his deep ebony complexion. His tooth enamel perfectly matches the thick ivory bangle that adorns his right wrist. White with an inner golden glow. The ivory, unashamedly displayed, lends to his warrior mystique. Placed on his arm as a young man, it is permanently fixed above his now adult-sized wrist bones. Even when dressed in a proper suit and tie, that bangle peeks out defiantly as he gesticulates. It begs: *go on, ask me about it. Perhaps I killed a rhinoceros in my youth, or helped take down an elephant that invaded the crops of my village. You won't know unless you ask me, but you won't, will you? You wouldn't dare. I've killed. Let's leave it at that.* He motions to the wood stump next to him. It's time to *ukwambaula*: to sit and talk over matters.

I find I'm having no trouble behaving as a proper Zambian woman should. I shuffle over to him, my eyes averted to the ground. I sit on the stump next to my guest and slump my shoulders in an attempt to shrink myself, secretly hoping I'll melt into the ground and disappear so this conversation won't have to take place. I am defeated, ashamed. I sit silently waiting for the bomb to drop.

Oh God, just let it be quick. Just rip off that bandage, one clean stroke, and be done with it. Say I'm no good, tell me it's over, just say it. Just say ...

"*Muli shani?*" He asks. *How are you?* The million-dollar question.

"*Bwino*," I reply. Oh, yes. I'm fine. About as fine as a person can be who is in the middle of a breakdown and about to be flushed out of Peace Corps. There's a name for people like me—ET. It means early termination. Worse than that, I'll be a "MED SEP"—someone who's been medically separated from the Corps. Someone deemed unfit to stay. I'll be sent home with my tail between my legs, floundering for some excuse other than "I got sent home because I'm crazy" when people ask me why I've come back.

We exchange more niceties, inquiring about the health of each other's families, how the crops are coming in, and so forth. I'm on automatic pilot, answering questions the way I have rehearsed time and again in our Bemba class. I wish language had been flowing out of me this effortlessly when I had been in my exam. I guess the pressure is off now. I've got nothing to lose, nothing to gain, by getting my responses right. Any bystander would think we are just having a chat, two human beings checking in with one another. But I'm waiting for the real drama to begin. I know this is just the calm before the storm.

Each polite exchange of words between us is a textbook example of social etiquette, as contrived as setting a proper dinner table. The napkin folded just so, the silverware laid out in ascending order, glassware to the right, a flower arrangement placed with care in the center. But soon he's going to do that trick where he'll whip the tablecloth out from underneath all our carefully laid out pleasantries. I wonder, will I still be left standing when my world is whipped out from under me? Or will I fly off into the unknown, spinning out of control, fruitlessly attempting to anchor myself back to a place that no longer exists?

"Excellent," he says. "You have come along well in your language training."

"*Natotela mukwai*," I thank him.

It has occurred to me that this might be the last conversation I ever have in Bemba so I'm milking it for all it's worth. I don't want to give up the language and I don't want to give up this place. My eyes search the yard in a frantic effort to memorize everything about our surroundings, the swept yard, the crackling exterior of lime on my little swaybacked hut, a young bunch of green bananas budding from the tree next to the bathing shelter, the dingy plastic bucket lying on its side by the open well, the *citenge* cloths pinned up on the clothesline. One of the *citenge*, a bamboo print on a chartreuse background, I recognize as one of my own. It catches a ride on the breeze and waves like a banner next to my hut.

A feeling akin to patriotism stirs in my soul at the sight of it. I chose this place. I chose to make a stand here. This is my home now, and no one is going to take it away from me. I am no quitter, and I refuse to be sent away from here as one. No matter how hard this gets I am not giving up on it, it's mine. Let them just try and make me leave.

"I have come to discuss our training program with you," he says. Now we're getting to it. We are going to talk his concerns about me not being a right fit. Well, tough! I begin mentally preparing my defense, *under stress, have exhibited model behavior up to this point, deserve a second chance to prove myself...*

"Some volunteers have expressed concerns about our curriculum, so I'm meeting with each volunteer to discuss any issues you might have ..."

My brain starts to fuzz out the actual words he says after "meeting with each volunteer." He's not here to yank my world out from under me. This is a routine visit. Each excuse and self-vindicating remark I had prepared in my mind shrivels up with the same warp speed I had conjured it. I won't need to defend myself after all. This small miracle, this bit of grace falls like a warm blanket over my mind and blots out every thought but "thank you."

I draw my attention back to my guest, knit my eyebrows together with concentration, and focus on his mouth until the words begin to make sense to me again. Asking him to repeat himself because I wasn't paying attention wouldn't be a very good way to repay him for not kicking me to the curb.

It seems that other volunteers, instead of berating themselves for being idiotic or incompetent, have shifted the blame for their shortcomings to the staff of the training center. Complaints range from deplorable living conditions to difficult course work to specific teachers. The multiple hours of language training each day has been deemed too taxing, the technical competency exams too frequent and time consuming. In short, things are just too hard.

"... it really boils down to expectations," he says. "We want to be clear about what your expectations of this program are."

"My expectations?" I trail off for a moment and collect my thoughts. "I only had one expectation, really. I expected that the Peace Corps would be the hardest thing that I would ever do in my life, and it is. This is absolutely the hardest thing I have ever done in my life. But I'm not complaining. I wanted it to be hard. I came here for hard. I love that it's hard. If I wanted easy, I would have just stayed home. So, rest assured, this program has lived up to my expectations. In fact, I would say that it has exceeded my expectations."

We sit in silence for a beat or two, eyes locked together. A slow smile splits his face. I have surprised him. My response has really tickled him for some reason. He lets out a chuckle and shakes his head in disbelief.

"So we have exceeded your expectations? I'm glad we haven't disappointed you," he says and rises to take his leave. "Since everything is fine here, I'll be on my way."

"Yes, I'm fine," I say, really meaning it for the first time today. "Everything is just fine."

❧ 6 ❧

All the Sweeties

I can't look my host family in the eye this morning. Not after last night. I call my goodbyes over my shoulder and try not to trip over my *citenge* as I scurry down the path leading from our farm down to the village marketplace.

I'm on my way to meet one of my friends for church this morning. I need to go to church. I'm a dirty, dirty ho-bag.

Some nights, once I close my eyes and drift off to dreamland, there's a line of men waiting for me as far as the eye can see. But last night, it was just the one man, one of the volunteers. Someone you would not expect to be such a Casanova. I've always seen him as more of a boy scout than a potential lover. Not only is he a good ten years younger than me, but I outweigh him by a lot. I'm pretty average at a size ten and a five-foot seven height, but I feel like a giantess next to him.

Last night, though, he proved to be anything but puny. He stormed into my hut with the strength of ten-thousand men.

The door was torn loose from its hinges and lay in a shattered wreck on the floor. He lifted me from my mattress on the ground and stood me against the wall, his hands gripping my arms like a vice. Something else was pressed against me too, pinning my hips against the wall. There was no mistaking what he had come for. And I wanted it, he knew I did. In fact, it was already happening, though I couldn't remember taking my clothes off. My hands tore wildly at his back, his shoulders, and the chalky mud wall behind me. A throbbing heat began to build deep inside me. *Oh yes, yes!*

Now this is when it got weird. My host father walked in through the open door and took a seat at my little desk in the center of the room.

"*Eya, mukwai,*" he said.

I thought, *Jiminy Christmas, you've gotta be kidding me. He's come in here to correct my Bemba? Now?* Casanova showed no signs of stopping, despite our guest, and so I decided I wouldn't care either.

"*Eya* ... ah," I replied weakly.

"*Eya, mukwai,*" he repeated. This means "yes," but more literally translates to "I acknowledge, respected one."

"*Eya, mukwai!*" I repeated with more vigor.

"*Eya, mukwai,*" he said more firmly.

"*Eya, mukwai!*"

"*Eya, mukwai.*"

"*Eya, mukwai!*"

It went on like this until the end, a final "MUKWAIIII-II!" exploding from me and waking me out of my dream. My throat was killing me. Had I really been yelling in my sleep? What must my family be thinking?

The thing is, I've never been one of those people prone to having sexy dreams. In fact, I've always been envious of people who claim to have wild, guilt-free sex with nameless, faceless strangers in the privacy of their own minds while they slumber. Any dream I've had in the past that even approaches sex ends with me pushing them away saying something completely weak sauce, like, *"Gee, you know what? We've only just met and I don't feel comfortable ... I mean, it's nice and everything ... and I'm really flattered, but I just can't."* I always get angry afterwards. I mean, that's my real life. Can't I at least let go once in a while in my dreams?

Well, it seems I have finally gotten my wish, with a vengeance. No man is safe from my voracious cerebral appetite for sexual fantasy. My brain stores images of every man I meet throughout the day, locals, teachers, fellow trainees, and through some process of selection unknown to the rational part of my mind creates a starring cast and scene for that evening's performance. It's been like this for months now, not every night, but nearly. At first, I thought it was just a passing phase, some outlet for unresolved stress. But the dreams kept coming. Visceral, palpable, all-consuming, Technicolor fantasies, the details remaining vividly in my mind down to the smallest minutiae long after the moment had passed. They are more real than reality.

It's the mefloquine.

A synthetic offspring of quinine, this controversial anti-malarial prophylaxis is the U. S. government's drug of choice for their employees in countries where malaria still exists. Though a significant minority of people on this drug experience severe side effects such as seizures, panic attacks, visual disturbances, and psychosis, it provides the highest level of protection against the malaria parasite. I guess their view is that it's better to send you home crazy than send you home dead. But since one of the listed side effects is "suicide," you might get sent home dead anyway. Seriously, it says right on the package "may cause suicide" like it's as trivial a concern as "may cause mild redness or swelling." More common side effects include dizziness, headaches, insomnia, anxiety, depression, and vivid—often terrifying—dreams. Although some people experience horrible nightmares of epic proportions, I have to admit, I am having the time of my life with this stuff.

Lifting my *citenge* a bit for some slack in my stride, I ascend the small incline up to the football pitch. The path that cuts across it diagonally is the shortest distance to the market and the easiest way to go if a game isn't in progress. There will be a match later today (there's one every Sunday afternoon) which will make traveling back this way next to impossible. The whole village turns out for these soccer matches. Skirting around the sidelines takes hours with all the polite greeting and chit-chatting that's required in such a social situation. There is no blending in when you are a curiosity like I am. I'm so white I glow.

This sounds like a cliché, but it is the god's honest truth. The other night, I visited with a friend until after nightfall and, consequently, had to walk home in the dark. I hadn't brought a flashlight with me, but there was enough light from the moon and stars to guide me down the little dirt path that leads back to my family's compound. As I passed by a neighbor's property a voice cried out in the dark, "Good evening, Ba Chri!" I stopped dead in my tracks. I asked her how she could possibly know that it was me. After all, I was in traditional garb, wrapped in *citenge*, padding along in the usual flip-flops at least fifty feet away from her house in the dark. She said she could clearly see the white of my face bobbing in the distance, so she knew it had to be me. Can't argue with that logic.

Descending from the pitch, I catch sight of my equally luminescent friend Ava. She's standing in the center of the marketplace, one soft pink hand clasped in her host mother's sinewy black one, the other hand engaged in a game of high five with a child.

"Up high, down low, oh, too slow," she says, whipping her hand out from under the child's intended target.

"You're cruel, you know that?" I tease her.

"And you're late," she counters.

"No, I'm not. I'm on African time," I say, although a paltry five or ten minutes doesn't really qualify for African time. I would need to show up in an hour or two. Or maybe next week. African time is often described as "elastic." It's a concept that takes a while to grasp if you aren't used to it. It basically means that dates, days of the week, and numeric hours are suggestions, not concrete identities in and of themselves. They are an idea of a time that is not *now*, and therefore, not observable, quantifiable or important. *Now* is what is happening, and if it isn't *now* it is something that doesn't exist.

I have found this vague conceptualization of time evident in the language as well. For example, the word *mailo* in Bemba means "yesterday." It also means "tomorrow." It is only within the context of a sentence that one derives the meaning of the word as "the day that happened before today" or "the day that will happen after today." This is no problem for the native speaker to comprehend, but nearly impossible for the linguistic novice to catch during conversation since a mere one or two letter difference in a single word will entirely change the meaning of a sentence.

Ava's host mom relinquishes the grip on her hand so she can greet me. We say our good mornings in local language while exchanging the Christian handshake. Yes, there is a secret handshake that the Christians use. I had to come all the way to one of the most remote parts of the world to uncover it, but Christians can and do get down with their bad selves and engage in some funky hand-jive action. It's a three-part shake, hands hinging on the space between thumb and forefinger. Clasp down, clasp up, clasp down. There's not a lot of shaking up and down nonsense, just the three firm positions. They say it is the handshake that Christians use between themselves because it allows them to make the sign of the cross together. It means they are greeting one another in the name of Jesus.

When I met Ava's mom and she learned I was raised in a Methodist Church, she became very excited and kept repeating "a Methodist from *America!*" and insisted that I come to church with her and Ava this Sunday.

Some deep part of me, my inner spoiled brat, I suppose, wanted to cry out that I couldn't go this Sunday because it's my birthday. What my preferred plan of action on handling my first birthday away from friends, family, and all that I have ever known wasn't quite clear to me, however. Sit in my little shack of mud and straw and mope all day? Maybe leaf through all my photographs of home and cry my eyes out?

The more I think about it, this human invitation may be divine intervention in disguise.

Besides, I've been hoping to get invited to church for a while. My host family attends the Seventh Day Adventist Church and I always have classes on Saturdays, so I haven't been able to join them for services. I'm curious to see how people worship here, but I feel too embarrassed to show up at a church all by myself.

Ava's host mom has decided to keep a hold on one of my hands and begins escorting me to a mud structure at the rear of the marketplace. I hold out my other hand for Ava. Hand-holding is an institution here. I get my hand held for at least ten minutes a day by various people. I kind of like it. Hand-holding is not considered a romantic gesture; it's just good manners. When escorting a friend, you hold onto them. It's almost always same-sex handholding, man to man, woman to woman, boy to boy, or girl to girl. Even though I see men holding hands every day here, I still haven't quite gotten used to seeing it. Especially because the way men hold hands is the way I'm used to seeing love-struck teenagers do it. Not simply one hand clasped in another, but fingers entwined, or occasionally, just pinkies linked together.

I lean over and address Ava sotto voce.

"I had another one last night," I confess in a sing-song taunt.

"Do tell," she replies in the same voice. "Details, woman, spill it."

"I can't do it right now, we're about to go in church," I say. "Escort me home afterwards and I'll give you the blow by blow."

"Whoa, that might be too much detail for me," she says.

"That was just an expression, naughty girl. Stop it before you make me blush," I say with feigned shock. I'm already blushing, though. We both are.

"The only blow I'm interested in is a blow-pop, honey," she says. "I cannot stop eating sugar." She releases my hand and turns out the pocket of her cardigan to reveal a giant handful of no-name, third-world quality penny candy. "This stuff is totally gross, and yet, not gross enough that I refuse to eat it. This is a sickness. I would do anything for sweeties. I would turn tricks on street corners for sweeties. Seriously, I might need some kind of support group. Is there a Sugar Eaters Anonymous? Maybe I should start one. Want to be a charter member?"

"You know I qualify," I say. She's seen me dump an entire week's living allowance on chocolate bars during our trips to town. And it's not even the yummy American so-sweet-it-makes-your-teeth-ache-just-looking-at-it kind. We're talking the closest approximation of chocolate the United Arab Emirates can come up with.

The thing is, the diet here is almost solely comprised of carbohydrates. You eat lumps of maize meal several times a day with small amounts of vegetables as relish. The occasional egg, reconstituted dried fish or peanut sauce is pretty much the only thing that keeps your hair from falling out. Dishes like chicken, beef, goat, or pork are rare for most people. It's just not something that the average subsistence farmer can afford. A special occasion like a wedding feast or a funeral gathering may warrant a goat, but it's a rare treat.

Anyone who knows anything about nutrition will tell you that a diet high in carbohydrates will only make you crave more carbohydrates. You are basically a sugar addict. It's easy to feed that addiction here, too. Nearly every village has a shanty where you can buy dry goods like soap, razors, toilet tissue, Vaseline, shoe polish, salt, cooking oil, and, of course, sweets. The sweets, or "sweeties" as they are usually called, are equal to the fifty-kwacha bill, about a penny. And when I say they are equal, I mean they are as good as money. If a vendor doesn't have proper change, he'll pay you the balance in sweeties whether you want them or not.

When we first came into the country and were introduced to *nshima*, we were told that even though it would seem strange to eat the same thing at every meal, after a few weeks we would get used to it. Then we would crave it. Nothing else would seem as filling or satisfying as *nshima*. I didn't believe it until it happened to me. The last time my host mom made me rice for dinner, I went to bed hungry. It didn't matter how much I ate; cooked rice just doesn't expand in your stomach the way *nshima* does. *Nshima* makes you feel full for hours. That's the beauty of it. It makes people who are nearly starved feel full enough to burst.

The mud structure at the rear of the marketplace turns out to be the Methodist Church. No sign, no steeple, no cross, it's just a large rectangular structure of mud blocks and straw. I've probably ridden past it on my bike a million times and never noticed it before. A woman sweeping the dirt yard in front of the church pauses and greets us with a slight curtsy and open-handed thump to the chest which we give in return. This is the "I've got my hands full, but I'd shake your hand if I could" greeting. She smiles and goes back to sweeping the yard with her twig broom. Traditional brooms don't have handles. You've got to stoop way down to the ground to sweep. Watching women sweep yards is like watching a speed skater in full stride: body bent over at ninety degrees, one arm tucked neatly behind the back, the other swinging in graceful arcs out in front.

We step through the doorway, or what might be called a doorway if it had a door, and give another chest-thumping greeting to a woman sweeping the interior. She's using a traditional indoor-style broom of soft grass with an ornamental woven handle. This kind of broom is meant to catch dust and sweep surface dirt out of indoor living quarters. It's much more finely wrought than the twig brooms one uses for outside sweeping. Those are scraggly and wild as tumbleweed. They clean the dirt by scouring it into submission; every living thing that tries to take root is scratched out of existence.

The lumpy floor clunks hollowly under our feet. The dirt here is hard as concrete, packed rock solid by the countless footfalls of the congregants. A few beams of sunlight dance on the bare expanse of wall at the front of the church where one would normally expect a cross or flower arrangement. I glance up at the latticework ceiling of saplings and straw to spot the offending holes in the thatch. There's quite a few, in fact. I send up a quick prayer for good weather to hold out until I get home; I hadn't realized that I might need an umbrella during the service.

The grass broom whispers in a brisk swish as the woman in front of the church sweeps off two long rectangular lumps of dry mud. I can't imagine what purpose they serve, but if the thorough cleaning they are getting is any indication of importance, I assume they will play some integral role. The church pews, ten on each side of the wide center aisle, are the only items not made out of mud. They are peeled tree trunks, about six inches in diameter perched about a foot and a half from the ground. Not a single nail or screw or even milled lumber appears to have been used in the construction of the building. Something about the whole set-up makes me feel like I've walked into a church in the animated town of Bedrock, as if I'll soon hear the crunch of stone tires rolling up to the building as the Rubbles and Flintstones come to join us for today's service.

Aside from the woman sweeping the pulpit, or rather, the expanse where a pulpit would occupy, there isn't a single body in the place. Looks like the whole congregation, preacher included, will be arriving on African time.

"Too bad I made us late," I say to Ava, my sarcastic tone booming in the empty space. "Shoot, we may even have to split up. I don't see how we are going to be able to sit all together in a packed house like this."

"Hilarious," she says.

I swivel around to meet her gaze.

"When do people show up? I mean, you've been here before," I say. "Was it like this?"

"Yeah, but I guess I thought it would be different this time for some reason," she says. "The one time I was here before we waited for about an hour for everyone to show up. I thought maybe it was just a fluke or something."

"And the service was *how* long?" I ask.

"About three hours or so," she says. "I'm not really sure."

I wander midway up the aisle and stare down at one of the skinny log benches.

"Goodbye, circulation," I mumble.

My hand waves to the pews on the right with a flourish.

"What do you think? Should we sit in the middle of things, or should we go all the way to the front so people won't have to crane their necks to get a good look at us?" I ask.

Ava's host mother clucks her tongue in disapproval, motions to the rear pew on the left.

"Oh, that's the men's side," Ava says. "We have to sit over here."

"There's a men's *side*? We're actually segregated?" I ask.

I've gotten used to the fact that women have a different social status than men. I'm even getting used to sitting lower than the men, talking without direct eye contact, and getting down on my knees when offering something to a man. Observing social etiquette is just polite, after all, no matter what I personally feel about the actual practices. But being segregated in church just feels wrong to me. I suppose I should just be grateful that there are benches on our side of the room since we usually have to sit on the ground.

I saunter back to the rear of the church and plop down on the last bench. The dry wood squeaks in protest.

"Happy Birthday, by the way," Ava says as she plunks herself down beside me, the wood giving out another strained squeal. She beams me a wide, cheesy grin.

"Your birthday?" Ava's mom asks with a cocked eyebrow. She leans over my shoulder conspiratorially. "I won't say to anyone. Don't worry." Our tree trunk pew bows with an agonized groan as she takes a seat on my other side.

"Don't worry?" I say. "Why would I worry?"

She goes on to explain, in her unique brand of broken English, that it is tradition in Zambia to surprise someone on their birthday by throwing water on them. When I ask her why, she's at a loss to explain. I can't tell if she's just having trouble translating her thoughts on the subject into English, or she honestly doesn't know why people do it. I don't know why we do half the things we do in our culture, so I don't blame her. I mean, who came up with the idea of giving "birthday spanks" with "one to grow on?" That doesn't make any more sense than dousing someone with water. I think the water thing almost makes more sense. It's like saying, "Hey remember what it was like when you were born? You were all wet and you were wondering what in the hell just happened to you!"

I had been debating this morning whether or not I should say anything to my host family about my birthday. Now I'm glad I held my tongue.

People begin wandering into the modest chapel, trickling in through the hole in the wall behind us in groups of twos and threes. No one arrives without being escorted by someone, it seems. It's like teenage girls who need to use a public restroom. No one goes in without moral support. Every new arrival makes the rounds inside the church and greets each person in turn, exchanging the cross handshake and inquiring about each other's health. Ava's mom makes a big deal out of me, introducing me to everyone as "a Methodist from *America*" like it's as unbelievable as "a Methodist from the *Moon*." Everyone laughs and shakes their head as if to convey they believed they'd never live to see this day. They go back in for seconds or thirds on the handshake or simply hold on to my hand for a few beats and keep shaking their head like they just cannot believe their good fortune.

One woman wearing a cacophony of colors enters carrying a beaten-up dining room chair and is followed closely on her heels by a young girl holding onto a tattered cushion. The woman places the chair a bit off-center in the expanse at the front of the church, takes the cushion from the girl and positions it on the seat. I am mesmerized by this woman's outfit. She's got no less than five prints going on, from her lime green floral headscarf down to her bright red and yellow rooster-patterned *citenge*.

"Hey, you didn't tell me this was a B.Y.O.C. event," I complain to Ava as I shift my rear on the skinny tree trunk beneath me.

"What? Oh ... bring your own chair?" she says. "That's not a bad idea. I think that's the minister's wife. They bring furniture from their home."

The wildly adorned woman steps outside for a moment and reappears with a small, water-damaged coffee table perched upside-down on her head. She gently places it at the front of the church and begins making the rounds to greet everyone. I shake hands with her, the minister, the choir and the whole congregation. I'm getting to be a pro at this hand-shaking thing.

The choir has assembled at the front, six women (five of whom have breast-feeding children) stand in front of the long mud lump on our side of the church and three men stand at the other. So this is what the lumps of mud are for—the choir loft. I should have figured that out. They are set up the same way as in most churches I've been to. I just wasn't thinking that a log of mud would be a desirable place for sitting. But since I've already lost feeling in both of my legs, I can see why this would be the preferable choice.

The choir begins to sing in a call and response chant, the congregation immediately falling into the refrain with unerring precision and pitch. The rich and exotic chords, like harmony and dissonance married together, send chills down my spine. There is no accompaniment save the clapping of hands and a shuffling stomp of the choir's feet. I rise up on my numb legs to stand with the rest of the congregation and clap in time with the rhythm.

Again and again, the refrain breaks over my body, making me feel totally alive. I am washed clean of every thought other than what is happening in this moment. I can't understand exactly what they are saying, but I have finally caught a hold of how they are saying the words and I join in. At first, I sing under my breath to make sure I'm getting the words and tune right, then eventually I sing loud and strong, my voice lilting on the highest notes of the chords with the rest of the sopranos. Several of the women in front of me send out a shrill ululation, sending a new batch of shivers racing from the top of my head to the tips of my toes and back again. I've never felt this alive at a church service before. I feel my spirit rejoicing inside me, leaping for joy.

The call and response song bounces back and forth in the small space like a beach ball bounding on a multitude of outstretched arms in a concert. It passes to us, we toss it back, it springs back in our direction again. The momentum of the song carries us along in a way that seems to make time stand still, or at least make the passage of time irrelevant. I can't tell if we've been at it for five minutes or twenty-five, and it doesn't matter.

Eventually the caller slows his pace and the choir responds in a final drawn out phrase of closure which we follow. More ululations of joy rise up as an old woman steps into the center aisle and performs what I can only describe as a "gratitude dance." She's bent over all the way down as if she's sweeping, but instead she's cupping her hands together in a silent clap while turning her body in slow circles. It's like she's thanking all of us for this moment we are sharing together to praise and glorify the Almighty. Even more than that, it is as if she is thanking the moment itself. Thanking that inexplicable feeling, that presence that descends upon you when something very right has happened in your life. When a feeling of pure well-being has conquered every other thought and old habits of feeling fear or anger or unworthiness or doubt have been given no quarter. That's how it feels right now. Like a broom of appreciation has swept away every thought but love.

My mood shifts to the more familiar mode of embarrassment, however, as Ava's host mom grabs a hold of my hand and escorts Ava and me to the front of the congregation. The minister introduces us to everyone, again emphasizing the arrival of the Methodist from America, and asks everyone to welcome us. I am expecting some kind of group shout of welcome, but instead the choir kicks up another song behind us and the congregation begins filing up the center aisle to shake our hands all over again. Everyone gets in a shake or two, the minister included. Even the choir gets in on the act, each singing voice performing an intimate serenade as they draw close to shake our hands one by one.

All the formalities taken care of, we settle back into our seats to hear the sermon. The pastor paces back and forth behind the little coffee table, his drab olive suit flapping around as he gesticulates. The other men in suits look the same way, like teenagers who have borrowed their father's clothes, belts cinching in the extra inches so the trousers don't fall off. These are the first world cast-offs. Suits of loud colors, jackets with overly wide or super skinny lapels, trousers with bell-bottoms. If there's one surprising thing I've learned about Africa, it's this: this is the land where suits come to die.

The pastor brings out his small Bemba Bible, the *Bibele*, from his jacket pocket and begins reading a long passage. It doesn't take long, a matter of seconds perhaps, for any confidence in my Bemba speaking abilities to be utterly squelched. I've had a lot of practice at greetings and small talk, so I didn't have any trouble understanding what was going on before, but now that the sermon has begun, I feel like I'm stuck watching an interminable foreign language film whose subtitles have stopped scrolling. Adrift in a sea of nonsensical sounds, I grab ahold of any familiar word like a life raft. *"Aban-tu," that's "people!" Yes, I heard that. That was definitely the word for "people."* After another long interval I hear the words for "we are going" and "thank you" and "road" and "yes."

I am catching about every hundredth word. Certainly not enough to make any sense of the sermon, but often enough that my brain lights up with recognition and keeps me on alert for the next familiar word. I feel a lot like a dog listening to his master, its ears perking up at any mention of its name, the commands it knows, or the phrase "go out for a walk." After almost three months of language classes this is where I'm at: dog-level Bemba.

By the time the pastor wraps up, my legs have gone far beyond the pins-and-needles phase and moved well into the unresponsive-lumps-of-zombie-flesh stage. I can see the congregation shifting in readiness to stand as a woman places a little hand-woven grass basket on the coffee table at the front of the church. It's time for the collection. A bundle of papers rustle as it passes hand over hand down the men's side of the congregation. It lands on the coffee table next to the grass basket; a magazine that looks like it's been through a war. I wonder what words of wisdom can be plucked from these pages. It doesn't look even remotely legible.

A series of slurps and pops are heard as the female choir members pluck the babies from their breasts and swing them onto their backs in their *citenge* slings. Boobs get tucked back into blouses as the choir stands in one accord and assembles up front for the offertory hymn. This is a first for me. I've seen synchronized rising, sitting, swaying, shuffling and clapping and all sorts of body movements from choirs before, but never synchronized baby-slinging.

One by one, the congregants begin to rise as the choir begins a new call and response. Afraid that I'll topple over on my zombie legs, I furtively grind my fists into my thighs to stir up some circulation before attempting to stand.

As if on cue, all the ladies within arms' reach turn around and look at us. Before I even get a chance to figure out what is going on, Ava's host mom unfurls one corner of the *citenge* tucked at her waist to reveal a small wad of bills and begins passing them out to anyone who asks with a raised eyebrow and open palm. I watch in amazement.

Though Ava's host mom is as poor as anyone in the village, she's being given a stipend from Peace Corps for hosting a volunteer so that she can buy enough food and supplies (like kerosene for a lamp) to keep her ward comfortable. She's brought a good portion of this money so that everyone would have the pride of being able to put something in the collection basket.

Witnessing this small act of generosity blows my mind. I almost feel angry at everyone for taking her money, for just expecting her to give it to them because she has some to give. But I can see that she is not upset to dole out her windfall. In fact, she has come prepared for this very situation. She expected people to ask and has come with enough to give.

I have been learning a lot about the "community mindset" of the Zambian people as opposed to the "individual mindset" of the American people, but this is the first time I am really seeing it in action. I don't know how to feel about it. It goes against everything that I have been taught is proper, polite, and appropriate social behavior. I know that this is no place for judgment, that the variance of social mores ranges as far and wide as human beings themselves do, but I find my mind furiously working to put some kind of a label on how I feel about what I've just witnessed. Like an internal pinball machine my feelings bounce from amazement to outrage to pity to confusion to anger to sympathy. Making no sense of anything, my mind settles on my initial feeling of amazement. It's not good or bad, right or wrong, just simply ... amazing.

I wait until everyone has finished staring in our direction before rooting out the kwacha note I tucked into a side pocket of my shorts. I make a mental note to use Ava's mom's method of tying money into the corner of my *citenge* in the future. I feel totally obscene reaching under it like this, like I've just shoved my hand down my pants to scratch an itch.

Rather than passing the collection basket through the pews, people are rising and walking up the aisle to give their offering. I stand and shift my weight from one leg to the other a few times to make sure they still work, then shuffle along in time with the music to give my offering. The men and women are still sticking to their side of the center aisle as they proceed, the women dropping their kwacha in the little grass basket, the men onto the decaying magazine.

Separate offerings.

I watch closely as a man opens his fist over the magazine to deposit his money, but nothing drops out of his hand. He lightly presses his palm down to the wad of bills and walks away. He hasn't lifted anything. No sleight of hand has been performed. He simply faked it. He offered a handful of air and no one seems to have noticed or cared.

Intrigued now, my eyes fix upon the two wads of money and watch the clenched fists alight on the offering piles and open up. Sometimes I see something drop out, sometimes I don't. I notice that everyone has the same technique for placing the offering. Hand down into the money, an open palm press and release. I suppose it helps to conceal the identity of who actually has something to offer and who doesn't. Seeing how no one wants to be singled out as one of the latter, it looks like it's perfectly socially acceptable to "fake it 'til you make it."

I drop my money into the basket and follow the offertory

conga line around the far side of the pews back to our bench in the back row. We sway and clap and sing the refrain until everyone has had a go at the offering table. A small party of ladies in the front row takes up the offering, scoots off to the corner, and sorts through the piles of crunched up kwacha bills. The choir entertains us with a short hymn as the ladies count and recount the stacks of cash.

With a nod from the tallying committee, the hymn ends and we settle back into our log benches, the creaks and snaps of dry wood resounding like a twenty-one cap gun salute. A piece of scrap paper is handed off to the pastor. Apparently, we are about to receive the results of the offering. Looking around at the congregants, you'd think they were awaiting the results of a presidential election. Everyone is on the edge of their seat eagerly anticipating the outcome. Smiles are all around.

The pastor reads the men's tally first: one, five. Polite applause is given to the men for their contribution of one-thousand five-hundred kwacha. Now the women's total: three, eight. Hollers and ululations go up as the women cele-brate their victory on the giving front. I'm reminded of games I used to play in school when the teacher would divide the classroom and pit the boys against the girls. A little friendly competition. A small victory has been won for the ladies today, and I feel ... well ... a little smug.

On that note we are sent on our way with a prayer of thanksgiving and a group hymn. We file out one by one through the opening in the back of the church, each one of us shaking hands down the line of those who have exited, then standing at the end of the queue so that we are in the line too. It's like a reception line at a wedding, except everyone gets to be in it. Once we're all out of the church and have had an opportunity to shake hands with everyone again, some people begin escorting their friends home while others remain behind to dance and sing in the yard. I nab Ava's hand and ask her mother if I can borrow her for an escort. She nods, shakes my hand goodbye, and retreats into the dancing free-for-all.

Ava and I weave through the busy marketplace. I've never seen the place so bustling with commerce. There are vegetables of every description, doughy fritters stacked by the dozen, cups of homemade "sweet beer," mounds of dried fish, little plastic baggies of cooking oil, knotted packets of salt. This must be the after-church rush. People have traveled from all over to come to church. Now it's time to socialize and buy things from their friends and neighbors and relatives and exchange gossip.

Surrounded by so many people, I feel unaccountably lonely. Some sort of nebulous, birthday-related melancholy won't quit dogging me. I can't help but think that this is the first time—maybe ever—that my phone won't be blowing up all day long with family members calling to sing "Happy Birthday to You." I realize Ava asked me a question and is waiting for an answer. I haven't heard a word she said.

"Sorry, hon. You know what? I'm not feeling so hot all of a sudden." The flat of my hand absently rubs against my sternum, trying to erase the dysphoria within. I feel the need to be away from all the people and the noise and the friendly banter of the crowd around us. "I think I'll head home and lay low for a bit. See you later?"

We part ways and I trundle off, past hawkers and hagglers, past the cheering bystanders surrounding the football pitch, past the rows of maize leading up to my family's compound, until I reach the solace of my little mud hut. I lay down on my cot, atop the cheap, scratchy linens, and try not to think about much of anything. Not my birthday, not my family, not my friends, not my discomfort. I just let myself breathe. A few minutes trickle by, then a few more, until the malaise subsides and gives way to numbness. A knock on the door breaks the spell.

"*Odi?* How are you doing in there, birthday girl? You feeling any better?" Ava and Kelsea (she, of the fifty-goat dowry) peek their heads in.

I smile, finger comb my hair and sit up on the mattress. "Strong like bull," I retort.

"In that case, prepare yourself for festivities." The girls enter with singing, not the usual "Happy Birthday to You" but with the opening lines of 50 Cent's "In Da Club" while doing their best—yet utterly laughable—attempt at rapping and popping as they make their way over to me. Kelsea hands me a homemade card, a birthday cake drawn on the front in crayon.

"Seriously, you guys, this is so nice. I can't believe you did this for me," I say.

But even as I say the words, I know that if it were one of their birthdays, I would do the same thing. Though we hardly know each other, we are all we've got out here. And I know the feeling of camaraderie we've come to enjoy over the last three months will only grow over time. These people are my family now. They're the only ones who can understand what it is I'm going through and why I will continue to choose to go through it. They are in the same boat. Heck, not only are they in the same boat, but they are rowing the same oar I am. Like bench mates aboard a Viking ship, we're relying on each other's strength to keep the momentum going.

"Okay, now for the goods," says Ava. She hands me a mound of hard candy in brightly colored cellophane wrappers and a packet of instant root beer powder, sans fizziness, to drop in my Nalgene. "That's if you're feeling brave," she laughs. "It could be god-awful. We didn't test drive it first."

"Oh, you shouldn't have," I exclaim. "You know how I can't stand sugar." I take the handful of birthday sweeties and immediately unwrap one to pop in my mouth. I roll my eyes in mock ecstasy to coax a laugh out of them.

"Okay, party time! I don't have much in the way of entertainment here, but I do have these bad boys if either of you ladies are feeling lucky," I say and wave a deck of cards enticingly.

We deal the cards and gamble and cuss and giggle. There's no bit of pleasure, no sugary treat or mefloquine-fueled dream that can compete with this. Having an unexpected good laugh with friends: this is the sweetness that makes life worth going on with, and it's worth celebrating another year of it.

❧ 7 ❧

Close Up

"**S**eka!" the photographer says to the child in my arms. This is the Bemba version of "say cheese," the command form of the verb "to laugh."

Click.

I don't know how I've managed to get myself into this situation. I don't know any of these children. I've never seen them or talked to them before. I've certainly never taught them at their school. Yet somehow, I have managed to be in their school photos, each child sitting on my lap like I'm Santa Claus.

Another child climbs into my lap. She smells like one of those huge logs of perfumed soap that Zambians use to wash everything. Dishes, clothes, kids. Doesn't matter. I hug her in a bit tighter and inhale the sweetness of her.

Click.

What a surreal moment. I didn't know what to expect

when the photographer waved me over to be in the school's group photo. I thought it was a lark at first, but he was dead serious. I figured, sure, why not? Throw a token *muzungu* in there for contrast. I've been here long enough to know that many people love to have their picture taken with a *muzungu*. It's the ultimate novelty photo. It's like pulling out a picture of yourself posing with Mickey Mouse from a trip to Disney Land. It's proof you were there and hung out with the big guy himself.

The perfumed girl slides down from my lap and two more children flock to me. These kids smell like most of the other children. It's a faint vomity/pee/sour milk aroma. They obviously have a younger sibling at home and are getting their clothes washed with the diapers and spit-up rags.

Click.

The photographer thanks me for my time; all the kids have been photographed. The teachers spend another half an hour or so holding onto my hand and thanking me profusely. What they are thanking me for, I'm not quite sure. Being born white?

Where I grew up, pointing out someone's race is deemed impolite. Only in the case of having to describe someone's physical appearance will you bring it up, and even then, you will refer to the person in the most politically correct terms. Why is it that race always seems to become the elephant in the room, when variations of physical appearance among people across this big and beautiful world are natural and so obviously present? I thought that coming here, being the minority for once, might enjoin discussion about my race and I would become the elephant in the room. I have learned, however, that the color of the elephant trumps all. From what I've experienced, being white invites discussion. I am reminded daily, either by words or by action, how very white I am. I couldn't forget my race if I tried.

I wave my farewells to the group and start off down the dirt path to the hostel where I'm temporarily hanging my hat. Our swear-in ceremony is tomorrow, so we've been corralled into a nearby housing block on the Peace Corps ceremonial grounds for convenience. These barracks are easily the crummiest accommodations I've ever stayed in. The little mud huts we've been residing in during training are luxurious compared to this place.

For one thing, there are not enough mattresses and pillows to go around, so several of us are camping out on the floor. There are no mosquito nets, no dressers, no curtains on the windows and no handles on the doors to the bathrooms (which, incidentally, are shared co-ed with an adjoining room). You open and close the door by grabbing the hole where the handle would be. Real private-like.

The worst part of the place, for me, is that we can't shower. The water pressure is so low that it can't make it up the spout that high. We have a trickle in the sink (cold only) and the john has to be flushed with a bucket drawn from an outside spigot.

Everyone has taken to calling the hostel the "hostile." The three nights we are spending here are more than enough to make us look forward to mud hut living again, even though it means saying goodbye to everyone we've lived with, learned with, and grown with these last few months. It's time to kiss our training period goodbye. We'll be all on our own after tomorrow.

We've spent the last two weeks at the sites that we will soon call home, scattered hundreds of miles apart from one another in eight different provinces. I'm one of two volunteers who will reside in Copperbelt Province. The other volunteer, Izzy, lives in a village called Mikata, fifty-three clicks northwest and uphill of me. Hours of hell on a bicycle, in other words. Though she'll be my closest American neighbor, I can't imagine I'll be knocking on her door to borrow a cup of sugar all that often.

The dirt road darkens with dampness as I enter under a thicket of tall shade trees. I pick my way down the mud path with care, lifting the hem of my *citenge* to the side so I can see the path clearly under my feet. There's always a small trail that bends and twists circuitously on a dirt road—the highest and driest ground marked by those who have traveled through successfully before you. If you don't follow the highly trafficked ribbon of road marked by bicycle tires and shoe prints, you are likely to sink right into the muck. You only have to make that mistake once in order to learn your lesson.

I'm learning lots of lessons here in the bush. Usually the hard way.

One lesson I've learned recently is that in a country of seventy-three languages, the local tongue can shift swiftly from a broadly understood common dialect to an obscure tribal one within the space of a quick morning jog. It turns out that the language I've been spooning into my brain day and night for the last three months will be of little use to me. My village, though located in a Bemba speaking province, is inhabited largely by the Lamba people. I don't know a lick of Lamba.

That is, I don't know how to say anything besides the old "how are you, I'm fine" routine. After being introduced to practically every inhabitant within a ten-mile radius, I've had some good practice at my Lamba greetings. I've smiled at and shaken hands with hundreds, if not thousands of the Lambas. I even had my picture taken with a few. My arrival is the biggest news to hit the place in years; there is a new *muzungu* in town.

I shade my eyes with my free hand as I step into the sunshine again and let the hem of my *citenge* drop back down. The road is wide and dry all the way up the incline to the front gate of the hostel. I hear a smash of bottles and a whoop in the distance up ahead. Sounds like we're having a beer cricket match today.

I don't know how much beer cricket actually resembles a true game of cricket, having never played the sport myself, but I'm pretty certain the similarity begins and ends with the fact they are both referred to as cricket. Beer cricket was invented by Peace Corps Zambia some years back and has enjoyed popularity among the volunteers and American military in Zambia ever since. The field is comprised of two goals (marked by empty beer bottles measured one Frisbee width apart) and a central cup of beer lined on either side by the dead soldiers of previous play lined across the field like a fifty-yard line. Two-person teams take turns attempting to knock down the bottles of beer in the opponent's goal with a skillful fling of the Frisbee (a vertically-thrown "hammer toss" being the most widely-employed technique). Fouls such as overstepping the throwing line, crossing the center divide to intercept the Frisbee or accidentally knocking down your own beer bottles during play result in a penalty. You must drink the full cup of beer in the center. Additionally, each player takes swigs from his own bottle before each new man is "at bat" or whenever deemed necessary during play.

Since I'm not adept at throwing or catching Frisbees, running fast, or chugging beer, I'm pretty much out of the game. I do like to watch by the sidelines, though. I often fulfill the role of the beer wench, filling the cup after penalties and bringing the players a fresh cold one when they drain their bottles. Well, a fresh one, anyway. They are rarely cold after the first half hour or so. Buckets of ice would be a great addition to the game, but are hard to come by out here in the bush.

I summit the hill in time to see the Frisbee sail through

the beer bottle goal without grazing either of them. The girls defending the goal cry out in relief and high five each other.

"Damn it!" exclaims Paul. "This is why you need to learn the hammer toss, man. None of this namby-pamby shit. You've got to hurl that mother! When are you going to listen to me?"

"Whenever you get off my ass," retorts Jason. "It's hard to hear what you're saying when you're all the way down there."

"Funny, that's exactly what your mother said to me last night," says Paul. He's sporting some kind of "lumbersexual pirate" look today, with a scraggly black beard, red bandanna cap, jeans rolled to the knee.

"Oh really, you want to know what your mother said to me last night?" Jason ruffles his spiky white blond hair with one hand while rummaging around for a clean cup with the other. The penalty for passing through the goal without hitting anything is a full cup of beer for both team members.

As Jason regales the troops with the myriad desires of Paul's mom, I check in with the opposing team. They're up ten points and hardly breaking a sweat.

"Well done, ladies," I say. "Give 'em hell." I turn to Kelsea. "So, I hear you'll be running with these jokers for a while, huh?" I motion over my shoulder to the bickering pirate and Billy Idol look-alike.

"Yep," she admits. "We're the Northwestern Province gang."

"Gee," I say. "Some girls get all the luck."

"Sure you don't want to trade sites with me?" she asks. "You can hang with the testosterone twins and I'll man your swimming pool."

She's referring to the crown jewel of my village, Lake Kashiba, which may quite possibly be the only safe swimming hole in all of Zambia. Assuming you can swim, that is. Lake Kashiba is, for all intents and purposes, bottomless.

A deep chasm fed by an underground aquifer, the lake has no inlet, outlet, or shallow end. This means no crocodiles and no schistosomiasis, the two biggest dangers of swimming in this region of Africa. It's quite small as lakes go—ten minutes hard stroke from one side to the other if you've got it in you. Fortunately for me, I was a competitive swimmer all through my youth. Swimming is one of the few things I do well.

"I appreciate the offer, but I think I'm stuck with my site now," I say with mock regret. "It will be hard work, all those laps under the hot, hot sun, but someone's gotta do it."

"Yeah, you're really taking one for the team," she says, and turns her attention back to the game. The guys have finished their penalty drink and have announced the game back on with a resounding chorus of "I love my Green Bay Packers."

We shoot each other a sideways smile and accompanying eye roll and say our farewells. Exiting the cricket pitch in favor of a less frenzied environment, I wander over to my quarters in the barracks. It has just occurred to me that I'll be on Zambian national television tomorrow and I've got nothing to wear. Nothing good, anyway.

I've packed one requisite dress for an official capacity, such as this will be, as specified by the Peace Corps' recommended clothing list. It's not sleeveless, not low-cut, and not above the knee. Unremarkable and unflattering, as I remember. I haven't had an occasion to dig it out of my suitcase until now. I wonder if it still fits.

I open the door to my room and gaze upon what appears to be the aftermath of an indoor cyclone. Open suitcases occupy nearly every surface of the room, the contents of which are strewn about in loose piles (to the trained eye) of clean, mostly clean, mostly unclean, and completely heinous. Rooting around the cleans in the bottom of my suitcase, I find the edge of the gauzy floral garment I'm after.

Not too badly wrinkled, I think. I strip down to my

skivvies and pull the dress on over my head to give it a trial run. The fabric flutters down and falls with a swish, waving like a flag from the bust down. I grab handfuls of fabric at the waistline. Who's gone into my suitcase and replaced my dress with this circus tent? I know I've been losing weight, but this is ridiculous.

I walk over to the mirror hanging above the sink and stand on my tiptoes to try and get a good look. It's worse than merely dumpy, I look like I might be heading into my second trimester. This might be my worst fashion disaster of all time.

The door opens and Ava comes in with an armload of *citenge* fabric tied in a plastic sack. She's returned from her final fitting with a tailor in town. She, like many of the other volunteers, has had a traditional Zambian dress made for the event tomorrow. If I had had the foresight to try on my dress earlier, I could have been in her shoes right now. Her fancy plastic Zam-shoes. Damn it.

"Tell me the truth," I say, my voice unnaturally high with panic, "does this dress make me look pregnant?"

"A bit," she says, then starts backpedaling upon seeing my expression. "Not in a bad way though. It still looks nice. Don't worry about it."

"Sure, there's no reason to worry about looking pregnant as long as it's in a 'nice' way. It's only national television, after all. I'm sure the country will be looking on thinking, 'look at all those brave young people about to go off into the bush ... and that older pregnant lady, now she's *really* got moxie!'"

"What're you going on about?" she says. "This is Zambia, land of ill-fitting clothes. You'll look more at home in this place than I will with this get-up." She holds her bundle of wildly colored cloth. "And you don't look old, either. Enough about that."

I slide the dress over my head, toss it back in the clean

pile by my open suitcase, and flop onto the *citenge* serving as my mattress. A moment later, a cellophane-wrapped sweet hurls through the air, skids off my bare tummy, and lands at my side.

"You're my real friend, Ava."

❧ 8 ❧

Lamba Lessons

I pause to tighten the *citenge* threatening to slip from my waist. Attempting to remedy the enormity of my one good dress, I cinched it with the wrap, but the fabric has proved too slippery for this to work well. I figured today would be a good day for a floral dress, even one several sizes too large. It's Easter Sunday. My first Sunday and first holiday in the village. My new village, that is. For the next two years, I'll be calling the scrap of earth allotted to the Chikuni family near St. Anthony's Mission "home."

St. Anthony's is home to many churches, besides the catholic mission for which it is named. I'm on "Church Row," it would seem. Beyond my family compound of Chikuni lies a Pentecostal Church, followed a few paces down the road by the Seventh-Day Adventist Church, then the Baptist Church and beyond that, the Hall of Jehovah's Witnesses. My hut is the only structure visible from the road that is not a religious institution for at least a mile.

I'd like to visit all the churches in the area to see how people worship here. I think it will be an interesting cultural observation, and besides, it's not like the commute will kill me. According to my new neighbors, the best choir can be found at the Baptist Church. No contest as to which place to attend first!

Unfortunately, I don't know how I am ever going to be able to show my face around there again. I really goofed up this time.

The preacher was on a rampage about the amount coming in at collections. He was doing his best to round up more funds, even going so far as to point out people in the congregation and site "ten-thousand kwacha, ten-thousand kwacha." Now, ten-thousand kwacha is only about two bucks. I thought, sure, why not? I'd put that much in the collection plate at home. No big deal. So I dropped it in.

I might as well have dropped a bomb.

Apparently, the preacher must have been talking about some kind of lifetime goal rather than a one-shot deal. The totals were announced. Men: four-hundred kwacha, Women: eleven-thousand and fifty kwacha. There were gasps and cheers all around. Everyone turned to get a good look at me, the rich *muzungu* who has come into their midst.

One of the pivotal tenets of Peace Corps service is to live within the level of society that you are aiding at approximately the same standard of living. If people live in mud huts, you live in a mud hut. If the usual mode of transport is a bicycle, you will ride a bicycle. Sure, some countries have a higher standard of living. If I was serving in an Eastern European country, I might have an apartment and perhaps a motorcycle to get around. But this is where I'm at. The lowest of the low-income groups of the world. People here are lucky to make two hundred dollars a year. And I just plopped two of those dollars into the collection basket.

Way to go, Brainiac.

I'm going to have a hell of a time trying to convince people that I don't have money to lend them, that I haven't come here to solve all of their problems with a handout.

Ten thousand. Ten thousand.

Why did that guy have to keep harping on that number? If only I understood more local language maybe I would have saved myself this embarrassment. The problem is, I hardly know any local language. I've only begun to crack the basics of the Bemba language. Now I've got to throw myself into a-whole-nother dialect: Lamba.

The tops of the mango trees lining my yard come into view as I crest the hill. This is my landmark for home. I pad along the little dirt path winding through the trees and pause to survey my village as it comes into view. If you didn't know better, you would think that one of the tidy homes of burnt brick with corrugated tin roof belonged to the rich and exceedingly philanthropic white lady. But no, the dumpiest hut on the lot is mine. Okay, it's not a dump. It's a fixer-upper. Besides, I wanted a mud hut and that's exactly what I got. A house made out of mud, painted with mud, situated on a mud lot. Mud to the max.

The size is just right, about the same square footage as a one-car garage, and it is fully stocked with all the furniture and household items I need, thanks to the former volunteer who occupied it. It just needs some cosmetic help. The white wash of mud on the exterior is cracked and flaking. A swath of red mud detailing the house's midline has been almost entirely melted off by last season's rains. What was once—I'm sure—a cheery, decorative border now leaves the impression that the house has been garroted and is bleeding to death. The roof is all but completely caved in on one side, the displaced chunks of thatch hanging mere inches from the ground. The pit latrine behind the hut is in much worse shape. It's missing half the roof, and one of the walls looks like it is auditioning to be part of a tower in Pisa. A cow wandered in there the other day, got stuck, panicked, and nearly took the whole thing down. Having that fixed is priority number one. Out of all the ways I'd prefer to die, being crushed, trapped and possibly drowned in a pit of my own waste is not one of them.

A greeting is called out to me from behind. I turn to see Bana Mpundu fanning the ashes in her fire pit with a small ragged sheet of metal. She's trying to resuscitate the coals leftover from the morning fire. Her infant naps soundly in the *citenge* sling on her back, the dead weight of his little leg swinging in time to the blows of her fan.

I greet her in reply and take a seat on an overturned bucket by her fire to watch her work. Bana Mpundu is my closest neighbor, but I doubt she'll be my closest friend. Her English is as good as my Lamba, which means it is non-existent. For the last three days since my arrival we have greeted each other and sat around in silence. Our favorite pastime, one that transcends the language barrier, is to watch "Boy TV." Her four-year-old twin sons, Jacob and Judah, are a constant source of entertainment. Today's episode of Boy TV has a guest star, the cereal box of the *muzungu*. Someone's gone fishing for treasure in my rubbish pit and has scored a prime piece of entertainment. The boys are taking turns wearing the cornflake box as a hat, smashing it on the ground, or holding it aloft and prancing around the yard like it's the Olympic torch.

Bana Mpundu stops fanning the fire pit and inspects the coals. The embers flicker with an amber glow; they have a life of their own now. She begins to build the fire by propping some small sticks against the glowing embers and bends forward to give them a gentle blow. I study her face as she watches wisps of smoke rise from the fire. Who is this woman? What village does she hail from? How did she meet her husband? Did she fall madly in love with him or was it an arranged marriage? I don't know anything about her and I don't know how to ask her these questions. I don't even know her real name. Bana Mpundu, the only name I have to call her, means "mother of twins." This is what she is, but not who she is. Then again, this is how the Zambians define themselves. You are only called by your birth name until you become a parent, then you are the mother or father of your children. Anyone who doesn't have children will go by their own name, the "Ba" prefix falling before the first name or sometimes the surname in the case of men. It seems you're only you until you procreate, then you're someone new. You are greater than yourself; you have multiplied.

Nearly everyone I have been introduced to is Bana someone (mother of someone) or Bashi someone (father of someone). Now if you've got six or more kids, which most families do, this can get pretty confusing since you can be called the mother or father of any of your children. Fortunately, people are usually referred to by the name of their first child. If I were Zambian, I'd be thinking long and hard about the name of that first child, since people would be calling me that for the rest of my life.

As it stands, I'm Ba Christine. Mother to no one. Unless you count the cat I've inherited. She kind of came with the house.

Moglie's her name. My little pest control specialist. She's a tough cookie and looks the part with her shrewd green eyes and tattered left ear. Her coat, even meticulously clean, looks like a mottled mess. She is the most indescribable color of cat I have ever seen. They call her the "white" cat around here, though she's anything but. She's a white-washed calico with tabby stripes inside the colored blotches. She's every color a cat's got in her. Maybe she's the white cat because she loves white people. She's a lap cat in a land where no one touches animals. Worse than that, it's a land where affection, attention, or adoration of animals is considered absurd. The day that a *muzungu* moved into the village was probably the happiest day in all of her nine lives. She's become my shadow during the day and my bed companion in the night.

Moglie's real owner lives just across the well from me. Bana Francisco. She's someone who I think I'll become very close with. She and Bashi Francisco have been schooled well in the English language and have helped me a great deal with settling in. In addition to being a noble, generous and bright woman, Bana Francisco also serves as the headwoman of our village. She's a powerful ally, and living in her village means I am considered part of her family.

This is one of the interesting and unexpected things about Zambia: though it is a paternalistic culture, the chief, headman or community leader is just as likely to be a woman as it is a man. Women are considered, on the whole, to be more honest than men, therefore more fair in judgment and less susceptible to corruption. This makes them a natural selection for an impartial judge, which is the main role of the headman: settling disputes.

Bana Francisco can be seen serving in this capacity several times a day. Whether it's for adults who have traveled some distance to seek her counsel or for her own brood of children squabbling in the yard during play, she is the judge and jury for any unsettled score. She's our own personal small claims court handler, the Judge Judy of St. Anthony's.

The wind changes direction and blows a gust of smoke in my face forcing me to cough.

"*Icushi*," says Bana Mpundu. She indicates that I should move over to her other side.

"*Icushi*. What does that mean? Smoke?" She stares at me blankly. I wave my fingers through the wisps of smoke rising from the fire.

"*Icushi*," she confirms. She points to her other side again.

"No thank you, it's hot. I'm going inside to rest," I say, and point to my house as I rise.

She shrugs her shoulders and says something in a tone of voice that sounds like "suit yourself," and goes back to building her fire.

As I reach my front door, a young man enters my yard and calls to me. We exchange the usual niceties before getting to the business of the purpose of his visit.

"I was told that you were very fat," he says while shaking his head in disbelief. "And indeed, you are huge!" He giggles with the joy of his discovery.

I look down at my body, as if to see what he can from his perspective. Even after my recent weight loss, I know I still look twice the size of these tiny Zambian women. Body weight is a measure of health and wealth in these parts. To them I am huge; the richest, fattest woman of them all. I will myself to take the compliment in stride and not descend into tears.

"Thank you," I say with a forced grin. "That's just what every girl loves to hear. What can I do for you Mister ...?"

"My name is Wesley," he says.

"Ba Wesley." I dip my head in acknowledgement.

"My mother, she is Bana Martha," he says.

I stare at him blankly in response. I've met so many Bana Somebodies that they've all melded together in my mind.

"That one, my mother, she is a nurse at the clinic. She said you are wanting someone to learn Lamba," he says.

I see the resemblance now. The oval face, high forehead, wide eyes, and easy way with laughter. He's his mother through and through.

"Yes, of course," I say. "Have you come for the job?"

"I can," he replies.

"You can ... be my tutor?" I ask.

"I can."

We stand in silence for a few beats. I'm not sure how to negotiate a price for this type of service. I'm hoping he'll throw out an offer first. The only number coming to my mind is ten-thousand kwacha. That two bucks is going to haunt me for a while.

"I also need more English. For school," he says.

"I see, so you would like me to teach you some English? Shall we trade English lessons for Lamba lessons?"

"Yes." He starts into a fit of giggles like I have told a hilarious joke.

"Okay," I say, and smile like I just got the joke too. "I can."

9

Happy Trails

F lakes of wood and graphite fly from the end of my pencil as I shave it with my ten-inch all-purpose kitchen knife. My tutor waits patiently while I finish writing down the last definition. We've been at this for a few weeks now, meeting in the shade of my *nsaka* to share language lessons with one another. This is done more in English than in Lamba. His language skills far outweigh my own.

"So, let me make sure I've got this straight. *Ukuposa* can either mean 'to throw something' or 'to braid hair' *or* 'to weave a basket?'"

"Yes. And can be sick," he says.

"I thought that sick was the word for pain," I say. "My head is paining, my stomach is paining ..."

"Yes, but this sick." He bends over double and pretends to retch.

"Oh," I say, "you mean vomit."

"Yes," he says, "to vomit. That is the one."

"That's funny, we say the same thing. The throwing thing. We call it 'throwing up.' Or there's 'hurling' which can also mean to throw something," I explain. "Even 'tossing' works. We might say you 'tossed your cookies.'"

"Tossed your cookies?" Wesley shakes his head. "Now I am learning some English!" He launches into his trademark fit of giggles.

I may be the first and only person to instruct a Lamba on a hundred and one ways to say "barf" in the English language. No matter what I do from here on in, at least I can say I've left my mark.

I look over my myriad definitions of *ukuposa* and remember with a stab of homesickness how my cousin can't stand to hear the phrase "throw up." We would use the code name "curl your hair" if the subject came up in conversation. I think it's funny that the Lamba word for upchuck actually *can* mean to style hair. What are the odds?

It seems that many of the words in Lamba have several definitions, like there just weren't enough words to go around so they had to double up on meanings. This is part of what the locals claim makes the language so easy to learn; there are very few words as compared to English. That might seem like simplicity to some, but I find that having words with multiple definitions to be the epitome of confusion. Misunderstandings are sure to abound. At least on my end they are.

Even subtleties such as wanting something as opposed to needing something don't exist in the language. You can't contradict yourself by saying that you want to do something but you really need to do something else. E.g. I want to go out and play but I need to stay in and do my homework instead. The thought here is that wanting something is the same as having a need for it. There is no difference in definition. When a man says he wants you, he also is literally saying he needs you. That must be a pretty persuasive argument to the women. Not that I'm worried about facing that kind of dilemma anytime soon. I'm more concerned about being able to hear the difference between "I would like to weave a basket" and "I've gotta puke." Unfortunately, there is no difference. Context is the all-important key.

Bana Mpundu calls the "sitting greeting" to us as she returns from the well. She's a balancing act of baby on the back, full pail on the head, and plastic jugs in each hand. We call the "working greeting" back to her as she vanishes into her home with her full load.

I'm getting good at the greeting thing. The regular "how are you" is always a good standby, but the way most people greet each other here depends on what the person is doing. If the person is traveling on the road when you meet them, you throw them a "So you are traveling, respected one." The answer is an affirmation "Yes, indeed, respected one." There's a laughing greeting, an eating greeting, a busily working greeting, a returning home greeting, a hey-looks-like-you-just-woke-up greeting, even a suffering greeting. There's no limit to how you can greet someone, just as long as you know the verb for the action the person you wish to greet is performing.

"So, that child, the one of Bana Mpundu," I say pointing to the infant strapped to my neighbor's retreating figure, "His name is 'Icoola,' right? Isn't that the same word for bag?"

"Yes, he is the bag," he replies.

"Isn't that kind of a weird name?" I ask, as if I'm some kind of an expert on the names of this region. Every name is a weird name to me. The traditional names are exotic by virtue of their innate foreignness, and the English names seem bizarrely out of place. In what generation and in what place had a certain European gentleman named Wesley come to reside in Zambia? And through how many mouths had his name been spoken through in order to land in this time and this place upon my tutor?

"It's very common," Wesley explains. "It's the child who comes after the twins. He is always Icoola. Let me explain." He rubs his hands together and looks up to the sky as if hoping to see the answer up there. "When the woman grows the children, in the body, we say there is a bag there. The children they grow in the bag."

"The womb, or do you mean the actual placenta?" I interject.

"Yes, we say it is the bag," he continues, as if this explains everything. "Now when the twins come out, there you have the children. The next time this woman can give birth we say, now here is the bag itself!" He holds his hands in front of him like a catcher at home plate and ogles the space therein, as if he has just delivered the bag-child in question. He looks up at me and breaks into another giggling jag.

I laugh with him for a moment too, then exchange my chuckle to an outcry of frustration. I slap the back of my calf vigorously. The worm in my leg has been more active lately. The tickling itch of it burrowing below my skin triggers an instant derailment of my peace of mind. It's been months of this now, my wellbeing a state of perpetual train wreck. If only I could sleep through the night, I might have better control of my emotions. Unfortunately, this is when my leg's little tenant is the most active.

"I seriously don't know what to do about this," I say to Wesley, pulling my *citenge* to the knee and turning my calf to him. "They say it will just die off eventually, but there's no telling when that is."

He leans forward to examine my leg more closely. The raised red line of meandering worm track has crazed my leg from ankle to mid-calf and back again. The worm used to enjoy making lazy circles in the sinewy region above the inside ankle bone, until one day it decided to make a beeline for calf country and made a straight shot to the top of the soleus muscle. I guess the high country didn't agree with him, or perhaps he felt home sick, for he's now doubled back and is carving a tunnel down the center of the gastrocnemius towards the heel. From a distance, it looks as if I handed a red marker to a kindergartener and asked him for a tattoo of a giraffe.

"Get medicine," Wesley diagnoses.

"I tried, but Peace Corps doesn't have any medicine for this right now," I explain. Part of me wants to launch into a sarcastic, *"Gee why didn't I ever think of that? Good thing I have you around to help me,"* but since sarcasm is really wasted here, I opt for the more straightforward, snark-free answer.

He furrows his brow. "Why Peace Corps?"

"Because I am required to go to their doctor." Again, the short answer.

He sits silently for a moment and ruminates on my response. I hope he won't ask why Peace Corps doesn't allow us to get treated at any of the local clinics. I wouldn't want to insult the level of competence and education of his nation's medical staff. Especially considering his mother is a nurse.

"You can go to the clinic," he says. "They can have the medicine."

I began formulating my rebuttal, then caught myself before opening my mouth. Why not go there? I work there, don't I? Am I really afraid to go for treatment at an institution that I help to represent? This is nonsense. If I needed oral surgery or an appendectomy, sure, I would haul my britches over to Lusaka and get some real medical attention. But for a de-worming prescription? Surely this is right up their alley. This is not a first-world concern, it's a third-world one. I might as well get third-world medical treatment.

Wesley watches me closely while I wrestle with my thoughts.

"I can escort you," he offers.

"You can?" I'm wringing my hands and looking up at him uncertainly, like a child looking for reassurance.

"I can." He rises from his seat on an overturned water bucket.

Looks like language lessons are over for today. I rise from my spot on the ground and roll up my grass mat. When I'm away from home I take everything out of my *nsaka* to indicate that I'm closed for business. Otherwise, I've got my little outdoor gazebo set for company, a carpet of grass for the women and a couple mud bricks and water containers for the men to perch on. I've ordered a set of four small, wooden stools from the local carpenter so that I can entertain in style, but they won't be ready until sometime next week. I'm looking forward to that day. I may even promote myself from my spot on the ground.

I secure the padlock on the door of my hut and give it a tug to make sure it's locked. Such a silly precautionary measure, really. Anyone could break in with a few solid kicks to any one of the mud walls, but at least it will prevent kids from entering in and pilfering things like sweets, books, and other objects of interest.

Wesley and I walk along in companionable silence on the dirt path towards the clinic. He only has two more weeks at home before he returns to school in Mpongwe. That's our boma: bureau of mercantile affairs. I think boma is some leftover British colonial term for not really a town, but close enough. Mpongwe is the nearest paved road, the nearest telephone line, the nearest public transport bus, the nearest fax machine. It is the closest thing to what might qualify as "civilization." It's also a full day's walk from here. Our language lessons are about to be over for good.

We call greetings out to each household as we pass: *you are working, you are washing, you are eating.* The only yard we don't yell into is the one belonging to Bana Luke. Her elderly mother is sitting in the *nsaka* in the yard. You never yell to an elder. It's considered rude and disrespectful. We stand silently on the edge of her yard until we catch her eye then pantomime our greetings with a bend of the knees and gentle thump to the chest. She taps her chest in return. We smile at each other congenially for a moment, then continue on our way.

The path winds through village after village until it empties into the rear of the schoolyard. The football pitch is currently buried under three and a half feet of grass. As soon as a tournament looms near the kids will be out in full-force with their slashers. The metal sticks with their curved scythe-like blade will swing like metronomes all over this field, each child operating as a single propeller blade of a massive human-powered lawnmower.

We thread our way through the tunnel in the grass the children have carved with the foot traffic of their daily commute to school. The path is only wide enough for single-file, so I walk ahead of Wesley keeping my eyes to the ground to look for snakes in the road. About ten steps in, something strong grabs a hold of my leg and sends me headlong into yelping, scrambling, downward-facing-dog position on the ground. I haven't been bitten. I've been tripped.

I bring myself to my feet again and assure Wesley I haven't been hurt, only frightened. On close examination of the path, we soon find the culprit. Hovering about a foot from the ground is a tidy granny knot joining the grass from opposite sides of the path. It seems I've fallen prey to a classic child's prank. Classic for Africa, anyway. Land of massively tall and steely strength grasslands.

"Kids," says Wesley with a shrug.

I look down the path and spot several more booby-traps, some already tripped with torn grass hanging from one end of the knot and some still fully armed. I turn from the gauntlet and look to Wesley with a cocked eyebrow.

"Be my guest," I say. My colloquialism is lost on him. He stands patiently, waiting for me to finish my sentence. "You walk first. I will follow."

He shrugs again and with no apparent care for snakes he blazes a new trail through the thicket of grass running parallel to the existing path. I stay as close to his heels as possible. As we near the school, the lessons of several classrooms float through the broken glass of the windows and mingle into a curious musical number. The ABC's are being sung to the tune of "Auld Lang Syne." A boy reads aloud from the board "twenty, thirty, forty, fifty." Another classroom parrots its teacher. "The girl goes to school. The girl goes to school. The girl has a book. The girl has a book." The word "girl" is being pronounced in that curious African way that is somewhere between "gal" and "gull" that I haven't quite mastered yet.

The myriad bits of rhyme and song and repetition remind me of that point in a musical or opera where people who have been singing their bit of song and story suddenly collide into a duet, then a trio, then a quartet, and so on until the original melody is lost in a lovely mess.

From the corner of my eye, a scrap of color beckons to me as we step off the playing field and onto the main thorough-fare of St. Anthony's Mission. It's a long strip of light yellow *citenge* lying like a shed snakeskin trampled and half hidden in the road. I swoop on it with the swiftness of a seagull at a neglected picnic basket.

Tucking the little treasure into my shoulder bag, I glance up at Wesley, hoping he hasn't noticed my second dive to the ground in as many minutes. He has noticed, though, and his face has exactly the look on it that I was dreading. The what-in-God's-name-are-you-doing-picking-up-someone's-old-band-aid-and-sticking-it-in-your-handbag look. That's what these are, really. It's possible the hem of a *citenge* got snagged on a bicycle chain or torn by a passing ox cart, but this scrap was most likely tied to a wound and fell off during play on the football pitch. These little bits of torn cloth are, aside from the cellophane wrappers of sweeties, the most commonly found roadside garbage in Zambia.

"For my welcome mat," I explain lamely.

I have to admit, it is a little disgusting the way I've been collecting these scraps. I do a whole sterilizing procedure with them, though. They soak overnight in a chlorine bath, then get scrubbed by hand with washing paste until every speck of filth is gone, then set to hang dry on the clothesline running from the roof of my hut to the monkey orange tree so that it can bake in the sun's rays. Then they are trimmed, twisted together, and poked line by line in half-inch intervals through an old mealie meal sack with a stick I fashioned just for this purpose. It's a long, tedious process, dependent solely upon what materials I happen upon during my walks. But it has been, on some days, the only reason to leave my hut. It's a game for me, my own little treasure hunt. The spoils may be the most pathetic treasure imaginable, seeing how even Zambians consider it trash, but since it gets me out of the house each day when I would rather hide inside my hut curled up with a book, its worth is beyond measure.

The treasure hunt forces me to socialize, practice my language, get some exercise, and explore new paths through the bush. I bring a pocket-sized notepad with me to map my route as I go. Bit by bit, mile by mile, I learn my new home. Along with the bits of cloth I gather new information, a group of huts on this path, a well over there, a burial ground behind that field. Each gets penciled into my map as I go, the paths spanning for pages on end. I learn the farms, the villages, the intricate spiderweb of footpaths connecting each habitation for miles around.

Besides, it gives me something to do in the evenings. I sit by the light of a candle, crouched low on a buffalo hide stool, the incense of a burning mosquito coil drifting in lazy clouds around my ankles. Inch by inch, I force more cloth to emerge in a thick shag on the topside of the sackcloth, the mat growing heavier on my lap with each passing evening. When I run out of scraps, I toss my homemaker persona aside and put on my cartographer's hat. I unroll my poster paper map on the ground, tack the corners with rocks, then with a candle in one hand and a pencil in the other, I transfer the details of the day's walk from my notebook to the growing radius of what I consider the "known world." Off in the far southeastern corner, beyond the Kafue River that marks the border of our district stands a notation in as frilly a script as I can manufacture: *Here There Be Dragons.*

It turns out I needn't have worried about Wesley's reaction to my bandage collecting habit; he has shrugged it off without a second thought. He's a man, after all, and weaving rag mats is women's work.

The division of work is quite clear in Lamba culture. Building the domicile is men's work: getting the allotment from the chief, clearing the land, and constructing the home from the foundation to the rooftop. You're basically done after that as far as housework goes. The occasional roof leak or structural damage is the man's responsibility, but beyond that, a man's main occupation appears to be that of a race-horse gone to pasture. His main purpose is to extend his family line while enjoying the comforts of life that others are compelled to provide for him. Not a bad gig if you can get it.

Women's work, however, is never ending. It includes, but is not limited to: drawing the water, foraging for wild edibles and firewood, tending the fire, cooking, washing dishes, sweeping the yard, house cleaning, laundry, tending the sick, rearing the children, washing the children, and washing the husband. I checked with my cross-cultural teacher and my language instructor to make sure I understood this correctly. Husband washing is part of the deal. This further strengthens my theory that when a man gets married, his arms and legs all but fall off, leaving the only functional appendage just below the belt.

The washing aspect of the marriage is actually a fascinating part of Zambian marital relations. This is a shared experience. After the woman bathes herself and her husband the ritual shaving is then performed. We are talking the "full monty" here, no hair from navel to tailbone. This is a real labor of love and an exercise in unflinching trust, for this is all performed with a single, naked straight razor blade and no shaving cream. This is considered an integral aspect of married life and is, above all, foreplay. Sex with the unshorn is considered unclean, if not outright vile. And shame to the widow of someone found unshaven when being prepared for burial. No matter what age they are, it is the duty of the mate to routinely shave their spouse in readiness of carnal pleasures.

As if somehow reading my thoughts on this subject, the village crazy man approaches clothed only in a raggedy pair of khaki cutoffs cinched with a piece of rope and asks me to buy him a razor. His request surprises me, not because he has asked me to buy him something intimate (people ask for personal things every day, even for the clothes right off my body) but he surprises me because I have never seen him talk to anyone besides his invisible and cantankerous companions. I look to Wesley to rescue me.

"Not today, Father. Let's buy razors tomorrow," he says gently in local language. Respect is always given to the elderly here. You address them as your parents and use the polite tense verbs, almost as if you are speaking to royalty, even if they are the filthiest, drunkest, craziest old people you ever met. I love this about the culture: respect beyond reason.

The old man turns and grumbles to his unseen adversary, probably about the stinginess of white people these days, and retreats to his usual place on a cinder block under the eaves of the grinding mill. The sour stench of homemade *munkoyo* root alcohol leaves an almost visible trail in his wake.

We enter under the canopy of the sprawling jacaranda trees, a quarter mile of flowering splendor leading straight to the front gates of the clinic. The long limbs reach toward each other above the road like soldiers performing the arch of sabers at a wedding, thousands of tiny lavender blossoms showering down like a ticker tape parade. It never fails to lift my spirits, this walk. It's not just pretty, it's Bollywood music video pretty. Each time I walk under the boughs I half expect people in bright costume dress and impossibly big smiles to dance onto the scene and burst into song. All in all, it's not a bad commute.

Just before the convent gates, the road splits. The main road bends to the left and on to the clinic while the right fork leads to the lake. The wedge of land between them hosts a curious evergreen grove. The pines stand in tight military formations, a forest of unnerving symmetry and perfection. It's not a forest so much as a fleet, the natural forced to behave unnaturally. It's as if the missionaries were making a statement about taming the wild beast and making order from chaos by the force of sheer will. That will being not their own, of course, but divine will. Missionaries are notorious for imposing their idea of civilization on those they consider uncivilized. This forest, to me, represents this idea with imposing, skyscraping magnitude.

Then again, maybe they were just trying to cultivate some decent timber and firewood. I don't know. One can only speculate on the intentions of the priests and nuns who founded the mission a generation ago. The skeletons of the original infrastructure remain: rusty water towers, defunct spigots springing from the ground at every village for a half mile, a reed choked swimming hole by the dam painstakingly measured and constructed for optimum fish farming. The comforts of modern living have one by one succumbed to neglect. The emancipation of Zambia forty years ago, along with the subsequent evacuation of the mission's inhabitants, was the kiss of death for the plumbing around here. Due to poor government funding, the Ministry of Health eventually allowed the Catholic diocese to regain control of the clinic's staff and grounds. But even with the combined financial contributions of both parties, nothing has been able to restore the mission to its former glory.

There are two receiving areas at the clinic, one serving as the urgent care facility and one open for regularly scheduled clinics. The under-five (years of age), antenatal, and underweight clinics are my domain. I am not here as a medical advisor, my decade-old bachelor's degree in biology hardly arms me with enough knowledge to be competent here. I am mostly an extra set of hands for the check-ups. I fill out forms, check blood pressure, record body weight, and dispense medication.

I've discovered there are two main jobs I do well. One, I locate and change errors in the patients' paperwork. There are almost always errors. Humans are humans, after all, and without the help of computer systems we are prone to miscalculate. Unless you are a freaky, triple-checking perfectionist like I am. And two, I serve as the indisputable second opinion. Though I'm not a medical professional, it seems my color trumps anyone's medical degree. At least as far as the patient's perception is concerned.

It works like this: if a woman is in her last month of pregnancy and the baby hasn't turned, she is advised to give birth at the hospital in Mpongwe in case there are complications that would necessitate a C-section. If she refuses this advice, I am called in. The nurse will guide my hands as I palpate the patient's abdomen until I can confirm that the head is not in a favorable position. Once I advise the patient to go to the hospital for delivery, I get nothing but a "yes, madam, thank you, madam, whatever you say, madam." It's quite a thing to wield that much authority over someone else's body. I think I've gotten a small taste of that god complex that doctors and surgeons fall prey to, but my well-entrenched imposter syndrome doesn't let any of that egomaniacal nonsense take root. No room at the inn.

My favorite times at the clinic are when I am called over to witness something small and lovely. Maybe I'll be asked to hold a newborn while the doctor attends the mother. Or a nurse will call me over to hear the faint tattoo of a minuscule heartbeat through the fetal stethoscope. My ear will press against the metal cone and strain to hear the faint tap, tap, tap of the tiny heart from inside the womb. It's like eavesdropping with a glass against the wall of an adjoining room, waiting to hear a precious secret but only able to make out the persistent drip of the room's leaky faucet.

I bid Wesley farewell at the entrance to the urgent care ward and adamantly refuse his offer to sit with me while I wait. Having served on the other side of this operation, I know how long these things take. There are three patients inside and six on the bench waiting to be seen. There's everything from burns to open wounds to cold sweats out here. I'll be lucky if I'm seen before nightfall.

I take a seat next to a woman with a colicky baby and prepare to settle in for the long haul, silently cursing my lack of foresight for not bringing a book to read. I decide to people watch instead. I study a young girl as she traces the designs on her mother's *citenge* with her forefinger. A woman braiding and un-braiding her own hair. A man rubbing his shoes with a rag until they shine. A woman mindlessly sliding her single flip-flop from foot to foot as she watches some boys play football in the field next to the mission. Her left foot eases into the right shoe making it jut out awkwardly to the side. It makes me want to laugh out loud for its elegance in summing up the situation I have just found myself in. I watch the shoe dangle from the proverbial "other foot" and wait a long, African-style wait to be seen as a patient in my own clinic.

10

It Takes Guts

I've been deluding myself, I realize. I wanted to believe it was some sort of stomach flu, or perhaps another case of food poisoning. But thinking back over the past twenty-four hours, a long spell of freezing cold, then burning hot, then somewhat normal, and now back to freezing cold, I can't deny the truth. Especially now that I am experiencing the telltale headband of pain with eyeballs that feel as if they could explode. It's malaria.

I finally got the blasted worm to die in my leg, and now this? Brilliant.

Fortunately, I know exactly what I need to do. The plan of action has been ingrained in me from day one, even before I stepped foot in the country. Number one: take my emergency ration of medication. Number two: get out of the bush, and find a phone to call the chief medical officer so the staff can be aware of my condition. Number three: report directly to the volunteer leader's house for recovery. Any deviation from this plan could mean death. The Peace Corps medical team cited several tragic cases to make this point crystal clear.

In training, it had all seemed like a rational plan. Now that the reality of the situation has arrived, this plan seems absurd, comical even. I have been incapacitated to the point of almost immobility with fever and cramps and vomiting. How am I supposed to travel to town, let alone undertake the journey to my leader's house in another province three hundred kilometers away?

I slide out of bed, take my meds, and compose a bush note to the sister-in-charge at the mission. I wait until I hear my neighbor drawing water from the well and pass the note to her, asking if one of her children can make the run for me. As evening falls, I hear the tap of a child's hand on the door. I open the door to find Bana Francisco's boy Mark with a note extended in his right hand, the left poised under the right elbow, as if the single slip of folded paper requires the effort of two hands to support it. We both dip our knees gently as I receive the note and I offer him a sweetie in exchange. I ask him to remain while I read the note in case I need to send a return message.

As I begin to unfold the note, he unravels the sweet, pops it in his mouth and tosses the cellophane to the ground. I am almost too sick to give him an argument about littering, it being perhaps my biggest pet peeve here in the bush, but after a second or two, I manage to give a hoot. I grab the rusty coffee can I use as a waste bin and ask him to pick up the wrapper and dispose of it properly. I may be barely functioning, but I am still here and therefore still "on." This is the hardest part about my job sometimes. There is no clocking out; it's a 24/7 job.

I finish unfolding the note and read the response from the sister-in-charge at the mission. It is carefully lettered in her distinctive thin, spiderweb-like script, a hand that is more used to drafting Korean characters than Roman ones.

"We leave for Luanshya in the morning. We will pick you at seven. God bless you."

I pack a small bag for the journey and crawl into bed to shiver under the pile of acrylic blankets and sleeping bags until they arrive. When the truck rolls up, I slide out of bed and the driver helps me into the back of the truck, where I share a thin foam mattress with two other infirm people bound for Mpongwe hospital. We struggle to keep our own small purchase of the cracked, white vinyl mattress cover as the truck bucks and rumbles on the uneven road. Anything less than a death grip on the mattress cover would risk becoming airborne and smacking your head on the roof of the covered truck bed. We still bonk our heads on sides of the cab as the wheels dip in and out of ruts in the road, our breath hissing sharply at each buffeting.

After forty minutes or so, we hit tarmac and the ride becomes less like assault and battery and more like a coin operated motel bed with "magic fingers." I use the brief stopover in Mpongwe to call the Peace Corps medical office in Lusaka and my leader in Serenje from a pay-per-minute phone stall on the main drag.

By noon, we reach Luanshya and the sisters drop me off at the coach station in first-class. I've only taken transport from the rattling tin cans in second-class with bench seats, never splurged for the full-size buses where I would have a seat to myself. It's four times the price and not something I can fit into my budget easily.

I buy a ticket for the coach and take a seat among the other passengers on a wooden slat perched on cinderblocks alongside the building. The bus is due to arrive in twenty minutes, I'm told. After my first hour on the bench, I realize this would be twenty African minutes, and settle in for the long haul.

An old man with a busted ghetto-blaster ambles over to join us on the bench. Instead of music, the boom box blares static and a high-pitched whine of frequency waves not quite tuning in. Faintly, under the clamor, a rhumba tune could be heard.

I turn to him and address him in my most polite Bemba, "Father, please turn off the radio. I have a headache."

He shrugs and turns it down to about half volume, so that the tune is lost and all that's left is static and squealing. He keeps it playing. No one complains. I know that this is absurd, not just because I am addle-brained with fever, but because it just can't make sense to someone like me. Someone who is spoiled with things called choices. I won't play a busted radio because its whole purpose as a radio is lost to me. Holding on to the radio simply for the fact that it is, in itself, a luxury item would not occur to me.

This is the exact reason people wear only one shoe, or a man will sport a broken watch or women wear a small length of broom twig through their earlobes. Status. It's an outward display of something that you have. You may not be able to tell time, but you have a watch. You may not be able to afford earrings, but you have pierced ears. But this business of the radio is taking it another step farther, when people have something to share, they share it. And this man has a busted radio with batteries that still have a little juice in them. According to this culture, he's being generous by sharing it with everyone else within earshot.

I am beginning to feel that more and more, I am putting the pieces together rather than puzzling over the things that I witness. Moreover, I am starting to understand what my place, as a *muzungu* lady, is within the context of this culture.

I am exempt from much of the rules of conduct, being a foreigner, but some things I cannot trump. I am not exempt from African time, from faulty public transport timetables, and certainly not from old men who insist on being polite by playing their crappy radios to the general public. I feel like patting myself on the back for finally starting to understand this place, but mostly I feel like tearing that thing out of the man's hands and smashing it to smithereens.

About every half hour I walk into the office, complain over the tardiness of the coach, ask if they have heard any news about where it is and when it might arrive (they haven't) then sit on the bench to shake, sweat, and do my best to ignore the squeal of the broken radio. Four hours later, a coach arrives and we board. After some time, we are asked to disembark and the bus takes off without us, presumably to a fuel station or repair shop. A minibus rolls up, of the variety found in the second-class depot. We are asked to board this vehicle, our full-size coach declared out-of-order.

By the time we pull into the transfer station at Kapiri-Mposhi, twilight is falling. I step off the bus and before I reach ten steps, a bus rolls in front of me to block my path.

"Serenje, Serenje, Serenje," the bus boy calls. "Direct to Serenje!"

About the last thing I want is to get on another transport, but the worse thing—the thing that comes in *dead last* on my list of things I want to do—is to find some crappy motel room here in Kapiri-Mposhi which is basically a slum centered around a bus depot, then try and find transport again tomorrow. One word gives me hope; it blazes like a beacon through the dust and the chaos surrounding us.

"Direct?"

"Yes madam, direct to Serenje. Direct. Come, come, come. We are going direct. You come with us," he insists and hops down to help me board the bus.

"You promise me it's direct?" I ask, still dragging my feet as he hoists my bag unto his shoulder and pushes me up to the first step. We're two hundred kilometers from Serenje, but if it's a direct shot, I still have a hope of making it to my destination tonight. "You promise?"

"Madam," he says, "don't worry."

I tap the driver on the shoulder. "Is this direct to Serenje? Seriously? I need to get there tonight."

"We are going to Serenje," he says.

Unassured but feeling completely out of options, I take a seat on the minibus and endure the twenty-minute starting and stopping of the engine and lazy looping around the depot in the hopes of picking up one last fare. Eventually they give up and take to the road. I doze in my seat next to a large teddy-bear of a man who smells faintly of soap—one of those large, pink, perfumey bars at the market sold by the brick. This is such a pleasant and unexpected surprise, such a change from the usual seatmate on a public transport minibus, that I nearly thank the man for his odor.

When the engine comes to a stop, I open my eyes to discover we are not in Serenje, but Mkushi, nearly another hour's journey away. The driver and bus boy take a break to stretch their legs and eat a meal. This is my seatmate's stop, and he bids me goodnight. I swaddle myself in an extra *citenge* and rest as best I can, but I am too cold to sleep. It's not just my fever, other passengers complain of the cold too, and one by one they begin to go off in search of shelter. After an hour or so, my sweet-smelling seatmate returns and asks how I'm holding up.

"I thought this might happen," he said.

I explain to him my situation, that I'm suffering from malaria, and I urgently need to get to Serenje for shelter and care. He bids me to wait, then searches the restaurants until he finds the bus boy. He sends him on an errand to root out the driver, wherever he is, and tell him the *muzungu* lady needs to speak to him immediately. After some time, the driver wanders over to us.

"You said we were going direct to Serenje. You promised me," I say. "We're all cold and we're tired of waiting for you to do whatever it is you're doing. When do we leave?"

"Ah, there's a problem, madam," he says, the smell of liquor powerful on his breath. "We won't be leaving for Serenje until tomorrow."

I assure him that the problem is his because I would now require my money back. We wrangle over price until a compromise is reached, and he stumbles back to the bar.

My seatmate escorts me to the nearest guesthouse, which turns out to be a nightclub with rooms for let in the rear of the building and a shared toilet out back. It is about the noisiest, seediest place I've ever seen, but I don't feel like I have a choice. Any other guesthouse is too far to walk to in my condition. I hand the night man the money for the room and he hands me a key. It's the kind of old-fashioned key that hasn't been used for at least a century in the States, like something Ben Franklin would have had strung on his kite string. My seatmate bids me good night and promises to see me to my bus in the morning.

"Be safe," he advises. "Lock your door."

"Wait," I call to his retreating figure, "you've been so kind to me and I don't even know your name."

"It's Oscar," he says.

"Goodnight, Ba Oscar," I say, "and thank you."

I close the door, lock it with the funny little key, turn off the light and surrender to sleep. When I wake in the night, the pain in my bowels is excruciating. It is urgent. I spring out of the bed and grope for the door handle in the blackness. It is locked. I need the key to open it. *Oh God, where is the key?* I flick the light switch. Nothing. No power. If there was ever a reason to cry, this is it. The worst, most horrific nightmare come true. But the situation is too painful, too desperate for tears. I feel my way to the pile of clothes and personal items I had laid by the bedside, feeling around frantically for the small metal key.

I have been warned repeatedly during my medical seminars and by more seasoned volunteers that we all would, at some point in our service, experience fecal incontinence. Malaria or not, they cautioned, it was going to happen sometime, and we should all just come to terms with the notion now and not feel like some kind of degenerate when it happens.

"If you get Giardia, you will shit your pants," said our chief medical advisor, her crisp British accent making the words even more absurd sounding than they were, like some kind of Monty Python sketch. "You will also belch sulfur, like you've a belly full of rotten eggs. You must remember this, for it will help you distinguish between this amoebic type of food poisoning from the more common bacterial sort, which will also make you shit your pants, all right? And then, of course, there's malaria and you're bound to shit your pants then. That's a given. Now let's discuss all the different varieties of diarrhea—yes there are types you know, don't look so shocked—so that you will be able to recognize and describe to me over the phone if it comes to that. If there is one thing I'd like each of you to be able to accomplish at the end of this class today, is that you will have a decent vocabulary of a fecal nature—a compendium of poop, as it were—at your disposal. For if you cannot properly describe the nature of your shit, there's not much I am going to be able to do for you when you call me long-distance, is there?"

At this moment I am certain of two things. One, that I am about to experience the kind she termed "explosive," and two, that I cannot, will not, *must not* experience this with my pants still on. With a determination I didn't know I had in me, I clench my hindquarters and search the pitch-black room with a renewed fervor. All the while solemnly whining, "This is horrible, this is horrible, this is a nightmare, this is horrible!"

Finally, after several torturous minutes, I find the key and feel my way along the bare cement floor to the opposite wall until I find the doorframe, the door, and at last the keyhole. Once the door clicks open, I sprint to the toilets. I leave the door open to let the moonlight in so I can find the toilet stalls. There are two johns, neither of them clean, neither of them has a seat on the porcelain base, neither of them flush. The water is out along with the power.

I brace myself for what portends to be the ugliest night of my life and pity every other guest that chose to take a room here tonight. Whether through choice or necessity, fate has dealt them a pitiable hand. Had there been a choice not even I would use this bathroom, for any reason, after my first bout in here. But I don't have a choice. At half-hour intervals, convulsions strike me, and I run to the toilet stall to hover in a crouch above the foul, seat-less commode, grasping the walls for support and letting the sickness pour out of me like water from a pitcher. I'm desperate to yell out in pain, but the last thing I want is for someone to come in and investigate what kind of trouble I'm in.

This is, hands down, the worst sickness I have ever had. The bouts of food poisoning have been horrendous, for sure. But they are no match against the sensation of having your blood cells actually explode at synchronized intervals. That's what these waves of fever are. It's the parasites bursting out of your red blood cells where they've been hibernating. They then reproduce like mad, duck into whatever blood cells are left and wait for the next signal to swarm. The cycle is so vicious, so effective, that malaria falls into the rare category of parasites that actually kill their host given enough time.

I had thought that food poisoning was bad, and it is bad to be sure, but nothing compared to this. Until now, the worst sickness I had ever had was about a month ago after eating a dinner of cold chicken at my neighbor Bana Luke's house. I know better than to eat cooked meat that has gone cold. I also know that to refuse the food that's been prepared for you when you've accepted an invitation to dinner is rude, and I cannot afford to offend or alienate my neighbors. I've only just arrived, after all, and I'm desperate to make friends. She offered me what she felt were the choice pieces: the neck, and a portion of ribcage with a tiny, shriveled lung clinging on the inside. She ate the feet and spent the meal sucking and chewing every bit of skin off the tiny bones. I followed suit, eating the lung, and gleaning every bit of skin and meat off the ribs and little neck vertebrae until only a skeleton remained on my plate.

I awoke in the night in alarm, just barely making it out of the front door before vomiting. I realized almost immediately that I was about to get just as sick from the other end of my body, and in the same violent fashion. I grabbed a flashlight and a roll of t.p. and made for the outhouse. Things quickly went from bad to worse as my flashlight lit upon something obstructing the entrance of the latrine. A snake was coiled at the base of the doorframe. Cursing my bad luck, I ran back to the house and searched for something to kill it. I grabbed one of the long lengths of sugarcane a neighbor had given to me as a housewarming gift and strode back to the outhouse to do battle with the snake. When I arrived, however, it had disappeared somewhere, which made every subsequent trip to the *cimbusu* a nerve-wracking one. Ever since that night, I have kept a stick ready for action, just outside the door of the outhouse.

In the morning, my new friend Oscar comes to see how I'm faring and to escort me to my bus. Miraculously, I feel fine. Emptied and sore, but fine. I've reached the eye of the storm, the curious calm that comes in between the waves of malaria. The bus won't leave for another hour or two he says, only two people have lined up at the depot and the driver hasn't arrived yet. Ba Oscar invites me to visit with his family while I wait. He escorts me in the traditional local manner with a hand behind my elbow. I have no idea why people do this. It's terribly uncomfortable. Nobody's elbow bends that way.

Ba Oscar lives only five houses from the bus lot. A tiny square of raked dirt with plastic jugs of flowers decorate the lot in front of the modest, cement block home. I sit with his mother and sisters on plastic chairs under the shade of the front porch's corrugated metal roof. We make small talk in Bemba while nursing enameled tin cups of milky, sweet tea. Oscar's mother brings out her small collection of family snapshots and shares with me their names and stories. She tries, repeatedly, throughout the storytelling to ply me with another cup of tea.

It's all so civilized, so full of courtesy and comfort that I can hardly believe this is happening to me after the horrors I experienced just a few hours previous. I had almost forgotten there was such a thing as wellness, and that I usually lived in that state of being. I am glad to notice that even in this place, this hard land where everything is a struggle, things can—from time to time—feel normal. There is family here, there are friends here. There's even a mother doing what mothers do best—encouraging her guest to take just one more helping of what she's prepared.

I realize in this moment that the danger of this bout of malaria has passed. I am in good hands. Not the hands I had been running to for succor, but good hands nonetheless. I'm certain I will make it safely to my leader's house to convalesce, even if Ba Oscar has to escort me there the entire way himself. When it's time to leave we exchange addresses and promise to write, and I offer my arm to my new friend, perfectly content to have him push my elbow the wrong way, just so I can enjoy his company a little longer.

Pyromania

I stitch the last bit of cloth in my welcome mat and hold it up to admire my handiwork. It weighs a ton. It's taken me a couple of months to finish it, with my picking up of spare dirty rags, laundering them when I had a decent collection, then spending the occasional evening threading them through the weave of the mealie meal sack. I bought only one object, a red polo shirt salvaged from a *salula* market heap, which I shredded and wove into a pattern in the center of the mat. A single red loop, the symbol of AIDS awareness.

I decide the final product is not too bad. I can tell what it is, but I wonder if it is as obvious to the untrained eye? I had envisioned that if this turned out well, I was going to suggest it as a fundraising project for one of the women's groups or the AIDS education group. The pickings would be slim as far as buyers would go, I now realize. Volunteers like me and other foreigners working in the health care field may be interested, but beyond that, no one would be willing put the sign related to AIDS at their front door. "No one can want such things," was the advice given to me by Bana Francisco when she saw me working on it one evening. I thought about what I've learned in regard to sustainability. Would this project remain viable without my help to connect to an expat population? Definitely not. And so, my fundraising idea was nixed even before the prototype was complete.

I get up and make my way to the front door, ducking under the clothesline of drying unmentionables strung up across the room. For some reason it is taboo to hang underwear on the line for everyone to see. Underwear isn't taboo in and of itself. In fact, I would go so far as to say that underwear is a craze out here. You'll find vendors in every marketplace hawking panties and briefs of every size and description, usually racy and impractical with zippers and sequins and bold prints. I've even had door-to-door underwear salesmen pass through my village on occasion. Once the undergarments have been purchased, however, they must never see the light of day again. You never even see children's underwear on the line. I can't imagine what the inside of some of these huts look like on washing day—it's not unusual to have ten or more kids per household. It's got to be wall-to-wall skivvies.

I reach the front stoop and plop down my mat. "Welcome," I call out to the crowds of no one in my yard. I step my bare feet unto the mat and feel the pile give slowly under my weight. As the last rays of the sun dip behind the mango trees and into the horizon, I realize something is amiss. Instead of the coolness that comes with the setting of the sun, I feel a renewed heat in the air. It occurs to me now that the smoke in the air isn't the usual wood smoke of the evening cooking fires. A thick haze has blotted out the last rays of the sunset, but the sky remains lit with an eerie glow. I step out to the road for a better view of the western sky. A wildfire approaches. The south side of the road is engulfed in smoke. Our village is on the north side.

I've been expecting this for some time now, but I feel panic rising in my gut all the same. This is the time of year called "fire season." It's not a question of *if* there will be fires to fight, but *when*. The grass, having surpassed even the tallest man in height, has fully matured, dried, and gone to seed. Our whole landscape has become a tinderbox and we, with our homes of earth and thatch, are sitting in the middle of it.

To prepare for this inevitability, I hired someone to slash all the grass in my yard. He's done a fair job so far; the wall of wheat-colored grass has been hacked back so that my bathing shelter and latrine are no longer engulfed in it. My neighbors have done the same, leaving me to feel positively exposed as I can now clearly see all the homes of the neighboring village and beyond. Now a quick pee in the night entails grabbing a flashlight, walking out to the latrine, and contending with the snakes and bats that insist on residing there, rather than just squatting somewhere in the back of my dirt yard. My hired hand has not finished slashing all the grass, however, and a good swath remains out by the road beyond my mango grove. The last bit of un-cleared land is, unfortunately, the land closest to the fire. If the blaze jumps the road—barely three meters wide—I could lose everything.

I run back to the hut and grab my few valuables—money, passport, meds—and place them outside the door so I can run with them if need be. I consider drawing a bucket of water but decide to run back out to the road and see if the fire is changing course. Maybe we'll be spared.

I stand in the middle of the one-lane dirt road and watch the blaze race towards us as fast and sure as an approaching cyclist. The roar of the flames is almost deafening now, with an occasional gunshot crack firing off as a tree bursts its bark.

It's a hot, fast burn. As the inferno approaches, it draws air to itself. My cheeks flush in the heat of the wind. My body is slick with sweat.

I prepare myself for the worst. I'm sure I can withdraw to safety if I need to, but what will happen if the fire crosses the road and my little hut burns down?

I think about it. What will happen? Not much. My things will go up in smoke, and it will be fine. My things are just things, they can be replaced. I imagine what that would look like: an empty shell of a hut with my brand-new doormat—half of it barbecued to high hell—adorning the threshold.

I think back on my things in storage in the States. What if all that went up in smoke? The answer shocks me: I would be glad. In fact, I feel so good at the thought of it, I begin to wish it in my heart. Twisted and crazy as it seems, I hope that the storage space will get nuked somehow. My things would be gone, and my attachments to those things would be gone as well.

I consider how I would feel about having nothing in this world, no possessions to be responsible for, no things to tie me down to a place. I feel lightness in my heart. I feel freedom.

Having come to terms with that, I decide to stand my ground here. If I lose everything, so be it, but I will do my best to protect what I've been given by this community. As I turn back to gather my water and heavy blanket to beat out flames, I see that my neighbors have all silently gathered behind me. Their grave faces glow in the light of the wildfire, each now as familiar to me as my own family. Bana Martha, Ba Patti, Ba Wesley, Bashi Beauty, Bana Francisco, Bashi Francisco, and Bana Luke. Each has an empty bucket in hand, ready to draw water if the need arises. They have come to stand beside me at the edge of the road. My only friend not here is Bana Ruby, who lives on the other side of the road. With her homestead in the direct path of the blaze, she will be fighting her own battle tonight. I feel amazed and touched that my neighbors are all standing with me rather than rushing to her aid. She has five children and her elderly parents to look after; I have no one to save but myself.

Wisps of burnt grass sail high overhead and drop into our village, some still alive with an orange glow. We stamp them underfoot as they land. Holding discourse is impossible over the din of the inferno, so we tap each other's arms and point to the areas in need of extinguishing. My skin feels tight and itchy, my lips and ears throb. I am baking. The onslaught lasts only a few minutes, the dry grass proving to be a highly flammable but inefficient fuel, like wads of paper tossed into a campfire.

I turn to look at my neighbors and see their forms retreating into the dark. They have left as silently as they arrived. None of the usual pleasantries have been exchanged. But this wasn't a time for pleasantries; this was not a social call. The fire is still burning, but it appears they know something I don't. I defer to their knowledge. They have a lifetime of experience with wildfires and defending their homes. Probably every year, every dry season of their lives.

In their stead, a stream of children arrives to keep vigil with me. We continue to stamp out stray sparks, but it seems clear that the real danger is over. This has become child's work, and it soon descends into play. Kids begin to dive on the sparks, rather than stamping them out. They cry out for their mothers—something along the lines of, "Oh mommy, mommy, help me! I'm burning!"

I want to scold them, tell them it's not funny. But seeing them goof around gives me a much-needed sense of relief. I feel grateful for our luck at having escaped tragedy, and I'm glad to have the chance to laugh about it.

I remember doing the same thing myself recently. A few weeks ago, my leader came to visit me with my closest volunteer neighbor, Izzy. We went to the lake for swimming and bathing and beer drinking. While exploring a rocky area by the shoreline, I slipped and fell into a small crevasse. I landed in a mass of shed snakeskin, several feet of bubbly grey-green tissue with long, whitish underbelly scales. Only one snake fits this description in this area, and its reputation is fearsome. I may as well have landed on the shed cloak of the grim reaper.

"You guys? We all almost died. For real. Check this out." I wound the skin around my torso and crawled out of the hole. "Black mamba."

Amid the gasps and curses, bursts of nervous laughter erupted. Soon all we could do was laugh at our crazy luck. We took turns holding the skin and pretending to wrestle with it in a losing battle for our lives. "Save yourselves!" we would yell, then taunt the empty skin of our adversary, "C'mon, you mother! Is that all you got? Huh? Is that all you—aaaaurgh ... oh God ... you got me that time ... dying ... dying!"

I have been told by locals that there is no point in running when you encounter a black mamba. It can easily outpace you. All you can do is pray that it won't attack, but that is unlikely considering its aggressive nature. Your last moments will be spent marveling at its speed, watching it rear up off the ground like a staff to deliver its killing strike, fangs first, the inside of its mouth black as death itself.

I had no idea how close a call I had to having an encounter with the inhabitant of that skin. A week, a day, an hour. There's no way of knowing. We lived that day, though. Lived to laugh about it, and it feels like it is time to laugh again.

I dive onto the ground with the kids. "Ugh! Mayo! Mayo! Oh, save me!"

The kids squirm on the ground in laughter, then join me in calling out for their mommies again. We extinguish the last of the embers in the grass with our imaginary death throes. I am probably burning little holes in my clothes, but what do I care? My clothes are already riddled with holes from sparks that jump from the brazier I use for cooking.

Once we feel our job is done, I pass out *citenge* to the kids. We tuck them around our waists in fat rolls and dance and sing until they are called home for bed in the customary singsong holler of their mothers. The sound, I muse, is not unlike that of fire truck sirens whining in the distance.

"OOOOooooOOOO!"

Fire trucks ... ha! ... as if we would need such a thing.

❧ 12 ❧

Unwritten Rules

Izzy and I have been hitchhiking every day for a week. If we are lucky this could be our last day, though most likely we'll have to overnight somewhere in Luanshya or Mpongwe before scoring a ride back to our respective villages.

I'm serenading my traveling companion to lighten the mood, breaking out my Motown favorites. I'm not holding back either. I'm belting it out, making up funny lyrics when I can't remember the real ones, throwing in dance moves. She's not having any of it, though. It's ten a.m., already sweltering, no shade in sight. Our heads are frying like eggs and our patience is running thin. We've been here over two hours and not a single vehicle has come by. Izzy slumps on a boulder at the roadside, grinding pebbles into the dirt with the tip of her sandal. She doesn't tell me to can it, but she doesn't acknowledge my antics either.

Tough crowd.

A buzz in the distance catches our attention. We study a smudge on the horizon and wait to see what emerges. The heat rising from the road plays tricks on the eyes out here; shapes vanish as easily as they appear. This bit of smoke draws closer, though, and the phantom smudge materializes into a semi chugging along in our direction, belching clouds of black fumes.

"Can we hitch on one of those?" I ask.

"Sure," she says with a shrug. "There's a mattress behind the front seats they use when they have to spend the night on the road. You kinda feel like you're on some magic floating sofa up there. The only problem is these things are slow-moving as hell. It'll take us twice as long as any other vehicle on the road."

"What other vehicle would that be?" I ask.

"Good point." She rises up off the boulder, stretches her back, and joins me at the roadside to try and flag down our ride. We stand with one arm extended out in the road, our hand flapping up and down to urge the truck to a halt. No one thumbs a ride in Zambia. The trick here is to act like some kind of wounded bird, one arm awkwardly sticking out with the hand flipping frantically, with the hope that you look so pathetic the driver will be overwhelmed with pity and pick you up.

The tractor-trailer blows by us as we continue to stand with our arm outstretched, frozen in defeat, eyes squinted against the cloud of smoke and dust churned up by every one of its eighteen wheels. I turn my gaze from the road, let out a wheezy cough, and spit as politely as possible to clear the dust from my mouth. I see another dark figure emerging on the horizon.

"Hold on," I call to Izzy, who has begun to retreat to her boulder. "Here comes another one."

"Hot damn," she says. "Rush hour."

Izzy is an experienced hitchhiker. I don't think I would have had the courage to try and hitch on my own. I have to admit, now that I've tried it, it's definitely the better way to roll.

Hitchhiking is not exactly encouraged by the Peace Corps staff, but it is mentioned as the most widely employed method of transportation by current volunteers. For one, it easily fits within our budget. When cash flow is limited, things boil down to "beer economics." If you don't have to pay for transport into town, that's two more beers you'll be able to buy when you get there. Also, the rides you can score by hitching are generally more roadworthy (not held together with spit, duct tape, and a prayer) and often get you to your destination much more quickly since it's not stopping at every village, marketplace, or bush-meat vendor along the way.

That's the beauty of a hitched ride. When you're sitting in a comfortably air-conditioned car (safely buckled in with a seat belt, of course) and having pleasant conversation with your host, you look at the guys selling fried mice on a stick or impala haunches or freshly skinned rock dassies with a kind of detached amusement. *Oh yes, isn't that interesting? Isn't that quaint?* Whereas on the local transport, you can be sure that someone is going to ask the driver to pull over so they can buy those mice on a stick, which they will then crunch on for the remainder of the trip. You can try and pretend that someone is eating pretzels back there instead, let that imagination and denial work overtime if it comforts you, but deep down you know the truth.

Izzy and I line up at the shoulder of the highway and pop our arm out to the road again like marionettes with only one workable string left. Our hopes soar as the vehicle slows and we see the passengers' faces—white faces. The joy is short-lived, however, as the Land Cruiser picks up speed and rockets by us like a silver bullet, the logo emblazoned on its side reduced to a blur of color. Probably a government vehicle or—more likely—some well-funded non-government organization (NGO). The NGO's tend to have way more mad money to blow on things like sweet rides.

"You've got to be kidding me!" Izzy exclaims. "I've never been passed over by muzungus. It's the unwritten rule, you know? White people don't leave other white people stranded in Africa."

I didn't know. But I'm learning now.

She paces along the road and tightens her bandanna cap as she rants on. "Not that I'm prejudiced or anything. I consider myself an equal-opportunity moocher. I'll take a free lift where I can get it. But I'm telling you, getting picked up by the *muzungu* is always the better deal. I mean, these guys with the tricked-out SUVs, they aren't just muzungus, they're *bwanas*. They are the bosses, the big-time *boogas*. They've got all the money in the world. They're foreign investors and landowners and CEOs of corporations.

"When they give you a ride, it's like 'let me take you grocery shopping' and 'here use my cell phone to call America' and 'let me give you a ride back to your village, it's no problem.' They feel incredibly guilty about having so much in a land where most people have nothing. When they see us living out there in the bush helping those people—you know, really taking the time to care for people who are suffering—there's almost nothing they won't do to make themselves feel better. Trust me, if you want to get picked up by anyone, it's a *bwana*."

I do trust her. She's got a lot more experience in these matters than I do. I've been taking copious mental notes on her advice on everything from where to eat, who to make nice to, which places can give beer bottles on loan, which missionaries will put you up for the night and even how to tell someone to get lost in local language. If I ever need to toss out the empty threat of beating someone if they don't do what I say, I am now fully armed thanks to her.

A rusted sedan rumbles down the road toward us and slows at our display of arm flapping.

"Score," sings Izzy as she jogs up to the driver's side window to talk with our potential chauffeur. She pops her head up after a few seconds. "Only to Mkushi, and five pin each," she reports. She crinkles her nose and shrugs her shoulders, universal sign language for "not what I hoped for." Not every ride on the road is a free one, but if you can't get a free one, sometimes a cheap one has to suffice. Five pin is half of what public transport would cost me, one American dollar all told.

"I don't care anymore," I admit. "That's fine with me."

We grab our gear and pile into the rear of the car. Greetings are exchanged in Bemba and English. The obligatory dialogue of people meeting on the road ensues, the "where are you coming from, where you going to, where's home for you and why did you leave it" conversation.

"You are returning from *Mutomboko?*" The driver sounds overjoyed at the mention of our previous destination. It turns out he is of the Lunda tribe, and the cultural festival we witnessed in Kasembe only a stone's throw from his home village. "You saw it then? You saw the big man go down?"

He's referring to the ceremony in which the chief re-enacts the battles and triumphs of his people. This all plays out like one of those breakdance movies from the eighties where gang wars are fought on the dance floor. Our hero, the chief, enters the arena with no weapon in hand, just an outrageously royal outfit of beads and feathers and dozens of meters of colored cloth worn as a full-length skirt obscuring what, I can only assume, are the traditional boogie shoes of his people. He conquers a warrior wielding an axe then one with a sword by virtue of the sheer superiority of his dance moves. The thing that made this year's ceremony interesting was that before the chief danced his way into everyone's hearts, he fell into a dead faint.

"Do you know why that happened? Why the chief collapsed?" he asks, his gaze locking with mine in the rearview mirror.

I assumed it was from the intense heat, massively heavy garment, and choking dust stirred up by the marching feet of thousands of sweaty onlookers. When the chief's sedan chair reached the top of the hill, I wasn't too surprised to see him swoon and slump back into the confines of the zebra skin carriage. What did surprise me was when he recovered five minutes later and danced his heart out.

The man is still looking at me through the mirror awaiting my response. Apparently, this is not a rhetorical question. I venture a guess.

"It was all part of the act?"

"No!" The man's eyes widen with disbelief, as if to say *how could you even think such a dishonorable thing of our great chief?* I want to explain myself by educating him on the legendary showmanship of James Brown, how by appearing overcome by the moment (or his own awesomeness) he swoons, heightening the emotional experience of the audience, making them cry out in protest and beg for more, but before I can break out my Godfather-of-Soul-defense, he turns around in his seat to lock my gaze. Apparently, I am the one who is about to receive an education.

"Witchcraft," he says, staring at me wide-eyed for a full beat before turning back to the road. "Someone was using witchcraft on him. But our chief, he is strong. He has overcome the bad magic. You see?"

"Wow," I look over at Izzy who has decided to sit this conversation out. "It's good that the chief is so strong. His people should be proud."

The man nods his head in agreement and seeming to swell with that pride, falls into silence for the remainder of our trip.

Piling out at the Mkushi turnoff, we see a familiar vehicle taking to the highway again. A shiny silver Land Rover. Muzungus. The words printed on the passenger door once blurred by speed are now legible, declaring the passengers missionaries from South Africa. We watch the vehicle proceed slowly, come to a halt, then reverse gear and back toward us. Izzy turns to give me a cocky grin. It says "I told you so" louder than words ever could, and the spring in her step as she jogs up to the vehicle shows me that she's regained her sense of humor. Yes, all is well. The unwritten rule of Africa, once thought to be broken, has been amended, and the universe breathes easy once again.

Once inside, we are greeted with a torrent of apologies.

"Well, we're not supposed to give anyone rides, against mission rules, you know. But it just laid so heavily upon our hearts leaving you on the side of the road like that. And when God put you in our path again, well, we just couldn't pass you by. Now, I hope you don't mind, but we were going to stop for a *braai* up ahead. Nothing special, just some jaffles and crisps and cold drinks. Oh yes, and chocolates. I have bags and bags of chocolates I simply don't know what to do with. You will let us feed you, won't you?"

Izzy turns to give me a justifiably smug look. I smile back wanly, trying to remain outwardly pleasant despite the crushing load of white privilege weighing on my heart. The generosity of these strangers may be unfairly portioned, heaped upon us through no merit of our own—save our skins —while scores of others have been passed over without a second glance. But I won't turn down their hospitality. Not a chance. When a gift is offered, you accept it graciously. You give thanks. You can wrestle with your thoughts later.

"Jaffles on the *braii*?" I say. "Well, I don't believe I've ever had the pleasure ..."

❧ 13 ❧

Lost and Found

Yesterday my cousin got married. I was the maid of honor. In absentia.

I did the best I could considering the thousands of miles separating us. Via massive packages of lengthy notes, magazine clippings, and sketches, I've been able to weigh in on décor, invitations, cake, venue, dress design, entertainment, wedding favors and the thousand little touches that make every wedding the full-blown migraine you never thought would happen to you because you weren't going to get sucked into all that crap in the first place. I've done my best to keep things light, sending her little bits of big-sister type wisdom:

· · ·

ARE YOU SAYING YOUR OWN VOWS OR DOING TRADITIONAL ones? Here are some nice vows in case you are stuck: Plagiarize at will!

"I promise to love, honor and cherish you for as long as we live. I promise to be obedient, except in the case where you ask me to do something I don't want to do, in which case, I'll do whatever I want. I promise to call you by embarrassing little pet names, but I promise NOT to refer to you as "the apple of my eye" because that just sounds so disgusting, and what does that even mean anyway?!? I promise you a life filled with joy and laughter, and not ALL of the laughter will be aimed at you. And even when we fight, I promise not to hold TOO much of a grudge because my love for you can overcome any obstacle. But I reserve the right to dredge up any past wrong you've committed since the day we've met so I can throw that in your face when I'm angry with you. And lastly, I promise to support you and adore you even though I'm always right and you're always wrong."

I've sent home a *citenge* for the bride and waist beads for her and all the bridesmaids to enjoy. This is a part of Zambian culture that you won't find in any guidebook but is pervasive throughout most of the tribes in Zambia and many other African nations. Women wear colorful strands of tiny, glass beads around the waist under their clothing, or sometimes in lieu of clothing altogether when they retire for the night. This is, in essence, lingerie and taboo to be seen in by any man other than your husband. I've had many discussions with women about the allure and significance of wearing the beads. Some consider it a vital part of seduction but are sketchy on the details of how this works, while other refuse to wear them or even to discuss why they won't wear them. Bana Francisco falls into this category, but since she is a strict Catholic and shies away from any traditional medicines, rituals, or ceremonies that lean toward the supernatural, I think that she might put the tradition of wearing beads in this category. The art of seduction is its own kind of witchcraft, after all.

I've been told that in some regions of Africa, hanging your beads by the entrance to the bedroom sends a signal to your husband. Depending on the color of the beads, or on tribal custom, the beads may indicate that the woman is menstruating or perhaps that she is particularly in the mood, so the husband is free to make advances. The beads serve as a "closed" or "open for business" sign.

In Zambia, however, they don't seem to follow any prescribed roles other than to proclaim, "I am your woman." The most elaborate answer I've received in regard to wearing the beads was from Izzy's neighbor, Bana Sipalo.

"If a man wakes up in the night and he feels something smooth in his bed, he might wonder what it is," she said. "But when he feels the beads, he can relax and know that it is his wife. Otherwise, he may think it is a snake!"

Though I pressed her further, she could give me no other information about why women wear the beads, mostly because she thought her answer was so hilarious that it required several more repetitions throughout the evening, no one laughing harder than she.

I've taken to wearing the beads, myself. Not the twenty to thirty strands the local women will wear, but I'll choose six or eight from my collection, choosing from the sets of pink, silver, ivory, celadon, and two shades of blue I have to suit my mood. Like wearing a fancy matching set of bra and panties, I feel I have a little sexy secret under my clothes.

My cousin has confided that she'll be wearing a strand of azure beads as her "something blue." Knowing that makes me feel that although I can't be there, at least I've made my mark.

It's not that I can't go home. I can. I could use my vacation hours and go on my own dime. I know other volunteers have gone home for weddings and other special family occasions. Whatever the occasion, volunteers all agree that breaking up a term of service with a home visit is, at the least, heartbreaking and confusing, or, at worst, the catalyst for a full-on identity crisis resulting in therapy and usually the termination of service. After careful evaluation of my mental state and ability to acclimate myself to third-world living, I can say with absolute certainty that I'd find myself in the latter category.

It became clear to me that I made the right choice in remaining in Zambia when I sat down to write the prayer and toast to be read at the reception. I took a blanket, notebook, and a day's rations out to the lake, hoping to sit in solitude, in a prayerful and solemn mindset until the right words revealed themselves to me. I had never written a prayer or a toast to be read aloud in public before, and I felt equally honored and daunted to pen such important missives.

No sooner had I settled into my favorite nook overlooking the lake when a party of boys emerged from the forest and planted themselves around me. My mission for prayerful contemplation soon became mission impossible. The half dozen boys in desperate need of a bath who were whispering and craning their necks to peer on to the page waiting for the next stroke of my pen hardly proved to be an inspiration. I knew they were just curious, hoping to catch a glimpse of my handwriting, the color of the ink on the page, or the manner in which I hold my pen—anything that could give them a clue of who I was and what I was about. But their agenda couldn't have been more different from mine. I wanted solitude. More than that, I wanted to revel in my self-pity. I wanted to be wretched and pathetic.

The urge to return to the family nest has never been stronger, and yet—paradoxically—I'm adamant about maintaining my self-imposed isolation. I've committed myself to this term of service and to see it through to the end. This job, this existence, has become the most important thing in my life. Each small achievement feels like the hardest won victory to date, each day topping the last. This bit of my life has become the thing I am most proud of.

It's only a shame that my emotional fortitude cannot seem to live up to the standards I have set for myself. This particular situation at the lake ended up with me chasing the boys through the woods crying out the Lamba equivalent of "Why are you doing this to me? Why can't you just leave me alone? Why? WHY?"

It's at times like these that I find it hard not to compare myself with the previous volunteer, the one who spoke perfect Lamba, the one who mastered all the local dances, the one who never told the kids to get lost at the lake. Instead, she'd make a game of it, asking the children to throw leaves and stones in the lake so she could dive in after them and bring them to shore like a golden retriever with a duck. But I don't fetch. And try as I might to look like I'm not having some sort of fit while dancing, my Rhumba is still a travesty.

My coping mechanism for dealing with disappointment is throwing myself headlong into household chores. Back in the States, I might detail every bit of tiled surface in a bathroom, scrub a stovetop until it looks as if it has never been cooked on, or vacuum the stairwell with small hose attachment. There's only so clean you can get a house made of mud, but considering the amount of angst I had over not being able to attend the wedding, I applied all the elbow grease I had to make it shine. I devoted the entire day to painting the walls and waxing the floors.

Normally I don't do this type of housework. Like many volunteers, I have hired help. This not only frees me up from chores so that I can concentrate on my work, but it allows me to spread the wealth a bit. It's not considered seemly to have as much money as I do (meager as my stipend is, it is still more than my neighbors make) so I am expected to hire people out for piecework in order to share what I have. I've got a handful of regulars that come by once or twice a month offering their services. Bana Francisco and Bana Ruby for laundry, Bana Joy and Bana Memory for yard sweeping and drawing water for the garden, and Hope for odd jobs like pulling weeds or smearing the house with a fresh coat of mud. I've even got the kids in on the act. When they come by asking for sweets, I hand them a jug to fetch water or a broom to sweep the yard so they can earn their treat.

Out of all my piece workers, Bana Luke has become my most reliable and indispensable hired hand. My right hand, if I'm being honest. I rely on her care and companionship more than she knows. We don't have a set schedule; she comes by when she needs some pocket money. Usually once a week she comes in to sweep the dust and termite tracks from the floor and walls, wash the floor with damp rags, then wax the cement and bring it to a high polish with a shining brush.

I love waxing day. I make sure I always have a supply of Cobra wax on hand, even if it means a trip to town to acquire it. The tin of wax claims to be lavender, which it is in color, but misses the mark in the fragrance category. It has a powerful but not unpleasant scent, clean but not caustic, unlike the handmade floor wax many of the local women make by mixing the leftover dribbles of candle wax with kerosene. This turns the dusty, mud-stained floor into a gleaming blend of olive and beige and mahogany, swirling and blending into one another, much the way a cup of coffee looks after a splash of cream. It's the same subtle kind of magic that happens when a handful of ordinary pebbles are dropped into a fish bowl. The water transforms the most unremarkable and worthless of objects into a treasure trove of fascinating colors in mysterious forms.

I tried to find joy yesterday in these little details as I worked, buffing the floors, daubing the lime smeared walls. Playing inspirational music from my discman, I turned the tiny speakers to full blast while I worked. I imagined my day as if I were starring in a movie montage, my homemaking routine resembling that of a karate kid workout: stroke up, stroke down, wax on, wax off. I was training to be quicker, stronger, better—but at what, I wasn't exactly sure. The movement just helped to push the grief to the back of my mind.

The one idea which kept haunting me while I worked, the thing that brought me to the edge of tears time and again, was the memory of my cousin and me setting out my aunt's teacups for company. This eclectic collection of antique teacups was from when my aunt got married, and each guest provided a china teacup and saucer for the bride. Though none of the pieces match, they complement each other in their uniqueness; each is a standalone piece of art. There are English teacups with floral motifs hand painted on bone china, Japanese cups with a silkscreened quality depicting stylized scenes of courtyards and gardens, Russian cups with bold geometric designs intricately laced with gold leaf. On special occasions, my cousin and I would take the delicate cups and saucers one by one from the china cabinet, marveling at each one in turn.

One day as we were choosing which cups to set out for tea after a holiday meal, my cousin told me, "When I get married, I want to have a teacup shower too."

I hummed in agreement, my mind on the same track.

"I just love these," she said holding a particularly delicate cup, the china nearly as thin as an eggshell, up towards the electric glow of the chandelier to let the light play through it. "So fun."

I'll throw you that teacup shower, I thought. And I meant it.

I had every intention of being there for her when she got married. But that future always seemed way off on the horizon. I never dreamed that future would involve a whirlwind romance and dash to the altar with a military officer about to be deployed to Iraq, and me living in a mud hut thousands of miles away from the big event. And never in my wildest imaginings would I have guessed the real reason for not being there: that I would be too frightened to attend.

I am fortunate enough to have company this morning, one whose tranquil presence feels like the perfect counterpoint to my disquiet. Sister Ignatius, a Korean nun stationed in St. Anthony's, meets me on the road to Lake Kashiba, a routine we have fallen into in recent weeks. She confides in me that in the wee hours of the morning, she'll steal away to the lake and take a private dip. But no amount of cajoling can convince her to go for a swim with me now. It's not permitted to see a nun out of her habit.

Sister Ignatius remains perched upon the high rocks enjoying meditation while I have my morning wash. My bathing ritual is to dive into the lake, climb out, suds up with Dr. Bronner's magic soap as best I can in my bathing suit and knee-length swimming trunks, then take another plunge. I take a few lazy laps to the middle of the lake and back. This is the one place I can be truly alone; no one would ever dare swim out to join me here. The waters are considered haunted —either by a "shadow-stealing monster" or by the spirits of a tribe who committed group suicide by tying themselves together and jumping in—depending on who is telling the local lore. I don't believe in the myth of a lake monster the way the locals do, but I'll admit to feeling a little creeped out when swimming too far from the edge if I'm in the water alone.

After drying off and resting a bit, we launch into a discussion of some projects I'll be running out of the health center in the next few months: an anti-AIDS youth group, a tuberculosis seminar, and a water and sanitation training. Like my friend Mirabel who teaches at the elementary school, she's young, full of energy, and speaks English well. These two ladies have become my favorite sounding boards; they understand the area and what problems I am up against. A session of brainstorming with them really helps combat the isolation I feel working out here on my own.

When the sunlight begins to fail and the shadows lengthen, we wander back up to the convent in companionable silence. As we reach the small statue marking the entrance to St. Anthony's Upper Basic School, Sister Ignatius turns to me.

"St. Anthony is my favorite saint," she says.

"Really? Why's that?" Not being raised a Catholic, I know doodly-squat when it comes to saints.

"He is the patron saint of lost things." She laughs in that way of hers that sounds like she's quietly hyperventilating.

I think how the two of us must look to the children peering at us through the school's broken windows: a Korean woman in a nun's habit and a *muzungu* American lady wrapped in *citenge*.

"How appropriate," I say. "There aren't many things in this place that look as misplaced as the two of us."

I wonder when I eventually do find my way home, what will I discover? Things will certainly not be as I left them, or if they are, I won't be seeing them with the same eyes. Right now, I feel—like people used to say in the 60's—that I am trying to find myself. Will I, here in the middle of Africa, find myself? So far, the things I have found out about myself are things I would have rather not known. Impatience, weakness, ill temper. Like the haunted waters of Lake Kashiba, I wonder what other monsters may lie hidden in my depths.

14

Don't Give Up

It's dark inside the police department, but it feels just as stifling in here as out in the sun. I lean my body against a filthy cement wall and enjoy the faint coolness that lingers there. I close my eyes and play a game in my mind while I wait for the clerk to arrive. It's one of my favorite games on a hot day: the cold fantasy game. I remember the sound of ice cubes plinking in a glass. Sucking a milkshake through a straw and stopping just before the point of brain-freeze. And my new favorite: the remembered exhilaration of swimming under Kundalila Falls, the sting of icy water pounding on my head and back and shoulders, my breath coming in shocked spasms.

The front desk clerk emerges from the back room with my bicycle and helmet.

"Thanks, boss," I say.

As he gently places the bike in the doorway, I notice the

tires have been wiped clean and every bit of chrome is gleaming. He removes a rag from his pocket and gives my helmet a quick buff before handing it to me.

"As usual, you've taken excellent care of my equipment while I've been away. You are too good to me," I say.

The clerk shrugs and blushes. A man of few words. I like that.

"I'll see you next time, boss," I say, and walk the bike out to the strip of tarmac that serves as the main drag for Mpongwe boma.

I wouldn't make the journey today except for the fact that I finally got a meeting set with the chief of my catchment area. If this wasn't so vitally important, there's no way I'd be on the road today. It's got to be over a hundred in the shade. And besides, I've got better places to be. I've been given a housesitting gig in Luanshya this week while my missionary friends, the Garfields, are out of town.

Meeting the Garfields has been one of the best things to happen to me since I arrived in Zambia. Not only are they good American company when I need it, but their association with the local Rotary Club has given me a much needed "in" as far as funding for projects is concerned. One of my initiatives, to provide each village with a source of safe drinking water, coincided perfectly with the Rotary Club's agenda for the funds they had raised that year. Lucky me. My neighbors thought I was a miracle worker once the drilling crews began casing their villages and dowsing for the best sites to install the boreholes. Now we are working in collaboration with my uncle's Rotary Club in California to raise funds for a carpentry school in my village.

The Garfields' home in Luanshya is like paradise to me. They don't have central air, but the ceiling fans keep the house bearable. And, of course, there are cold drinks in the fridge and a swimming pool to cool you off. Stepping foot in the Garfields' home is like stepping onto American soil. An unofficial, but very real embassy.

I could be there enjoying the lap of luxury for two more days, but duty calls. I need to meet with the chief. This is one of the first things a Peace Corps volunteer is instructed to do upon entering residency in a chiefdom. You arrange a visit through the headmen, bring gifts suitable for the occasion such as a couple of white chickens or a goat, and introduce yourself. Your presence will not be a surprise to him or her (there are women chiefs out here) as Peace Corps has already obtained permission for your residency in their chiefdom, but you must go as a courtesy.

Within my first few days of arriving, I should have had an audience with the chief, but all my efforts at arranging a meeting through the headmen failed. I only recently chanced upon one of the chief's aides and was able to book an audience on my own.

I begin pedaling home, taking one last mental stock of my cupboards before I ride away into the bush. No, I don't need anything from the shops. A truck's horn blares as it nears my bicycle, the occupant's hand outstretched to me. It's Father Mulenga heading back to the village. I reach out my hand and wave in a desperate attempt to get him to back up, load my bike in the back, and take me with him, but he mistakes the gesture for a greeting and waves more enthusiastically back to me as he rides away. I mutter a few disparaging comments under my breath and continue on.

Soon the tarmac gives way to dirt roads, then smaller and smaller pathways. Minutes pass slowly, painfully. There is no shade on the road. I sip water at intervals. Sometimes the trip only takes me two hours, sometimes up to four. Today feels like a four-hour day.

After my first hour or so on the road, I hear the rumbling of an approaching vehicle and I pull over to allow its passage.

The driver slides to a halt at my side, engulfing us in a puff of dust. I squint my eyes and hold a bandanna to my nose until it clears. It's Sister Ignatius from the Mission.

"*Muli shani?*" She laughs in her silent, gasping way. She likes to practice her local language skills with me even though mine are about as poor as hers.

"*Na katala,*" I reply. This can be literally translated to "I'm soft," but it means, "I'm exhausted." This sends the sister into another fit of air-sucking giggles.

I look in the back and notice the truck bed is empty. She either just delivered a patient to Mpongwe hospital or came out to do some shopping.

"Do you think I can put my bike in the back and hop in with you?" I ask.

"Sorry, not allowed," she says. Her foot has moved from the brake to the accelerator mid-sentence. She is rolling away. "Too bad for you, but you're not too far. Good luck. *Mwende bwino!*"

I would normally return the "travel well" greeting, but my mouth has dropped open in surprise and is refusing to work. I watch, slack-jawed, as the truck and its dusty shadow fade away into the horizon. I continue standing there, staring into the distance for a while. I feel as if I've blown a fuse somewhere. My mind and body have stalled, and I wait for a reboot. It comes in a torrent of angry thoughts.

Sorry? Good luck? Not far? Sure, if you think anything under 20 clicks isn't far, then, yeah, this is a breeze. It's a million bijillion degrees out here. It's hotter than the sun and I've only got half a Nalgene of water left. What kind of a friend are you?

I know it's not really her fault. It's clear that the head sister has been laying down the law again. No free rides to villagers. You'd think that since I work voluntarily for the mission at the clinic that I might be entitled to some perks, but no.

I really wish I had company. That would make this ride easier. Just having someone to talk to, or even ride silently beside makes the trip go faster somehow. On the ride out I had my village counterpart Mr. Chisembe with me. Even though I was pathetic and had to stop for water about ten times and even took an emergency break to buy dough fritters from someone who had set up shop along the roadside, I still felt the ride went by faster and easier with him there.

I don't know what it is about bike riding that exhausts me so much. It's just not my sport, I guess. Riding with Mr. Chisembe made this evident to me. He's much older than me, somewhere in his early sixties, and he has AIDS. Yes, he's probably been riding a bicycle his whole life, but the thought that someone in his condition is better at this than I am, and that he kept asking me what was wrong and why I was so tired, well, that just felt beyond embarrassing.

If he hadn't told me he and his wife had AIDS, I would never have guessed. They are both active in the community, very charismatic, well dressed, and they look fit. Not what I've seen in the TB wards at the hospitals at all. They are living with AIDS. Really living. They have both taken ownership of their lives, their choices and their future. They openly discuss the life they lived which led them to this place. The well-off city people they once were. The husband a traveling merchant, with a girl in every port, the wife turning a blind eye to his indiscretions and choosing to stay in her comfortable lifestyle instead of insisting the husband change his ways. They are both paying the price now.

As I reach the turnoff for St. Anthony's at Mpatamato, I see the chief's aide riding his bicycle towards me. I take a rest and greet him as he nears.

"So, are you going to escort me to see the chief tomorrow, or should I come alone and meet you there?" I ask.

A mix of emotions flash across his face: fear, embarrassment, anger. Nothing good. I can tell in an instant he's forgotten to arrange my audience with the chief. I remember the day I made the appointment with him. He had started drinking "Whiskey Black" with a friend. I wonder how many he had that day.

"This appointment for tomorrow, it is not possible. It can be another time," he says, and cycles away without another word.

Well, now I'm pissed. I could be enjoying the comforts of a home in Luanshya right now, floating in a swimming pool and drinking a Fanta. But no, I'm out here sweating in the sun, miles from nowhere, and for what? I consider turning back towards Mpongwe, but it's too late now. I'm closer to home than to town, and besides, I'd only buy myself another day before I'd have to make this trip all over again.

I can't believe that guy rode away without even an apology. I could plotz. Does he know what I've given up to be here? Does anyone? Does anyone even care what I am doing out here?

I take a swig of hot water from my Nalgene and begin pedaling for home. The road is on a gentle downward slope for the next few kilometers, so I ride slowly and with little effort. I concentrate on the contours of the road, making sure to follow in the groove of other cyclists. During the rainy season, the road becomes carved into crazy forms by truck tires, oxcarts, and people on foot. The water itself has a hand in the destruction of the roadway as it claims certain portions for rivulets to run or for deep pools to collect. There are large swaths where the silt has washed away leaving deep, gravelly ruts that can unseat you from the bicycle in a hurry should you slide into one by accident.

I soon find myself riding through a field of large termite mounds. This barren place always reminds me of a graveyard, the rusty lumps of earth like headstones and mausoleums rising out of the ground.

The last time I rode this stretch of road from the Mpatamato junction it was still in the hot rainy season. Which also means flying termite season. They're a tasty treat if you can catch enough of them and fry them in oil. They're popcorn in bug form, really. During this season after each rain, the winged termites swarm out of their mounds and take to the air, presumably to escape the influx of ground water and dry themselves. This is when you'll find children poised over the mounds with nets and pots to trap them and fry them up. But on the day that I rode through, there were no children in the field, and I had the unfortunate timing to arrive just as a shower ended. The termites swarmed up out of their homes and straight at me. My wet skin became a death trap. The termites' cellophane wings became plastered to me, their little bodies writhing in a fruitless attempt to extricate themselves.

I'm not one of those insect-phobic types—far from it— but having my skin covered head to toe in wiggling insects gave me a major case of the creeps. I admit it. I hopped off the bike and did the dance. Anyone who's ever walked thorough a big spiderweb knows *the dance*—it's universal. Your feet pop off the ground in a futile effort to run away from your own body as your hands attempt the equally impossible task of swatting every inch of skin at once.

Though horrible at the time, the memory now strikes me as outrageously funny, and I begin laughing so hard that I have to pull over to the side of the road and stop the bike. I let the laughter flow, then a few tears. When they subside, I stand still, stuck in neutral again. I wait and stare into the distance. I don't want to go on.

I hear the rumble of another truck approaching. I stay where I am, not bothering to turn my head to see who's approaching. A battered yellow truck passes by, rolls to a stop, then backs up towards me. The driver, a Zambian man with a handsome, broad face rolls down the window and smiles.

"I know you," he says. "I exactly know you!"

"Really?" I look over at the stranger once more. "Exactly?"

"You are the Peace Corps volunteer, yes? Is that not exactly it?" he asks. My raised eyebrows answer his question in the affirmative, so he presses on. "This is how I know: you are riding out here with this hard basket on your head."

"Ah, my riding helmet. Dead giveaway."

A volunteer a few years back had an accident while riding her bicycle without a helmet. Tragically, the blow to her head proved fatal. Wearing a helmet had been mandatory even then, but since that incident, we now have to sign affidavits swearing that we won't ride without one.

"In my village we also had a Peace Corps. He was just like you, this Peace Corps, always riding up and down, up and down, all over every place," he says. He leans out the window a bit and looks me square in the eye. "Like you, he was always working hard to do good. These people here, some of them, they cannot understand this about you. They cannot know why you are here. You can tell them and try to make them understand, but they cannot. But me, I know the Peace Corps. The Peace Corps is not like these NGOs. The Peace Corps, they know us. They live with us. They always do good for us. These NGOs are not good. But you, you are good. You are good all the way in your heart. That is why you are here. That's why you cannot give up."

He gives two solid thumps to the side panel in farewell and puts the truck in gear. I manage to say thank you, though my throat is nearly closed up with emotion.

"Don't give up!" he calls once more as the truck rolls away.

One thought overwhelms all others. One crazy, way-out-there thought: this man is an angel.

I don't think of angels as celestial beings, necessarily. I believe that if there are angels, they are among us, that they are us, and we become one when we let spirit guide us. I know one such angel very well. I call him Dad.

As I stand astride my bicycle and watch the last puffs of dust fade away, I remember a story my father shared at the dinner table one night when I was a child. He had just returned from a business trip and was regaling us with the story of his journey. There had been a woman traveling with young children, he said, standing at a boarding gate weeping uncontrollably. The children were fussing and wailing with angry tears, and the mother, at her wits end, had given up trying to console them and joined them in her own crying jag.

My dad, ever the Boy Scout, had asked if he could help her. They had been traveling all day and their last connecting flight had been cancelled leaving the woman stranded and paralyzed with despair. My father took care of rescheduling her travel arrangements and even seated himself with her and the kids to help her out and see her home. She kept repeating, "I can't believe that you are a real person. No one is this nice. You are an angel, I'm convinced." He protested that he was indeed a real person, just a normal guy from South Jersey who was on his way home to his wife and kids. "I don't believe you," she said. She handed him her contact information, "But on the off-chance you are a real person, call me sometime and let my husband and I take you out to dinner or something to thank you for all your help."

"I won't call her," he said. "I've decided that everyone has the right to believe in angels. I don't want to take that away from her."

Beyond this, I don't know if I believe in angels, really, but at this moment I feel energy run in electric waves from the crown of my head to tips of my toes and back again. If ever I needed a pep talk, today was it. Also, if ever I needed a ride, today was also it, so I don't see why my angel couldn't have offered me a lift. I shake my head and laugh at myself for being so cynical. It doesn't matter to me whether this man was mortal or celestial. Either way, it feels like a miracle at this moment. I close my eyes and breathe. *Don't give up. That's what the man said.*

I mount the bike and push off.

"Don't give up. He said don't give up. Don't give up. He said don't give up," I repeat the mantra over and over. Sometimes out loud, sometimes under my breath, sometimes only in my head, but I keep it going until I reach home.

15

Crush

The first thing I notice is that he's whizzed in his pants again. Poor Old Tata. I'm not sure what he suffers from, probably cerebral palsy. I'm not even sure if he can walk or if a family member helps drag him places. I always find him here on this stretch of sidewalk, sitting on his slab of cardboard. I stand over him for a few more moments, breathing shallowly, pushing the stink out of my nostrils with each exhale. Today I've brought him a fifty-kwacha bill and a few dough fritters from the market wrapped in newspaper. The gifts are sitting in his lap, hopefully not soaking in the dampness there, and his gaze is focused lovingly on my face. His hand pats my breast as if it were the head of a child.

"Thank you, thank you," he says.

He's not trying to be fresh, it's just as high as he can reach from the ground. It's not like breasts are a sacred or taboo thing here, anyway. I stand with him for a few more seconds, letting him pat me until I can't take the stink anymore. The whole point of me taking the time with him is to make him feel like a human, and one that is cared for. I am there to show him he is not invisible. Not to me. And for that I have become his "White Angel."

When I visit with Old Tata, I am reminded of the stories my father used to tell me about his years working in Philadelphia. "Filthy-delphia" we call it, a childhood mispronunciation which stuck, and for good reason. The streets are grey and rank, littered with homeless and their portable nests of cast-off clothes and blankets. Among all the bums, Dad always had one or two that were "his guys"—the regulars on his route who would be the recipients of his spare change. You can't help everyone, he would say, but you can't just turn a blind eye to the squalor around you either. It eats a person up in some ways, wearing permanent blinders as you walk down the streets, ignoring all the huddled forms on the edge of the sidewalks, feigning deafness to every plea for help. So, he would choose his guys. That was his deal with himself, the compromise he could live with.

Sometimes one of his guys would go missing, maybe he froze to death one night, maybe he took up on a new street corner. You just try not to think about it, he would say. If one of his guys would go missing, he would choose another. It could take time to find the "right" one. Someone not too strung out, not too visibly agitated or unstable that could easily become a danger to him. Eventually he'd find one on his route that suited him, and his spare change would flow back to the street again.

I don't know how I settled on Old Tata. There are plenty of people hard on their luck out here, the majority of the country really, but something about the man spoke to me. Maybe it's because this one, literally, did speak to me.

I've got a weakness for Zambians that speak English well. Although, I'm not sure just how good his English is since he spends most of his time simply agreeing with me, letting me talk at him. I don't know what it is about him. I just find myself babbling. The weather, my travel, how much mail I got that day. It doesn't matter what the conversation is about, he just wants to listen to me talk to him, and I like seeing him get such a kick out of it. Anytime he sees me approach, his face alights with joy and his limbs quake with a renewed fervor. I don't know how Old Tata got his education, but through the spasms and the bubbles of saliva, there are discernible English words there. "My White Angel," he says, "How was your travel? Have you come far today?"

I try not to go for the quick cash handout when it comes to him. Some days it's a packet of grilled cassava root or a fried sweet potato sprinkled with salt. Some days it's only a crumpled kwacha note, or some old sweets scrounged from the bottom of my purse, but I never walk by him without some kind of gift. Maybe it's childish, but if I've got nothing to offer, I'll walk blocks out of my way to avoid seeing him. He's my adoptee, my own little piece of woebegone that I have chosen to love in this rundown boma called Luanshya.

But this town wasn't always so bad off. The copper mines had once made this spot one of the most affluent on the continent. When copper was king, Luanshya was a model of colonial British living, the "garden jewel" of Zambia. A seeming paradise, really, if you had the fortune to be born with the right color skin and a skewed sense of entitlement. The remnants of class distinction still linger today. Upon boarding a taxi bound for Luanshya, you'll be asked which destination: first-class, second-class, or third-class. If you ask a taxi to drop you in first-class, this is where you end up, right in front of Old Tata's cardboard nest between the post office and the butcher shop. Nowhere particularly classy by today's standards, but that's what this part of town is called.

This used to be the white-only part of town, the mining company's corporate suburbia. Each roadway, though pocked and crumbling, is paved in generous width. Driving on them, one can see deteriorating estate homes and overgrown English gardens that speak of a former glory long gone and not likely to be recovered. The economy boomed then, the kwacha being 1:1 with the pound during the British occupancy, rather than the 7000:1 it is now. First-class is now a dismal destination: dirty roads, rundown shops, labyrinths of shacks selling cheap, China-manufactured goods and bootleg videos.

The bus depot lies in second-class, formerly the Indian part of town. This is the more industrial section, where shops of wholesale goods stretch on for miles. And third-class, that was where the native population lived and shopped. If a third-class citizen wanted so much as to step foot in the first-class section of town, he needed papers.

But Tata doesn't need papers now. He sits on his bit of stained cardboard, his withered legs tucked in to allow others to pass by on the grimy sidewalk. First-class all the way.

I say my goodbyes and dart off to the post office. I scan the little brass P.O. boxes lining the outside of the building until I find the right number. While I wrestle my ill-fitting key into the lock, I say a quick prayer. *Please let there be something good!* I swing open the door to the tiny letter chamber and do a little internal dance of glee when I see the treasures inside. Among the handful of letters, some small yellow index cards are peeking out. Packages. Several of them. My joy becomes tinged with dread. How am I going to carry them all?

I bring the slips inside to redeem them and sift through the letters while the postal worker searches the cluttered shelves for my packages. On top are the weekly letters from my dad, I can rely on those, thank goodness, and there are three: news from home. A letter from the Eastern Province: news from a volunteer. And a letter from America in unfamiliar handwriting. I look at the return address and feel my cheeks grow hot. A cute guy. No—a *dreamboat*. One that I've liked for years. One that I wrote to more than six months ago, but never really expected to hear back from.

Three packages plop on the counter, one small (*I can fit that in my backpack,* I think), one medium (*I'll have to carry that*), and one rather large (*nowhere but on the top of the head for you*). I sign for the largesse, fork over the customs fees, and load myself up like a pack mule. If there's one thing I'm grateful for having learned here in Africa, it's how to balance things on my head. I'm not so good that I'm completely hands free; I use a finger or two to steady the load and improve my balance (or maybe just my confidence), but it's a skill I use pretty much every day.

The letters will keep until later. I love having something to look forward to, and since I only get mail about once a month, I want to stretch out the joy of having new letters to read for as long as I can. I may open half tonight and save the rest for another day. The letter from the dreamboat, I might open that one last, just so I can savor the giddiness I feel at having received it.

I make my way slowly down the steps and out to the street, taking in everything underfoot with my peripheral view. There's no looking down when you've got something on your head, and a trip-up spells disaster. My pace is reduced to the typical African shuffle, and as I shuffle, a strange man begins buzzing around me like a bee. His eyes are attempting to fix mine, but continually dart to my chest and to the various other parts of my female form, sizing me up.

"You are abstinent, madam!" he blurts out. His eyes bulge

with disbelief and a fervor I find unnerving. "That is very fine. That is very good indeed."

I freeze mid-stride and stare back at him. My first instinct is to go on the offense, strike out at him for his cheek. Who is he to talk to me about my sexual practices? How dare he? I am oscillating between outrage and incredulity, wondering how he could possibly know about my dearth of sex life. Part of me wants to argue with him. Tell him it's not true. Tell him about the guy l let feel me up not ten minutes ago. But I stand by mutely until he explains himself.

He crooks a finger to the pin affixed to the breast of my fleece jacket. It's a twist of red ribbon—the symbol for AIDS awareness. Instead of actual ribbon, mine is fashioned from tiny glass beads, the handiwork of a women's group dedicated to raising AIDS awareness and erasing the stigma attached to the disease.

Wearing the red ribbon means you understand the facts and bitter realities of living with HIV or AIDS, either first-hand or secondhand, and are willing to engage in conversation about it. Only the bold few will wear the ribbon, but the symbol is found on billboards across the nation, often extolling the ABCs of prevention. Abstinence. Be faithful. Condoms. Any of these methods may prove effective, but none of them, as I have been informed (ad nauseum) by my community, are part of the culture. It seems that abstinence, far and away the least popular of the ABCs, has become equated with the symbol of the red ribbon. At least in the mind of this particular gentleman, anyway.

"I am also abstinent, madam! Yes, it's true. I know!" He says with a head shake, as if he himself needs the convincing.

I scan the features of his craggy face: the huge, watery, jaundiced eyes, the equally yellowed stumps of teeth, the raggedy graying hair matted with filth as if he had been napping on the roadside, and the enormous cancerous-looking mole on his left ear lobe sprouting a few long hairs like some grotesque earring.

"I'd like to say, on behalf of all the women of the world, *thank you*. You have no idea."

He nods and smiles widely, completely missing the insult. This gives me the courage to continue on with my barbed compliment, just to satisfy the perverse pleasure I feel in this moment.

"It's a real sacrifice you are making on our behalf, but we'll manage somehow," I say with a sigh.

I don't like the way he's looking at me. It's that hungry look of a man that feels he's made some small victory with a woman and feels encouraged to go farther—wants more than what he's been given. It's as if this talk on abstinence has gotten him all fired up to try and get somewhere with me, as if the strange opening line he handed me might turn out to be the best pickup of all. We've got something in common now, and who knows where that could lead?

I make some hurried excuse to part company with him and head to the supermarket. Shoprite, the Mecca of Peace Corps volunteers Zambia-wide, has been singing a siren song of chocolate bars and cheese slices begging to be eaten since I set foot on the road to Luanshya at dawn this morning. I check my packages with the guard at the front of the shop, tuck the claim ticket in my wallet, and step into the air-conditioned glory of semi-civilization. I linger over every shelf of goods, enjoying the un-African-ness of the place. The whir of the refrigerated display units, the harsh blue light of the overhead fluorescents, the clickety-clack of the cash register keys, even the insipid elevator music—it all sets me at ease somehow. I pretend I'm back in America, shopping for my well-appointed home with all the modern comforts and conveniences I took for granted while I lived there. Light bulbs, bathroom cleaner, a clothes iron, meat, dairy, beer. I look at them all lovingly and move on to the items on my shopping list: a tin of milk powder, a small block of cheese, a stick of butter, apples from South Africa, and as many chocolate bars as my budget and conscience will allow. Most staples I can get in my village: eggs, rice, cornmeal, flour, sugar, vegetables, even bread when the dirt roads are navigable enough to allow the safe passage of a delivery truck. A trip to Shoprite is for special indulgences, uniquely *muzungu* items: golden syrup for pancakes, sun-dried tomatoes for pasta, liquid dish soap in the squeezy bottle, all at exorbitant prices. I pay it. Gladly.

I redeem the laminated claim ticket for my packages, stuff the precious few groceries into my backpack, arrange my box juggling act, and head for the minibus depot in second-class. It's not a terribly long walk, maybe a kilometer, but long enough that the straps of my backpack feel as if they've dug permanent furrows into my shoulders, and the hand steadying the box on my head has lost all circulation. I pile into the rickety deathtrap we call public transport, situate all my belongings on my lap and under my feet, and massage the pins and needles out of my right arm.

As we rattle along the road to Mpongwe, I gently finger the zippered pouch containing my letters. *Not until I get home,* I chide myself. *Something to look forward to ...*

Rolling into Mpongwe, I can barely believe my luck when I see whose truck is idling by the bus depot. It's Father Mulenga from St. Anthony's. A final bag of ground maize is being loaded into his truck bed from the grinding mill. The operator of the *cigayo*, dusted head to toe in a fine, white corn powder, is chatting it up with the priest as he climbs into the cab. I sprint out of the minibus, with my jumble of packages, crying out for him to wait and take me with him back to our village.

That's the thing about going to town. You never know how and when you'll be able to get home again. If you want a ride back, you could be stranded for days in Mpongwe waiting for it.

The Father nods and tells me to climb aboard. The cab is full, but I can hitch a ride in back, he says. I perch upon the mountain of mealie meal sacks. The grain is warm from its trip through the grinding mill. Almost uncomfortably toasty, really, but the air is so crisp that I find it enjoyable. It's kind of like standing a little too close to a bonfire, your face is roasting, but you can't make yourself walk away for some reason.

It's not just the sack of grain that's burning—the idea of that un-read letter from the dreamboat has my brain in an obsessive frenzy. I can't wait any longer to read it. I unzip the pack and fish around wildly for the right envelope.

I had hoped he would write. In truth, it was a lying awake in the middle of the night kind of hope—the fervent wish of a teenager's heart. But now that the letter has come, I fear what it will say. It will probably be breezy, a "hey thanks for writing me" letter. But I am hoping he signs it "love" or with Xs and Os or says something, one little thing, that would let me know he kind of likes me. A small thing that I can dream about later.

I freeze after the opening line, "My dearest Christine."

Overload. I've hit the jackpot on the first line. What could the rest of the letter say that can possibly top that?

But it does top that.

Every sentence sends more butterflies aflutter in my stomach. Every word is a revelation. He tells me about the first time he laid eyes on me. Remembering every detail of what I was wearing, he describes the wave of excitement and nervousness wash over him, his hope that he might someday know me, and the disbelief in his own good fortune when I was introduced to him later. "It's like this," he explains. "I have a crush on you, and it's a schoolboy thing not to have told you earlier. And have I really said anything so terrible or embarrassing that you shouldn't read it? No, I don't think so ..."

In the midst of a hungry second reading, the truck spurts to life. I press the letter to my chest, lay back against the warm sacks of grain and watch the clouds of dust billow out behind us as we retreat into the bush.

The trip is a blur until I reach home and the solace of my mosquito net. I read the letter over and over, tracing my fingers over the best parts, until my stub of a candle sputters and dies. I light another and read the letter some more.

16

Chiaroscuro

P lunk.

A bucket hits water deep at the bottom of the well and wakes me. As I hear the bucket being drawn up again, hand over hand on the old rope, my awareness rises, bit by bit, from the murky depths of consciousness it has been submerged in. Other noises begin to present themselves, fuzzy, nonsensical sounds that gather in volume and clarity as my brain categorizes them. There is the chattering of birds, a tinny song pumping from a neighbor's radio, the banter of ladies gathered at the well. I roll toward the window and a bright shaft of late morning sun strikes me in the face like a slap. With a moan, I pull the blanket up to my eyes to dampen the fierce red glow of light through my eyelids. It's late.

Generally, I am up at dawn with the rest of the village. It's what's expected. At first light you rise, you make fire, draw water, wash, clothe and feed your family. Having no family of my own, you think that I'd be exempt from this routine, but if I'm not up and stirring by seven-thirty, you can bet there's someone knocking at my door or calling into the little hole in the wall by my bed asking if I'm sick. Not wanting to own up to being lazy, I thank them, grudgingly, and haul my sorry self out of bed. But no one has come to wake me today. And though I'm grateful for the reprieve, I can't help but wonder why.

I crack open one eye to peer at the clock by my bedside, but my gaze falls far short of its goal. It can't seem to get past the hand gripping the blanket near my face. A hand spattered with paint.

The events of the previous night come flooding back. Embarrassment roils around like a snake in my gut. *Holy freaking cannoli. I may have lost my mind this time. For real.* A fit of nervous giggles threatens to take a hold of me, but I squelch them with a groan, a full body stretch and brisk rubbing of my face in my hands. I am waking up. I am going to face the day and all its consequences. Just what the consequences are for vandalizing someone's livestock in the middle of the night could possibly be, I have no idea.

And why would I want to make the cows of a certain Mr. Bashi Webby look like New York subway cars? Because they are bothersome, ruinous, thieving creatures that make me forget entirely that there is such a thing as animal rights, or that I am a supporter of them for that matter.

It's just that something had to be done. That much was clear. And at one o'clock in the morning, I had done something that I felt was a bold, proactive move in the war against crime. At the time it seemed logical, even brilliant, but now in the harsh light of day, I see my actions as any onlooker might—the folly of a person gone completely insane.

The thing is, these damn cows have been a nuisance, not just to me, but to every household for miles. The owners refuse to tie them up at night, which allows them to wander into anyone's garden and feast on their hard-won labors. I wonder if it's not simply a lack of courtesy on the part of the owners, but a deliberate attempt to avoid the cost involved to provide decent fodder for their livestock. But the owners have refused to own up to their irresponsibility, claiming each time that it is the work of some other cows. Namely, that of Kodak and Spectra—a photography aficionado's cows—which are tied each night about twenty yards from my front door.

His assertion might have been plausible had I not witnessed the intruders with my own eyes. Kodak and Spectra are medium-sized cattle, fawn, with short horns. Bashi Webby's cattle are massive black and white creatures crowned with impressive long horns that look like they could gore you straight through. Now, I don't know a lot about cows. I claim no expertise in the field, to be sure, but I can tell the difference between brown cows and black and white ones. I can also count the difference between two cows and four, and the insistence of Bashi Webby that I am not seeing what I have seen, that I have been mistaken time and again, is absolutely maddening.

Our village has been a favorite target for midnight snacking by these unbridled bovines. Mostly due to the fact, I believe, that cattle are by instinct herd animals, and they enjoy the company of other cows. During these social visits we've lost three crops of sweet potato leaves, several flowering shrubs, rows of string bean plants, a host of beet greens, countless cassava leaves, and two tender, young banana trees. And that's just our collective yard in Chikuni village. Goodness knows the total damage they've done to the neighborhood over the years. Last time they plundered my garden, one of them stomped on the edge of my chicken house, breaking one of the supporting beams of the thatched teepee. The chickens made it out alive but now the structure is listing and needs to be totally rebuilt, so I figure they owe me for that too.

I woke in the night to a strange and unwelcome cacophony of sounds coming from my garden: clomping hooves, wet slaps of a fresh cow pie plopping to the ground, and the murderous ripping of plants being torn from the earth. But beyond the chomping of vegetables, the increased thumping of my heartbeat, and the exasperated groan that escaped me, the sound that changed everything, the one too subtle to be heard, was the snapping of my temper. The proverbial straw had broken the camel's back and all the anger I had in me flooded to the surface, pumping hot and urgent through my veins.

"Muthafu-cryin' out loud! What in the ever-loving hell are you two jerks destroying now?" I donned my headlamp, shoved shoes on, and stormed outside muttering a string of nonsensical, scatological curses under my breath.

Now, if one were to look inside my head—no, even further than that—inside my personality, and witness a visual representation of what was occurring, the scene might have looked something like this: an arena, much like a boxing ring, with one aspect of personality standing center stage talking in the big shiny microphone dangling from the rafters. They are the one calling the shots, putting words in my mouth. The other aspects of personality, the fragments that all combine to compose my temperament, sit in the audience. The usually dominant personality, the mild-mannered gal, closely resembling Dorothy from *The Wizard of Oz* and not given to swear words much stronger than "poop," had abandoned center stage. She had become a weak, huddled mass cowering against the ropes, alarmed that she may have somehow contracted Tourette's syndrome. Pure rage had taken her place, a writhing, growling beast, ballooning to monstrous proportion, ready to smash the crap out of anything within reach. Personality aspects like reason, pity, and fear remained fixed in their seats, simply watching the beast grumble obscenities and bark orders into the microphone. The rage had only one agenda: to wreak havoc.

Back in the physical world, this new, hyper-enraged version of me scoured the hut for an instrument to do battle with and landed upon the remnants of my house-painting project. In an effort to spruce up the place, I've been painting over the termite track-stained, lime-smeared walls on the inside of the hut. Using powdered oxides and pigments, I created a lavender hue for the bedroom, a pale sky blue for the sitting room, and a delicate shade of mint green for the new bathroom.

I seized the bucket of paint and strode out to meet my intruders. There under the mango trees, armed with only a paintbrush, a can of blue goop, and an angry alter ego calling the shots, I embarked on the quixotic mission of sending the cattle home to their owner looking like giant Smurfs.

Now, the thing about cows, especially when they aren't tied up, they don't take too well to being painted. After a few pathetic and unremarkable looking dabs on their hide, I switched to the dip and fling method with the brush. The paint began to run low, but my frenzy remained unabated. I ran inside, giggling maniacally, grabbed another can of paint, this one lavender, and a small cup for paint chucking. The splatters became more pronounced and impressive, so I employed this method until that can of paint ran low too.

The cows meandered from the garden to the front yard and back again, not enjoying the beauty treatment, but not making much of a fuss about it either. When they retreated to where Kodak and Spectra were, cozying up to them and smearing them with paint, I decided to call it quits. Sweaty, exhausted, and wearing at least as much paint as the intruders were, I tore a branch from the mango tree and urged the intruders to flee the yard, whistling a sliding two-tone song as the herdsmen do.

Once the cows were well on their way down the dirt path back to their owner's village, I crawled back into bed. I lay there for a long while waiting for my adrenaline to wear off, muttering and cursing to myself. Eventually, I sunk into a muzzy black hole of dreamless sleep. The kind of deep slumber that I'm sure people with a clear conscience enjoy on a regular basis. I wouldn't know anything about that.

Now it's time to face the music. I slide out of bed, tie a *citenge* over the waist of my nightgown, and slip on my flip-flops. Checking my look in the hand mirror on the doorframe before I duck outside, I am shocked to see the state of my hair. Besides the usual morning rats' nest of a hairstyle, the whole mess is flecked with lavender and blue like crazy, whimsical dandruff. Brilliant. I tie a bandana over my hair, and then tie a second *citenge* around my waist. Respectability, that's what I need. If there ever was a two-*citenge* day, this is it.

I unbolt my rickety front door and step into the sunshine. The morning seems obscenely bright, and I shield my eyes like someone with a hangover.

The chatter at the well stops instantly. It seems that the music should stop too, a record screeching to a halt the way it does in movies, but the song blaring from the spent speakers of Bashi Mpundu's radio is the only sound to be heard. I recognize the song instantly as the controversial hit *"Yakum-boyo"* by Danny, Zambia's premiere pop artist. Controversial because *yakumboyo* means "from behind" which, as the lyrics explain, is how one man explains to his friend how he came into his newfound wealth. He is, in essence, renting out his rear end to the highest *muzungu* bidder. And this, the anthem of the black man taking it up the wazoo for the white man's pleasure, is what I've emerged from the house to, as if it's my theme song. I have the hysterical urge to run inside and put on a third *citenge*, perhaps one that can cover every visible piece of me that proclaims me to be a *muzungu*, or perhaps one just big enough to crawl under and die.

They watch me take in the scene of the crime. Something about their silence tells me that they aren't wondering what happened here; they already know. They know in the way that people know in a small town. The way that, although you might not remember every indiscretion you have made, others feel a compulsion to take it upon themselves to remember and to pass it on.

Signs of the previous evening's shenanigans are all too evident in this light. Pastel splats decorate the dirt lot of our village, the trunks of the mango trees are smeared with it, random bit of leaves are stained with drips and sprayed with castoff. It's as if two Easter bunnies had a deathmatch in my yard. But instead of jellybeans and marshmallow peeps left behind as spoils of war, this battlefield is riddled with cow patties. Lots of 'em. In the dark, I had not seen the retaliatory strikes of my adversaries. But apparently, cattle do not suffer vandalism to their persons without having the last word.

I scuttle off to my *chimbusu* on the far side of the yard, partly for my morning pee, partly just to hide. I linger in the little hut, tossing ashes into the pit and sweeping out the space with a small bundle of dried grass until I hear the ladies at the well say their farewells and start for home.

Moglie jogs up to the *chimbusu*, mewing her greetings. This is our morning ritual, and although I don't totally understand it, I enjoy the comfort of the routine. Especially now that I am having a very un-routine morning. She waits outside the door for me to finish in the latrine, then situates herself between my legs for the slow march back to the hut. My morning escort service. Her tail, as usual, is tucked under my *citenge* and is pulling me back to my mud hut, presumably so that I can feed her a handful of tiny, dried fish for her breakfast.

Just then, the owner of the cows in question steps into the yard to discuss the situation with Bana and Bashi Francisco. And by discuss, I mean scream at the top of his lungs. The words are civil. There are all the usual niceties, but "good morning," "how did you sleep," "how is your family's health" are all exchanged with ear-splitting volume. Zambians don't use sarcasm in their language (which really burns me as most of my comments aimed at cleverness miss their mark entirely) but I think that I might be witnessing the cultural equivalent to this type of verbal assault. It is never appropriate to immediately launch into a discussion of why you have come to visit someone; custom dictates a lengthy exchange of pleasantries. But phrasing the pleasantries in an unpleasant way conveys a full disregard for the content of the discussion.

The conversation quickly evolves to the matter at hand, and though the language is well above my cognitive abilities, it is clear that I am witnessing a master duel of verbiage: quips, insinuations, insults, and veiled threats woven through the highest honorific form of the Lamba language: every pronoun translating to "respected one", each command verb with the polite suffix indicating "if it pleases you, honored one." I stand by, slack-jawed, watching Bana Francisco and Bashi Francisco take turns with their opponent, thrust, parry, remise, seconde, riposte. And through it all, not a single finger gets pointed in my direction. Not so much as a glance toward the *muzungu*, the one standing in the yard of what looks like Jackson Pollack's African villa.

Part of me wants to throw myself in the middle of the argument and take on all the blame that I so richly deserve. No one else can possibly be held accountable for this. Who is the only one in the village that could possibly afford paint, and furthermore would waste it on such a bizarre errand? Who is the only one cracked in the head enough to think that this could possibly have been a good idea?

But deep down, I know why I am not being implicated. I can't be blamed. I'm the *muzungu*. I don't like it. It's irrational and unfair and incomprehensible to me having been raised in a land where we are told all men are created equal, but I know that it is just how things are here. This is not my land, not my laws, not my mores.

The discussion ends with Bashi Francisco belting out in English, presumably for my benefit, "The law will decide! The law will decide, sir!"

Luckily for me, Bana Francisco is the law around here. As the headwoman of our village, she handles the local disputes. It is no small comfort to me in this moment that the woman I call *mayo*, my mother, is what amounts to the local sheriff.

As Bashi Webby turns to leave them and march through my yard, I urge the headwoman over to me with a few flicks of my hand. I want to face the man and have my say, but in order to do that I need a translator and Bana Francisco, for all of her modest protesting that she doesn't speak English well, is the person who understands me best. I have an idea, one that might turn this whole situation on its head, and I need her help to execute it. I may be crazy, that much is clear. But I might also be crazy like a fox. Bana Francisco translates my query.

"You are angry with me, sir?"

"My cows have been painted, madam. Painted!" His eyes bulge comically.

"And you believe they were painted here," I say.

"Yes, of course. The insult! Painted cows!" he exclaims.

"So you do not deny it was your cows, untended and untied, that came here in the night. Come see here." We pick our way through the minefield of paint splatters and cow pats to the back yard. I point to the ravaged garden. "And look here." I show him the chicken house, which had been damaged earlier, but seeing it there collapsing in on itself makes for a more impressive argument as to the destructive nature of the nightly visitors.

Bashi Webby now stands mute. He cannot now turn it around and say that someone else's cows had perpetrated these acts. He has already admitted that his cows were here, and this is where the great insult occurred. I cock an eyebrow and smirk at my translator. We now have him in a catch-22.

I stride closer to the man (the cat still remaining absurdly under my skirts), squint my eyes, summon my inner Clint Eastwood, and lay down the law for him in my best, slowest Lamba, *If I see your cows in my garden again, I am going to paint them again. Understand?* I refrain from calling him a punk, mostly because it would be insane, but also because I lack the vocabulary.

Suddenly contrite, Bashi Webby concedes, "Yes, respected one. I will leave you now. Remain well." He isn't yelling anymore; his voice is barely above a whisper.

Wanting to partake in the game of insincere civilities I missed out on earlier, I call out jovially to his retreating figure.

"Cisuma, mukwai. Mwende bwino!" Very well, respected one. Please travel well.

I turn to Bana Francisco and see she is smiling a small crooked smile, her eyes cast downward to the ground. A smile of triumph. There aren't many victories a woman can claim over a man in this society, and this small, crazy bit that we are chalking up on our team as a win feels pretty satisfying. I reach over and give her hand a squeeze. She squeezes back.

The sky rumbles and darkens ominously in the eastern sky. Looks like we're in for a heavy rain. Clean yard, clean trees, and clean cows in a matter of hours. And maybe, if I'm lucky, a clean slate.

17

Farmhand

My legs ache as I ride up the final stretch of road to the Bothma farm. It's a fifteen-kilometer ride through the bush from my village, not impossible but not something I'd do every day just for kicks either. This visit is long overdue; they've been inviting me out to visit the farm since I arrived in St. Anthony's more than a year ago.

Mr. and Mrs. Bothma are white South Africans who became expats at the end of apartheid. They come complete with all the baggage one could expect from members of a disgruntled ex-privileged class, and I try to keep that in mind when the subject of race comes up in conversation. And somehow, it always comes up, try as I might to steer the conversation away from it. Part of me wants to yell at them, tell them their ideas are disgusting and that I never want to talk to either of them ever again. But when I feel that way, I can see how hatred breeds more hatred, and I don't want any part of that. And besides, I don't see how making enemies of these people could steer either of our lives in a positive direction.

It's also hard to hate someone who has been unfailingly kind and generous to you. They've often acted as a fairy godmother, bringing me my mail or groceries from town when heading back into the bush, and they've never ridden by my home without stopping to ask if I'd like a lift out to Luanshya. And that is only peanuts compared to their most recent act of generosity. They took it upon themselves to modify my mud hut to what they consider a more acceptable standard of living. They have given me a bathroom.

For the last month, I've had a team of workers at my home digging ditches, laying bricks, pouring concrete: the works. Thanks to the generosity of the Bothmas, I can now take a hot (albeit brief) shower in the privacy of my own home. By means of a plastic container fitted with a showerhead, and secured by a block and tackle, I can heat water over the fire, pour it in the plastic reservoir and enjoy an indoor plumbing miracle for about a minute and a half. This luxury can only be topped by the toilet—an actual porcelain john— that flushes by means of pouring a bucket of water directly in the bowl. Both of these modern-day wonders drain through PVC pipes into a fortified underground pit by the mango grove. The most miraculous part of it is that after smearing the outside with mud and thatching the roof, it looks completely unremarkable from the outside.

What prompted this generous donation of labor and materials was the Bothmas' uncanny ability to swing by whilst I was bathing in my grass shelter. Nearly every encounter with them involved me calling to them over the flimsy screen of thatch while I finished washing my hair, or emerging wet, wrapped only in a *citenge*. They have been continually scandalized by my near nakedness out here in the bush, and mentioned on more than one occasion that I can't live like "these people."

I've explained time and again the rationale of the policy of my volunteer organization, about keeping the same standard of living as the people you are working with. It's just as much about experiencing life in a different culture than it is about providing aid. But this concept is just unfathomable to them. And I can't help but wonder, if I were an African American serving at this post, would they still tell me I can't live like "these people," or would they consider me to be one of them?

Late yesterday afternoon Mr. Bothma popped by on his way back from Lusaka.

"Why don't you come for a visit this weekend?" Head ducked under the thatch of the roof, a hand leaning against doorjamb to hold him up in a stooped bow, he reminded me a bit of Gandalf paying a call to Bilbo at his hobbit hole. "I've just taken the missus to the airport. She's down to Jo'burg to help our eldest daughter with her wedding plans. I'll fly down next weekend for the event, but I'll be bored out of my mind 'til then. Say you'll come stay for a couple of days, eh?"

I congratulated him on the news of his daughter's impending nuptials. He has two daughters living in South Africa, I remembered, one two-years younger than me, and the other only a year behind. Spending the weekend alone with Mr. Bothma and his racist ideals isn't really my idea of a good time, but I couldn't think of a reason to refuse especially when asked pointblank like that.

"That sounds nice," I said, politely but noncommittally.

"It's settled then." He thumped the doorjamb once and climbed back into the truck. "I'll see you tomorrow." Leaning out of the open window he called, "I'll have a fire going under the donkey so you can have a proper bath when you arrive, if you'd like." He tipped his head and accelerated down the dirt road.

I don't know why setting fire to a donkey would get me a proper bath, but since there's nothing in the world I would like more than to get clean, I say torch it. Set a whole team ablaze if you have to.

As Mr. Bothma comes into view, I see him tending the fire, as promised, under a large metal water basin with a pipe leading from its top into the roof of the house. I imagine a disclaimer posted beneath the basin: *no animals were harmed in the lighting of this donkey.*

"Howzit," he calls and waves a greeting.

Mr. Bothma is wearing the usual Afrikaner gear: polo shirt tucked into high and tight shorts (the kind not seen in the U.S. since the early eighties) and canvas *tekkies* slipped on without socks. He's got to be pushing sixty, considering he's got daughters about my age, but he looks more like a rugged forty-five. In fact, if you were to roll up Indiana Jones and Crocodile Dundee into one man, you'd get Mr. Bothma, at least looks-wise. A lifetime of outdoor living has left his arms and legs tan and muscular, his sandy hair only barely high-lighted with grey along his temples.

"It's going good," I say and unbuckle my bike helmet. Sliding it off, I run my hand over my sweaty, matted hair. "I'll be even better once I wash out this rat's nest I'm passing off as a hairdo."

He chuckles and leads me to the bathroom. He tells me to relax and take my time, and I assure him that won't be a problem. It's the getting me to come back out of the tub that'll be difficult. I soap, scrub, and rinse three times until the water runs clear, then I draw the water to neck high in the deep claw-foot tub and soak until I'm waterlogged. I run my hands over my body, still trying to free the dirt in the small crevices of my hands, elbows, knees and feet. I can still see dirt at the roots of the short blonde hair on my legs and wish I had thought to bring a razor with me as well. Even though my host is not a native Zambian, there is still no way I will consider asking him for a razor, considering the sexual implications of shaving in this country. And razors, like toothbrushes, are items much too personal and "cross the line" of sharing, as far as I am concerned.

Eventually I emerge, rosy and pruned, and he invites me into the kitchen for some refreshments. He introduces me to a different kind of tea, as like to South Africans as a cup of earl grey and a scone might be to the English. He prepares "tiger's milk." A chicory coffee steeped in milk, sugar and a generous dose of spirits. The sweet, boozy mugs of hot milk are served with rusks, a slightly sweet, dry biscuit. I dip the biscotti-like cookie into the drink for a few seconds and raise it to my mouth.

"Longer," he advises. "You try it like that, and you're gonna break your teeth."

I dutifully re-dunk my rusk. "You're serving me refreshments that could maim me? You're some host, you know that? What's next? Are we going to go rest on a bed of nails? Juggle chainsaws? Brush the teeth of your pet croc out in the Kafue there?"

His eyes light up like a kid watching a fireworks display. I've discovered he's the kind of guy who enjoys teasing banter, so I lay it on thick for him.

"I don't know about that," he says, "but I thought we would take a ride out on the Kafue, yeah. I have a small boat we can take out. See if we can catch ourselves a few *snoek* to fry up."

I have no idea what *snoek* are, but a fish fry of any sort sounds like heaven to me so I agree. We walk through the garden of towering canna and out to the riverbank where the tiniest speedboat in the world lies docked. It's a one-man job, he says, but if I wouldn't mind sharing the seat with him, I can steer the boat while he works the engine. We slip off our shoes and wade into the river to board the craft. It's a tight fit, to be sure, but I nestle in between his bare legs and grab a hold of the tiny steering wheel.

The hope of catching fish soon becomes lost as the engine roars to life and we thunder across the muddy waters. I steer the boat prudently at first, looking out for stumps, rocks, and crocodiles, but soon cave in to the fun of it all and make wild passes at each shore threatening to topple us both. Like kids on a roller coaster, we laugh and whoop and holler until we can hardly breathe.

Returning to shore empty-handed but happy, he sits me down on the veranda and asks me to relax while he devises some entertainment. I glance around the yard while he's in the house and see a lineup of solar panels hooked up to car batteries. The house has light fixtures, kitchen appliances, stereo, TV and all the other trappings of a modern home. It didn't occur to me until now that I haven't heard the expected whirring of a generator at the farmhouse. It's solar panels that allow them to live off the grid in such style.

Mr. Bothma emerges with a harmonica rigged around his neck, an accordion, and a grin a mile wide. He launches into a zippy Afrikaner folk song, alternately singing and blasting out a melody from the harmonica. He is very skilled, and I tell him so during my standing ovation at the end of his concert.

He opens the sliding door to the music room so I can peek in. There's a small organ, a fiddle, and several guitars lining the walls. The whole family plays instruments, he tells me proudly. I conjure romantic images of the family gathered about playing waltzes and jigs and two steps, family concerts that no one will dance to because there's no one left out here to witness it. How very Swiss Family Robinson meets Von Trapp family, I think. Kind of whimsical, but kind of sad at the same time. It's not that they are actually stranded out in the middle of nowhere; they've chosen isolation for themselves.

At dusk he lights the *braai* and prepares a mixed grill showcasing all the meats available on the farm: choice cuts of pork, steak kebabs called *sosatie*, and homemade *boerewors* sausages. He prepares *pap*, which turns out to be nearly identical to *nshima*, though he swears it's different. He lays the table with cheeses and an assortment of pickled vegetables and a bottle of wine. We eat and talk and drink and play cards well into the night.

The next day I awake to a feast equal to the night before. A breakfast of rashers, pork chops, fried eggs and homemade yogurt with muesli. And all throughout the day, cup after cup of tiger's milk with stone-hard rusks.

He encourages me to take another spin out on the river, but I question his sanity considering the antics of the day before.

"No worries," he says, "what could go wrong?"

"Oh no," I say. "Famous last words. I can already see where this trip is going," I tease him.

The trip quickly descends into the same shenanigans as the day before and we terrorize the wildlife for all we're worth. As we peel around a bend, the engine sputters and dies. We are miles from the farm and the current is taking us in the wrong direction. I hear a muttered flurry of curses in a guttural tongue, which I assume is Afrikaans. We manage to grab a hold of some reeds and pull ourselves to the shore. The scrub is thick along the shoreline making land travel impossible.

"What now?" I ask.

"I've got a mate who owns a farm only a mile or so back. We can walk it," he says. "He's not at home, but there's a decent road connecting the farms we can travel on."

I start leading the way up the bank with him towing the boat behind us.

"Watch out for the flatties now," he says, "There may be some resting along the bank here."

"The flatties?" I ask.

"Yeah. The flat dogs," he says. "The crocodiles."

I look down in the opaque brown water swirling around my knees and wonder how I am supposed to look out for anything down there. The best I can do is move slow and look out for movement in the water.

"Tell me about your friend. I didn't know there was another South African living out this way," I say.

"Oh, he's from Northern Rhodesia," he says. "Zimbabwe, now. Yeah, he's a secretive sort. Not surprised you've never met. He doesn't get out much. He's a bit maimed, you know. Missing half his arm. He'd been out on the river one day with his family when some hippos capsized the craft. The family swam to a small island in the middle, but were stranded there. So he decided to swim over to the shore for help, but got bit by a flattie. Took his arm clean off. Family thought he was done right there. Watched him drag himself up on the bank, boneless as a half-cooked rasher, stump of an arm just gushing. He hears his family screaming and crying and carrying on out in the middle of the river, looks up to them, and what does he see? His own bloody arm waving to him like it's drowning. The flattie taking it down in gulps.

"The man, he doesn't scream. He doesn't cry. The shock is on him. He just knows he's got to go get help, so off into the bush he goes. He walks and walks, doesn't even know where he's going but he knows he can't give up. He's got to save his family. There's nothing he can see, just flat bushland that goes on and on. There's no high ground, so he decides to climb a tree to see if he can see sight of a road, a telephone wire, a tin rooftop—anything. Anything that can point him to help.

"Now, how the hell do you climb a tree when one of your arms has just been ripped off? Hell if I know, but the man does it. Not without incentive, mind. Soon as he picks the tree he thinks he might be able to haul himself up, a crazed water buffalo charges him. Imagine that? Man is standing there doing nothing but bleeding to death, otherwise minding his own business, and this ornery bugger comes charging at him like he's been personally wronged. Just charges in for the kill. Well, who knows what that water buffalo was thinking but he wouldn't leave that tree. He paced around and around that trunk, all through the day and night, forcing the poor man to cling to that tree for his life up there—and him just hanging on with that one arm! Turns out that buffalo may have saved his life, though, because the smell of all that blood drew in a lion, and he was just itchin' to have a go at what was left of that man. Imagine that? A damn crazed buffalo pacing the ground below you, a lion hunkered down on a ridge beyond that, just waiting for an opening. Waiting for a chance to charge up that tree and haul you out of it.

"It goes on like that all through the night. By the morning, someone happened upon the family stranded in the river. They brought them ashore and tracked the trail of blood to find the man. Well, to recover what was left of him, anyway. They were just looking for remains at that point. They'd no hope to find the man alive and well. Assumed he was long dead after seeing that crocodile make off with his arm. But there he was, clinging to the tree top, arm tied in a tourniquet with his belt, the water buffalo still pacing underneath him. They fired a few shots to chase off the buffalo and brought the man down. Lost the forearm, of course, but he was no worse for wear otherwise."

"Okay," I say, slowly pronouncing the word with about three extra syllables. "That is—hands down—the most amazing story I've ever heard, but do you really think that's the kind of thing I want to hear *while wading through crocodile-infested waters?*"

He only chuckles in response.

One slow step after another my foot plunges into the riverbank, knowing each step could spell disaster, death, or dismemberment. After fifty yards or so, we both feel as if we've pressed our luck as far as we could.

"I think we should get out and try to beat a path through the bush," he says.

Not needing to be asked twice, I jump out of the river like it was hot lava and pick my way barefoot through the thorny underbrush. When we finally reach an opening to the road, we tie up the boat and walk easily on the open ground.

"*No worries*, he says. *What could go wrong*, he says," I tease him as we walk up the sloping driveway. We clap each other on the shoulder and laugh. Continuing up the drive, our arms remain around one another as we hike in companionable silence, taking turns using the other as a leaning post every few paces to pull thorns and sharp pebbles from our bare feet.

It's dark when we return home, so we retire to the family room and eat leftovers rather than cook. We drink wine, listen to ballads by Neil Diamond on the stereo and play board games until we can't keep our eyes open any longer.

I hug him goodnight and, as I pull away, he presses the small of my back with his hand firmly to guide me to his room. I dig in my heels and stand fast. He's looking at me intently, cocking an eyebrow as I meet his gaze to make sure there is no mistaking him. He's asking a question, hoping to be understood without speaking aloud, and I give him my answer just as firmly with the same silent body language. I stand solidly in place and say, "I'll see you tomorrow." Emphasis on the last word. I smile to try and reassure him that I am having a good evening, that he's done nothing wrong and there's no reason for either of us to become angry. I spin out of his embrace and retreat to the daybed in the library I've been using as the guest quarters.

As I step into the library, I realize something for the first time. There is no door on this room.

I lay awake, heart pounding, praying that I won't see his figure darken the doorway. Would he attempt to make advances on me, and if I don't accept, will he become angry? Will he hurt me? I am trying to piece together what I know about this man to see if this would fit his behavior, but I don't know enough about him to know if he has a dark side. I've been too trusting, too open, and as a result have now become too vulnerable.

It occurs to me that his invitation to stay the weekend while his wife was away may not have been happenstance, and his advance on me not just a spur of the moment idea inspired by alcohol and excitement. Perhaps all weekend long he had been trying to seduce me. All the affection I had mistook to be avuncular now makes me cringe.

I sleep fitfully, lying awake for long silent stretches and listening to the noises of the night hoping and praying that the creaking of floorboards won't be among them.

I awake to find myself unmolested by anything but the bedclothes, which have wound themselves around me like an anaconda from my constant tossing and turning during the night. The sky is dark and grumbling; we are in for another storm.

I beg off breakfast, claiming an urgency to be on my way due to the impending rains. My backpack clangs as I hoist it on my shoulder. I forgot I'd brought some handlebar extenders I wanted Mr. Bothma to help me with. My fingers have been going numb during long rides, so I got these to keep my wrists at a better angle.

"Do you think you can attach these to my bicycle? I don't have the right tools or the strength to crank these on," I say, handing over the metal bars and clamps. "I really need a dad to do this for me. I was hoping you could help me out."

"Dad?" he says, his shoulders visibly drooping. "You think of me like a dad?"

"Yeah, of course I do," I say and flash my most innocent smile.

He's not looking at my smile, though. He's still staring down at the twisted mass of metal in his hand, frowning. "Dad," he whispers and trundles off to the work shed to retrieve his tools.

He hauls my bike out of the garage, and I sit a good distance away and watch him wrestle with the clamps and his thoughts.

As I watch him work, I realize I will never be completely free from the incident. I have spent the weekend with this man alone. His workers have seen us laughing and carrying on together. The gossip network has no doubt been actively exploring every possibility of what this could imply. It's not that people are out to think the worst of me, but this kind of behavior is typical of married men in this country. It is not unusual, or even particularly looked down upon for a man to have mistresses. In the case of Mr. Bothma, who is by far the biggest *bwana* they know, they would consider it a waste of power and influence if he did not. The next richest man in our area, Mr. Chibawe, by comparison, has nine wives and more mistresses and illegitimate children than I can count.

When the new handlebars are attached, I hop aboard the bicycle and make a slow loop around the yard to test the feel of them. Satisfied, I say heartfelt but hasty thank yous and goodbyes astride the bicycle—making no move to disembark to offer a handshake or hug. I'll never embrace this man again, and the look on his face tells me he knows it. He waves me off and I push off down the road, just as the first fat drops of rain begin to pelt the earth. I pedal hard through the downpour, trying to gain as much ground as I can before the mud becomes impassable. It's only a matter of time before I have to disembark, kick off my shoes and carry my bicycle above the ankle-deep sludge of mud and cow crap.

The show tune "I Dreamed a Dream"—one of the ballads Neil Diamond crooned to us last night—comes to my mind as I push myself faster and harder away from the farm. I begin humming under my breath, then singing aloud, then belting for all I'm worth. I need to get out all the nerves, the disappointment, all the pissed-off-ness of being a human—in particular, being a woman—and all the ridiculous string-pulling it requires to make friends, stay safe, soothe hurts, or press for advantage. Managing human relationships is exhausting. I pedal harder, singing loud and strong as I fly down the slope of the long driveway. I commiserate with the trees and the earth and the rain. The farther I get from the farm, the more certain I am that I won't ever return down this road to visit the Bothmas again.

❧ 18 ❧

No Refunds

A bead of perspiration runs down my cleavage and drips into my sweat-soaked bra. The air is still and stifling inside the parked minibus, and the eight of us sitting inside waiting for the ride to begin are cranking out enough B.O. to rival a boxing gym. We've been waiting here for hours. The sun has started beating against a sign at just the right angle to cast a blinding glare in my face. It reads "Kapiri-Mposhi." Not "Welcome to" or "You Are Entering." Just what spot on the map you're occupying. But in my mind, I flesh out the rest of the sign.

Kapiri-Mposhi: The Backass end of Nowheresville

Kapiri-Mposhi: The Pimple in the Armpit of Zambia

I take in the squalor surrounding the bus depot: scantily clad prostitutes, drunkards with their cartons of cibuku beer, gangs of filthy children trying to hock everything from sweets to pumice stones, slimy potholes laden with piss and vomit.

Kapiri-Mposhi: Land of Disenchantment

Kapiri-Mposhi: Run. Run for your life.

In my mind there are only two good things coming out of Kapiri-Mposhi: the chance of hitching a decent ride and a junk food meal at the quickie mart. The convenience store at the fuel station boasts a wide selection of cold drinks, a deep-fryer cranking out a constant supply of crisp samosas and french fries, a novelty ice cream freezer chest, shelves of imported snack foods, and a refrigerated candy display case. When I arrived this morning, I indulged in two cartons of chocolate milk, fried chicken and chips, a Snickers bar and a Bounty bar. At least a month's worth of grocery money on a single calorie-laden meal.

I camped out in the little quickie mart, casing the joint, waiting for a decent looking vehicle to pull up to the pumps. But after two hours, my patience wore thin. I gave up and bought a ticket for public transport. Clearly my worst move of the day, because I've now been in Kapiri-Mposhi for five hours and haven't made any progress on the trip whatsoever.

I'm embarking on my quarterly sojourn to the provincial meeting in Serenje where all the volunteers in our province gather to share our collective reports and progress. After three months of being on our own out in the bush, we've got plenty to share with each other. It's not an all-out bitch session, but letting loose our tongues and our hair are integral aspects of provincials. Once the requisite meetings are held, minutes typed up, and reports handed in, preparations for the party begin. What ensues is basically a costume party on steroids, comparable to any frat party in the history books. Anything goes: sex, drugs, and rock 'n' roll on a scale that only entertainment-starved American kids could dream up. Cakes and pies are baked, vats of alcohol infused Jell-O are molded, smoldering fire pits are stuffed with whole pigs and goats, and cases upon cases of beer are retrieved from the marketplace, each carried on the head with extreme care. Special arrangements need to be made with the purveyors of alcohol weeks in advance, in fact, since the event of provincials has literally drunk the town dry on several previous occasions. Needless to say, this has not endeared us to the local population.

I've never been much of a partier, but insanity to this magnitude is the polar opposite of normal village life, and therefore a welcome change. It's a chance to dump everything that you've been holding in for the sake of propriety. It's a chance to be selfish, gluttonous, amorous, even ruinous. I haven't been to a provincial where at least one thing didn't get utterly destroyed. A piece of furniture, a relationship, a reputation. My indulgences are a bit more tame than most. I bake, fry, stew, chop, and sauté anything I can get my hands on. There can be anywhere from twenty to thirty mouths to feed, so I cook for fifty. Then I dance. I dance until I am too tired to go on, then I nap, get up, and dance some more.

The only dance I'm doing right now is a fidgety chair dance like a hyperactive child forced to sit through a long church service. The sugar rush has long worn off, and I have crashed headlong into agitation and crankiness. Suddenly, as if a switch had been flipped, I am done with this. Done with this place, done with this transport, done with this sitting around and going nowhere. I shrug on my backpack and march over to the ticket area under the signpost.

I hand my receipt back to the ticket seller. "I can't wait anymore," I say. "Give me my money back. You can sell my seat to someone else."

He looks up at me from under the brim of his baseball cap. He smirks, leans back in his chair and slowly slides the brim of his cap around to the nape of his neck while looking me up and down. His sweaty face shines like it's been oiled.

"No refunds, madam, sorry." He doesn't look sorry, he

looks smug. He has the look of a man who enjoys being in a position of power, and this gig he has as ticket seller at what might be the crappiest run-down bus depot in the nation is his piece of the pie.

Now, not only am I done with this, but I am not leaving without getting my money back. There will be no reasoning with me now, no compromises or bargaining. I have gone beyond reason. I have traded in my adult mind for that of a headstrong toddler primed and ready to go thermonuclear if I don't get my way, pronto. One way or another I am getting my money back.

"I'm not asking for a refund," I say. "A refund would imply that you provided me with some kind of service—a service that fell so short of expectations it would require compensation. You haven't provided me with any kind of a service. You haven't given me anything except hours of delay. Just give me my money back. You'll rebook the seat. No harm done."

"Just sit back down, madam," he says. "The transport is leaving soon." He dismisses me with a wave of his hand. "Very soon."

"The hell it is!" I burst out. "And even if it were pulling out this minute, I am not getting back on that transport. You'll give me my money back and you'll give it to me right now." I hold out my hand.

He lifts up the huge roll of money representing the day's earnings and with a sneer, stuffs it down the front of his pants, as if this is some kind of impenetrable vault, and the matter now closed.

"I am getting my money back, if I have to shove my hand down your filthy skivvies and get it myself!" My hand lunges toward his pants to prove I'm not kidding. He leaps out of the chair and starts running, both hands clutching the wad tucked in the crotch of his jeans.

"No refunds!" he cries over his shoulder as he dashes into the crowd.

I sprint after him, hands outstretched to grab him and bring him down any way I can. "Get back here and give me my money!" I manage to nab the brim of his baseball cap. He slips the hat off his head and keeps running. "Give me my money back, you cheat! Give it back or I'm going to kill you! You understand? *I am going to kill you!*" We weave in and out of the lines of minibuses, bystanders parting the way and shouting. I can't tell if they are shouting encouragements, or admonishments, or simply crying out in alarm. I can't hear anything over the sound of my own voice shouting about how I am going to tear this man limb from limb with my bare hands. He jumps up into one of the large vacant minibuses, and as I hop into the vehicle in pursuit, I see him leap through the open rear window. I am not following him. Not that way. I notice a shoe on the floor of the bus by the window and take comfort in the knowledge that even if I lost the chase, at least I'm not running around in the filth with only one shoe on. I collapse in a seat and crush the creep's baseball cap in my hands. I give up.

A man runs up to the bus and cries, "Here's your money, madam! Please take it!"

I stare back in amazement. "He gave my money back? He gave up?" Perhaps the loss of a hat *and* shoe is more than a man can bear out here.

"No madam," he explains, "it's my money. Just don't kill him! Please! Don't kill him!"

Stunned into silence, I look from the man's tortured face to the fistful of cash and back again. This man, this kind stranger, believes he is actually buying a man's life. I don't want to tell him that it was only a figure of speech, that I wasn't actually going to kill the ticket guy. Instead, I show him that I am taking his offer seriously by weighing it in silence. Eventually, I exchange the stolen baseball cap for the proffered cash. Leafing through the kwacha notes, I see that it's the full amount of my fare, all seven pin worth. I got it. I got my money and I can walk away.

"Okay," I say to the man. Not *thank you*, not *I couldn't possibly*. I say "okay" and I walk. I walk all the way to the junction, more than a mile uphill, hating myself more and more with every miserable step. The worst part is, I know the man never would have offered me the money if I were not a *muzungu*. The rules of reason and decorum have been bent in my favor, and I was complicit in the bending of them.

When I arrive at the turn off, I reach into my pocket and pull out the wad of bills. Seven-thousand kwacha. About a dollar fifty. This is worth threatening a man's life over? Even in jest? I feel despicable. If I were my supervisor, I would not only can me and send me packing on the first flight back to the States, I'd have me committed for a psych evaluation.

I wait on the corner and stare southward to the scene of the crime. I pray to God that I'm not still standing here when that minibus finally does roll around the bend. Wouldn't that just be the cherry on top?

After a long spell, a minibus emerges from the north and flicks on its turn signal. The rusty tin box glides around the corner on bald tires and slows to a crawl in front of me. The bus boy hangs out the open sliding door and calls out the destination of the voyage. I am the only one lingering on the corner waiting for a ride, but he calls out to the world like a freak show barker at a carnival, trying to entice passersby to experience the horrors and fascinating spectacles inside the tent flap. "Serenje, Serenje, Serenje ... Mukushi, Serenje! Yes, madam, yes! Serenje!"

I stand by mutely. My head, seemingly of its own accord, is shaking "no." The bus continues to creep along, an inch at a time, not willing to stop but not willing to pass me by either. My feet remain fixed, my expression pained. Trading in one lousy minibus ride for another? I've got to be out of my mind. But this one is at least moving.

I cave. There's no other option. There's no chance of getting to Serenje before nightfall and I'm desperate not to be passed by, or worse, picked up by the bus that I vacated at the depot. I climb in and see there isn't an empty seat. The bus boy taps one of the rows of passengers, and they scoot over to provide space for one butt cheek on their bench. I perch on it kitty-corner praying that someone might soon disembark.

The busboy holds his hand out for the fare, but I tell him that he'll get it in Mkushi. There's no way I'm paying up front for a ride again today. He shrugs and bangs twice on the vehicle roof to tell the driver to get going.

The minibus rattles as it accelerates to its top speed, around 35 mph. There is a small hole in the floor by my feet, and as I watch the tarmac skitter below, I ponder the concept of roadworthiness. In the U.S., the smallest car malfunction, even a burned out blinker, is cause to take the vehicle off the road. Here, if the car rolls, it's ready to ride. This is especially true of a long downhill run, when even fuel is not considered a necessary part of a vehicle's roadworthiness. There is a long stretch of hilly road ahead and I wonder if I will be experiencing the on and off stretches of silent free-fall later.

Last time I rode in a minibus on this stretch of road, the driver hit the brakes to avoid hitting a stray goat. This subsequently caused all four rows of benches to slam to the front of the bus. None of the seats had been bolted down. The old man next to me started crying, "OH! OH! MY LEGS!" It took us a minute or two to excavate ourselves and haul the heavy seats off of him. Fortunately, his bones weren't broken, but boy, did that driver get an earful from me. I take a moment now to look under the seats to check for bolts. These, at least, look secure.

Suddenly, with a deafening squeal, the sliding door of the minibus flies off the side of the vehicle. We all stare wide-eyed at the gaping hole as the wind pelts us in the face. The driver slows to a stop and reverses to retrieve the stray piece of his vehicle.

No one says a word, but every tongue in the bus clucks with disapproval. *Tsk, tsk, tsk, tsk.* We sound like a percussion section manned entirely by maraca players. During the rest of the two-hour trip to Mkushi, the occasional reprise breaks out among the passengers. A solo, a trio, a quintet. The bus driver says nothing in response. He has no defense.

As we roll into the dirt lot in front of the Mkushi market-place, my eye is caught by a couple of busboys animatedly acting out a drama for a crowd of onlookers.

"Give me my money back, you cheat! I'm going to kill you!" The words, though heavily accented, are unmistakably my own. The man playing "crazy *muzungu* lady" rips a baseball cap off of the other man's head and chases him about in a tight circle. The man playing "skeezy ticket seller" falls to the ground while "crazy *muzungu* lady" then proceeds to merci-lessly beat the man with his own hat.

"Ah, no! No, madam, noooo!"

I slump down in my seat. The mortification is paralyzing. And under the mortification, anger is seething. I'm not angry that people are making fun of me. I fully deserve it. I'm angry at myself for being such a horse's ass. What really goads me, though, is that the news about me has traveled faster than I have today.

I've never felt so disgusted with myself. I've come halfway across the world with the intentions of helping those most in need and serving as an ambassador for my country. And this is what I end up doing? Running around screaming and handing out empty death threats to the very people I came to help?

I decide there is no penance worse than remaining on this minibus until it fills up and chugs into Serenje. I fork over the fare to the busboy and settle in to watch the re-enactment of my insanity again.

"Come back here, you!"

"Argh! Madam, no! No refunds! No refunds!"

❧ 19 ❧

The Lengths We go to for Love

Mirabel and I have collaborated on projects for nearly two years, mostly centered around the school where she teaches, but it's only been the last couple of months that we've grown close as sisters. The pregnancy she has been hiding has now become evident and her world is starting to crumble. It's clear that the man she recently started dating is not the father, as she is already nearing her second trimester, and he has rescinded his hasty marriage proposal.

"It'll be okay. You'll see," I tell her.

Mirabel smiles in a lopsided way that shows me she disagrees, then gives my hand one last squeeze before she turns and walks back to the school grounds.

"Listen," I call to her. "Why don't you come over later and we'll talk more? I've got some new magazines from America we can read and I got some popcorn from Mpongwe. Let's have a girls' night."

She turns and smiles, this time broadly, and accepts gratefully.

I step inside the grounds of the health center and walk to the large meeting *nsaka*. The poinsettia trees are in full bloom, giving the place a bit of holiday charm. Even though it's nearly February, it still feels like Christmas every time I see them.

It's two o'clock, or "fourteen hours" as it's known here, military time being the standard. It's time for the monthly Neighborhood Health Committee meeting. I know that I'll be one of the only people here, but in order to illustrate my commitment to follow through with my word, to say as I do and do as I say, I continue to show up on the dot at each scheduled meeting. I duck into the *nsaka* and am glad to see my three faithful counterparts, my rocks. These are the legs upon which anything I build here will stand on when I leave. I smile at each one in turn, Mr. Chisala, Mr. Kabeya, and Mr. Chisembe. I haven't seen Mr. Chisembe in weeks. Another round of infection he couldn't fight off left him hospitalized in Ndola. I fear his battle with AIDS may be lost before long.

I offer my hand to him in greeting and hold on to him for a few minutes as we talk. Holding hands with your friends when greeting or escorting one another is one of my favorite things about this culture. I rely on this small bit of human contact each day to keep me sane. I study his features with care; he seems to have aged ten years during the month he spent in the hospital. His skin looks looser on him somehow, and the creases of his brow and his smile lines have deepened. Much of his hair has gone to silver and the stubble on his chin gleams in contrast with his dark complexion.

Next, I greet and hold hands with Mr. Kabeya, who doesn't look much better than Mr. Chisembe these days. His wife miscarried a few weeks ago. He is still waiting for her to return from her exile.

This exile is not a punishment, but a tradition. It is one of many long-held superstitions intended to keep the world of spirits at bay. The world of the invisible is always recognized to be close at hand—ghosts, medicine, witchcraft. People often apologize to me for this, thinking that being from a Christian nation I would be unfamiliar or repulsed by such beliefs. "You may not have witchcraft in America," they say, "but we in Zambia, we have witchcraft."

There are some times when this does come off a bit embarrassing for them. Like the time when the police arrested a crocodile for a crime and held it in the Luanshya jail for weeks, just waiting for it to shapeshift back into a man. The were-crocodile is a popularly held belief in this part of the world. Eventually they emancipated the poor reptile, realizing they must have captured the wrong one, as this was only an ordinary non-shifting crocodile—not a man at all.

That kind of magic I have a hard time getting behind, but the simpler, everyday rituals I find fascinating.

I went with all the other women in my village to visit Mr. Kabeya's wife after her miscarriage. It was a purely women's affair, no men in sight. The *nsaka* in the yard had been draped with *citenge* to make a tent that provided shade, and perhaps, a shield from prying eyes. The women filtered in one by one and greeted the would-be mother with the suffering greeting. Unlike a funeral, there was no wailing or drinking or story-telling. We sat in silence, an occasional whispered conversation breaking the lull. We just sat with her in her grief. I didn't know until later that the grief was not all about the loss of the child. She was about to lose everything that could give her comfort. After that day, the woman would go into exile for a month or more. She would be brought to her parents' village and would sleep in a separate hut, and have her own cup, plate, and utensils which would be shared with no one else. No one would sit and talk with her, no one would visit her.

Superstition holds that if one is to have close contact with a woman who has just miscarried, if they eat a meal with her or sleep in the same room with her, the spirit of the lost child might haunt them. This would be the only social gathering she would attend, and the only emotional support from her friends and neighbors. When she returns, she will be considered clear of the incident. No one will likely speak of it again.

After we had sat for a while, an old woman came into the tent with a large leaf of *imposho*, a local variety of aloe. She broke it open and milked the leaf to allow the thick juice to ooze forth. The tent became perfectly still as we watched the ritual. She eased down the mother's shirt and rubbed the leaf on her back, then on her chest drawing a small pattern I could not make out. Then she rubbed the leaf on the backs of her hands, her palms, and the tops and soles of her feet in the same pattern. The old woman exited the tent and called the husband and all the children of the household to come forth and she anointed them in the same fashion. I had first thought the ritual to be for the mother's healing, but I soon realized it was a form of traditional medicine for warding off the spirit of the unborn child.

For Mr. Kabeya's sake, I hope his wife returns soon. He's looking thinner every day.

Next, I greet Mr. Chisala who looks quite well. His young wife, who I would guess to be about forty years his junior, had a baby last month, so he's pleased as punch. Mr. Chisala has been the Chairman of the committee since its inception seven years ago. Though he's retired, I think this volunteer job must keep him as busy as he ever was back when he was a landowner. People still tell stories about back in the day when Mr. Chisala was the "big man"—the richest farmer in the chiefdom. He's now one of the humblest people I know. His hut and possessions are no more extravagant than anyone else's, certainly less so than mine. I've at least got small wooden stools for my guests to sit on, whereas he only has a tree stump, a couple of cement bricks, and an old tractor tire to perch on. He's been my most important counterpart, ever cheerful, ever willing to hold a meeting no matter how far we may need to travel.

The man who was supposed to be my village counterpart, the Environmental Health Technician at the clinic, transferred to another province shortly after I arrived. His replacement lasted all of two months, the next fellow for six months and we are still awaiting his replacement. I've barely got the names of these guys down before they are out the door. I've learned not to get too attached.

There was never going to be someone as good as the first one that left. Ba Mubanga and I met and clicked right away. It was clear that we were attracted to one another, but two things stood in our way: Firstly, he had a relationship with the previous volunteer, Susanna, and I do not relish the idea of stepping in as a replacement *muzungu* girlfriend. I'm having a hard enough time trying to fill her shoes around here as it is. Secondly, he was leaving. His transfer request had been submitted before I even stepped foot in the village.

I still get letters from him, though, and he's proved to be a wonderful pen pal. They are not love letters, per se, just letters of friendship laced with admiration. I send letters back to him in the same tone. If he had decided to stay in St. Anthony's, then who knows? Things might have gone differently for us. As it stands now, we enjoy a nice correspondence and I like having someone to tell my stories to who knows all the places, the players, and the situations I am faced with. Unlike the dreamboat back in California, Ba Mubanga is someone who truly understands what I am up against out here.

Mr. Chisala rises and hands me an envelope. "This has arrived for you. It was sent to the mission."

This letter isn't written in the familiar, cramped script I expect. Not from Ba Mubanga, then. This is in a hand I don't recognize. The postmark is smudged but looks to be sent from Serenje. I tear it open and read.

HAI CHRISTINE,

I'm glad to have this chance of expressing my heartfelt Love for you. It is really hard to believe that I'm everyday down to Loving you, deeper and deeper since the time we met on twenty-first December when you were on the way to Dar-es-Salaam.

My heart always rejoice when I take a glance at your beautiful face, your hospitality and care. I do care about you always although we haven't discussed anything concerning Love affairs. I'm always and shall always be by your side. It has taken me time and effort to realise that I'm in Love at first without knowing yourself. The beginning of, any relationship, I wasn't so serious but I'm serious all this! I want us to be serious for Love is just between two people.

When people are in Love, not everyone around them is happy. Some people will try to destroy our Love. But be stead/bold and we will reach the end. You have become planted in my mind. I always think and dream about you. Please take care, this world is not fair for young Lovers. Remaining to hear from you.

Yours Loving friend,
Binwell

. . .

THE UPPER RIGHT-HAND CORNER READS "20.00 HOURS, IN HURRY REPLY SOON" with an ornate box drawn around it, a bit like a child's drawing of the sun. Apparently, not only am I supposed to remember this guy that sold me a train ticket for a trip I took more than a month ago, but I am supposed to reply in all haste so I can put this poor guy out of his misery.

"What is it? Good news?" Mr. Chisala prods me. Being wracked with spasms of silent laughter, I can't answer. He continues the conversation without me. "Yes, it is good news I think. See, she is crying now! Tears! Actual tears of happiness! Yes, this is a good letter. She has been waiting for this one, and now it has come. Happy news. I can tell."

"A love letter," I finally manage to say as I catch my breath. I wipe tears from my eyes with the hem of my *citenge*. "Unfortunately, the love had an expiration date, and I missed it. My loss, I guess."

"Is it from Mr. Newton?" he asks.

"Mr. New—ew, no. Thank goodness. Just some stranger," I say.

Ba Newton is a water and sanitation trainer I inherited from a former volunteer in a nearby catchment area. I have no problem with his training methods or the price he asks for providing his services. My hang-ups with him are all based on his lack of understanding and respecting personal boundaries. On previous visits with me, he would remove things from my hut without asking, like my Walkman, sunglasses, bandanna, etc. and wear them around the village. The last time I saw him, he had arrived in the middle of the night in a rainstorm. I received him, hauled his muddy bicycle back into the bathroom to keep the living area clean, then stepped back into the main room to find him completely shucked down to his skivvies. After a stunned silence followed by a heated argument about when and where one should doff their wet clothes when visiting a lady, I packed him off to the neighbors faster than you can say, "I see London, I see France."

"I don't want to talk about Mr. Newton," I say. "I know he's coming to lead the training for the Water and Sanitation group soon, and I am happy to do all the budgeting and planning and everything for it. But that man is not going to stay with me again. Not ever. One of you can take him," I say. They give each other "knowing" looks. Clearly, they think we've had some sort of affair, but have had a falling out. The thought repulses me, but I don't even want to protest my innocence. That will probably only confirm their suspicions. I don't care what they think as long as they get the point. He's not ever stepping foot inside my house again. Period.

One by one the other members of the committee arrive, and we begin the meeting. We're budgeting for the next quarter, which means everything needs to be perfectly measured, documented, and boxed in perfectly straight lines. Arguments erupt over which side of the ruler has the straightest edge, whose penmanship is best, and which order the names of the committee members should be listed in. I serve as referee for the little spats and try to keep everything on track, insuring essential items make their way into the budget and not fretting over the minutiae.

"Okay, everyone listen up, now. Next item: saladi. How much saladi should we budget for?"

Silence falls over the crowd. Visions of fritters, crispy *kapenta* fish, and heaps of greens swimming in greasy tomato *supu* dance in our heads. A question of this importance requires serious thought. Like any good dish, we give it time to simmer.

The St. Francis of St. Anthony's

"Ba Chri, I have a surprise for you. Your most special friend has come to visit," calls Bana Memory as she knocks on the door.

Who on earth could this special friend be? And why have they come calling at the ass crack of dawn? I slide out of bed, rub the sleep out of my eyes, wrap a *citenge* around my night-gown and open the door.

No one else appears to be standing in the yard, just Bana Memory with a mischievous glint in her eye and something hidden behind her back. Her hand swings forward and presents me with a grey ball of fluff. Two large golden eyes stare up at me. "Your owl!" she says between guffaws. "It is your most special friend."

I can feel myself blushing as I join her in laughter. I take the proffered bird and tuck him under my arm like a little Nerf football.

"Oh, Mwacuula, how did you get here?" I croon to it.

Bana Memory laughs even harder "You have even given this one a name? It is Mwacuula?" She bends over laughing like she is going to fall down. The whole naming thing is doubly absurd to a Zambian. First off, no animals get names except for cows and dogs. They are working animals and can obey commands directed at them, but no other animals would need a name. Everyone here knows that. And secondly, the name itself is pathetic. In local language it means "you are suffering." But the first time I saw him, he'd been kicked around and left to die on the road, so I thought the name suited him.

She tells me that on her way over to my home, she found a group of children teasing the bird, holding it by its outstretched wings and walking it down the lane towards the school.

"I told them that if you knew what they were doing to your owl, you would beat them. You would beat them hard. Kwa kwa kwa!" she says, batting one fist in the air to pummel the invisible brats.

I close my eyes and pinch the bridge of my nose. With my eyes still shut I say, "Uh, thanks, that was ... nice ... of you." I look down at my feathered friend and stroke its head. Poor little guy. It's really been living up to its name. "Bana Memory, how do you know about my owl? I never told anyone about it."

"Everybody, they know," she says with a flip of her hand and walks off.

Yes, of course they do. I haven't whispered this to a single soul, but it doesn't surprise me that everyone knows. That's the way of things here. What is there to talk about except your neighbor and what they do? The fact that I never told anyone about the owl is irrelevant. Whatever you do, people somehow know.

Only once did someone pass me by when I was with Mwacuula, someone I didn't know. But it's clear to me now that my care for the bird would have seemed so remarkable to this stranger that it would have made an interesting story, one that surely everyone would know by now.

I had come to feed the owl some regurgitated mouse guts (compliments of one of Moglie's kittens) and found Mwacuula covered in filth, stinking of piss, and his bad eye caked with mud and closed shut. Someone, or maybe a group of boys, made sport of the poor thing again. I brought back a bucket of water, a washcloth, and a clean towel to dry him in. That's when the stranger saw me visiting my little friend. Who gives an owl a bath? Crazy *muzungu* ladies, evidently.

I've kept my care of the owl quiet for a few reasons. Mostly because people here detest owls. They are about as admired as the snakes and vermin they feed upon. Since I've always had a fascination with them, I was shocked and saddened to hear that this was the general consensus in this country. When I asked people why, I always got one of two responses. Number one, according to local superstition, they are thought to be the harbingers of death. It's said if one alights on your rooftop and hoots, it means someone in the home will die soon. And number two, they just plain scare the crap out of you when you are walking on the roads at night. They lie in wait on the roads for snakes and mice to cross, and when you draw near, the only warning you get is a brief flash of eyeshine before it whooshes straight up and over your head.

I've always loved owls, perhaps partly due to the fact that I had a painting of owls in my room as a young girl. It seemed to me that they were always looking out for me, perched in the frame above my dresser drawers. The few times I've seen an owl in flight have been nothing short of magical. They seem to hold all laws of time, space, and gravity at bay and fly in what appears to be slow motion, their wings cutting the air in uncanny silence.

Beyond my sheer admiration of the actual bird, I have my own silly devotion to the image of the owl. I have a strong memory of recovering from a stomach flu once while on holiday at my great-grandmother's house. I had the usual comic books, ginger ale and saltines by the bedside table, but what gave me the most comfort were the little dolls of owls on a shelf by the bed. Covered in silky rabbit fur—one doll in snowy white, one in brown—the tender softness of the little owls imparted a feeling of well-being that nothing else could.

I decide to take Mwacuula back to his nesting place right away. Normally, making fire and brewing coffee is the first order of business, but I don't think it's a good idea for me to keep him here in the village. I don't want him getting used to people. Not even me.

I start up the road toward the Kaundas' maize field, where the owl's burrow lies. This road, a long stretch of nothing close to no one, has become one of my favorite places to wander in the evenings. Bana Francisco introduced me to this pathway as a shortcut to our new fish farm. It was here that we found our first animal orphan. We were returning from a long day's work of digging ditches for diverting water to our fishpond site. We found a baby goat lying prostrate in the heat, all motor functions beyond panting having abandoned it. We took turns carrying it home, about a kilometer for each of us, found someone who had a lactating goat to be its nursemaid, and sent word back in the direction we had come that the goat had been found. It all got sorted out after a few days, once we'd all caught heat for goat stealing. Gratitude runs in short supply here sometimes.

It was only about a month later in virtually the same spot that I found Mwacuula. It was just a ball of grey fluff on the path, of such an odd form and size that my brain was racing to try and categorize it. A rock? A plastic bag? A hedgehog? As I neared, a little beaked face swiveled around and focused on me with one golden eye. The other was swollen shut. Someone had kicked him in the face. He didn't move or cry out. He just stared at me with beak open and tongue fluttering in a desperate pant. I thought, *what is it with this stretch of road? It's like the damn Bermuda triangle for baby animals.*

He really was just a baby, still covered in fluffy down-like feathers rather than adult plumage, but he wasn't tiny by any means. This chick was nearly as big as my cat. I wondered just how old it was and how big the egg it hatched from must have been.

I wrapped the chick in my *citenge* and brought him to the shade of the nearest tree, a gloriously large and spooky looking tree called a false baobab. This turned out to be the right move, for as I neared it, I discovered the owl's burrow there in a hollow chink in the trunk.

Until today, I never touched Mwacuula with my bare hands. This was something my mother taught me when I was a girl and we discovered a bird's nest in our yard. She told me to look with my eyes and not with my hands because the mother bird would smell the scent of me and would abandon the nest. I don't know if that's true, but I think it's a good rule of thumb to not touch wild animals with your bare hands for any reason. I always used tongs for feeding Mwacuula and towels for washing and drying him. Part of that being the no-bare-hands rule, but since he has quite sizable talons and beak, self-protection definitely factored into that decision.

Now that I've broken my rule, I figure I'll take it a step further and really investigate. Since the kids were playing with it and I know it's been kicked around and abused before, I decide to give it a physical and see if anything feels dislocated or broken. I'm no doctor, but I've been a bodyworker for years, so I have some palpation skills and know a thing or two about anatomy and physiology. I am amazed by how light and hollow the bird feels, like one of those toy gliders made of balsa wood. I carefully stretch and prod his little body. He's gained a bit of height these last couple of weeks and his adult plumage is beginning to show. After a thorough exam, I decide that against all odds, he seems no worse for wear. The eye has healed well and he doesn't even smell like pee anymore. I am beginning to think he just might make it.

When we reach his burrow, I gently tuck him back into the little hole and promise to return later with more water and dried fish pieces. The stores are almost depleted.

I head back the way I came, opting out of my normal walking route around the Kaundas' maize field and back. My ritual of an evening walk has become an important part of my routine, part of what keeps me grounded. It is my time to be alone and sort through my thoughts, which often drift toward the dreamboat in my hometown who's been writing me love letters. This daydream time, this time away from prying eyes, is when I carry on imaginary conversations with him. He's a great listener, the version of him I hold in my head anyway, and he finds me endlessly fascinating. He listens to all my concerns, all my daily drama, and eases my fears just by being there.

As my time here draws closer to the end, my anxiety grows about what waits for me when I return. Out of everything, the one shining hope I am holding above all others is that this might be it—that he might be *the one*—a companion I can build a life with. Most people fear ending up alone, but I find I've always operated well as a one-person show. The real challenge for me would be to add someone else to the mix. Making room for a "we" instead of just "me" is something I've yet to manage successfully. I know I am probably kidding myself, putting way too much imagination and hope into a relationship that may never take off, but I can't shake the feeling that this romance—for good or ill—is meant to teach me a vital lesson about love. *All aboard the S.S. Dreamboat, full steam ahead.*

I take a slow, African-style stroll home. The sun is barely up and already it's scorching. We've had temperatures in the 100s for weeks now, it seems. I've decided I'll wear this little nightie with the *citenge* as my outfit today. It's too hot for real clothes or even undergarments. I'd feel self-conscious, but other women sometimes wear nightgowns as dresses too. For them it's just like any other garment. Since I've lost a good fifteen pounds after my second bout of malaria, nothing else fits me properly anyway.

I am starting to gain the weight back, slowly. And my hair —I lost a good bit of that too, but it's on the rebound. I thought I must have had a severe case of head lice from the way my scalp was itching. I finally went over to Bana Francisco last week and asked her to have a look. She told me, without even bothering to inspect my head, "No, Ba Chri. It is not that. Your hair is growing back in. That is why you itch." I felt mortified that she noticed how much hair I had been losing (a side effect of the once much-loved, sexy-dream-inducing mefloquine which I have had to stop taking) and even more embarrassed that she has noticed my hair growing back in. Clearly, it was so obvious that everyone has noticed and already discussed it amongst themselves at great length. Taking my small hand mirror, I stood out in the sun and had a look for myself. I could not deny that she was right. There, glinting in the sunlight, stood prickly new growth all over my scalp like fine cactus spines.

When I reach home, I start the fire, put the kettle on and go inside to wash. I dampen a washcloth and run it over my face and body to take the dust off. Water is too sparse right now to bathe properly. Our well dried up. First time it's happened since it was dug seven years ago, they say. The

Kaundas' well still has water, but it's murky as heck and takes a good day for the silt to settle enough to consider drinking. Maybe I'm a priss, but brown water that I can't see through just isn't suitable for cooking or cleaning anything. The borehole at the school is the closest source of decent water right now. It's about a kilometer away, far enough that I only fill my small ten-liter container. I don't want to carry anything heavier than that on my head for that long of a haul.

I pull on the same nightie and *citenge* once again and sit under the shade of my *nsaka* to cook my morning meal. Once I get a good fire going in the brazier, I set the kettle on for coffee and measure out water, mealie meal, powdered milk, sugar, and ground peanuts into a pot to make porridge. I watch the children play as I cook. Little Caleb Kaunda is running up and down the yard with a little car his father fashioned from a pink plastic Maheu drink container and shoe polish lids for wheels. He's pushing it with a long stick shoved through the top of the car—Zambian-style remote control. The rest of the Kaunda children are in a bicycle-rim-rolling contest against the Chikuni twins. Kids seem to have the energy to play in any kind of weather. The fact that I don't want to do anything more strenuous than read novels makes me realize how far from childhood I really am.

It is times like this that I feel lucky my mother instilled in me a fierce love of reading from a young age. Novel reading has become my sole occupation on these scorchers. The other day had been so sweltering that I stayed glued to the grass mat on my concrete floor, just lazing and sweating, novel in hand, occasionally moving to a fresh spot on the concrete to soak up the cool. When it became dark, I moved from the floor to the bed for the evening session of lazing and sweating. That's when I noticed a lump in my shirt. Stripping off the t-shirt, I saw the lump was still there, just inside my bra. Turning the fabric out to investigate further, I was surprised to see a cockroach flip out and hit the floor, then skitter under the bed to take refuge. Since then, I've gotten into the habit of checking my clothes for unwanted guests before I tuck myself into my mosquito net at night.

You know you've reached a pretty sad state of affairs when patting yourself down for roaches is the best you can come up with for a personal hygiene ritual. "Achievement unlocked" on not sweating the small stuff. Go me.

The Bun that Broke the Camel's Back

No one would ever accuse me of being beautiful when I'm angry. I'm not at all like those movie actresses you see on the silver screen with blazing eyes and a furious blush in her cheeks, causing the leading man to stumble mid-argument and gush, "God, I love it when you get angry," before enfolding her in a passionate embrace. No, I become a trembling wretch with blotchy skin and quavering voice. I sweat uncontrollably. My nose and eyes go red, puffy, and leaky. The angrier I become, the more pathetic I look. In truth, I think it's safe to say that any argument I've ever won has been out of pity. A force to be reckoned with, I am not.

The cause of my most recent episode? The bread truck didn't arrive yesterday. Though I've had morning buns on the agenda for this Water and Sanitation training session for months, the universe didn't get the memo. The kitchen staff had to resort to cornmeal porridge for the morning's breakfast.

The training group has been complaining about the food for days, though it's by far more food than they would receive at home. Each meal has two or three kinds of relish with the *nshima*, at least one of them protein. I know for a fact that sometimes these guys are reduced to eating their *nshima* with nothing but a side of salt to dip it in. But somehow this chicken and beans and eggs and fish and greens just aren't up to the standards they are used to, they claim. When the buns got nixed from the menu, the crew decided to boycott the meal altogether. They sent a messenger to the kitchen where I sat enjoying my porridge and coffee with the cooks I hired.

"They won't come," he said simply.

I looked at the giant pot of sweetened porridge on the fire, enough to feed two dozen men. I had brought a loaf of bread from home and made small sandwiches of butter and honey for a treat. Pots of milky, sweet tea and coffee sat on the stove.

"And why not?" I asked, trying to keep my voice level. I didn't want to shoot the messenger.

"They say porridge is for children and sick people. They don't want it," he said, and walked away.

I looked again at the huge pot of porridge. What a waste. I complimented the cooks and told them how much I enjoyed the porridge. "Please bring the rest over to the clinic. We will give it to the patients," I said. The cooks shared a look as if to say they doubted even the sick people would eat it, but they agreed to do as I asked.

As I stormed over to the meeting hall, I thought about that line mothers always hand to their kids when they are being picky about their food, "There are starving people in Africa that would give anything to eat that." The longer I live here, the more ridiculous that sounds.

My mind stockpiled all the chastisements and insults I wished to heap on the men, and as I opened the door to the training, I let it rip full blast, f-bombs dropping where they may.

Not that that means so much out here. English is used infrequently, and curse words are considered novel rather than offensive. Commonly heard after someone sneezes is, for some unfathomable reason, "Oh, shit" rather than "God bless you." But using English curse words means something to me. It means that I am beyond my limit and I have resorted to name-calling like a child. I even called them a big bunch of crybabies, except I was the one choking on my own tears as I said it. They sat dry-eyed with shocked, innocent expressions.

"Do you know what a volunteer is?" I asked. "A volunteer is someone who chooses to do a job for no reward. They do the job because they wish to serve their community. Not for money or power or recognition or even a free meal. Because let me tell you, if you are just in it for the food, you had better rethink why you are here. I did not come out here from America and bust my hump for the last year just so you could get a fat *amabun* and a cup of tea this morning." Chairs squeaked and groaned under restless bodies as the men endured my tirade. "I am a volunteer. I can choose to work with whomever I like. And right now, I choose to not work with you."

I motioned to Newton, who, at that moment, closely resembled a deer caught in the headlights of an oncoming truck. He stood frozen in a half crouch, wide-eyed, barely breathing, the stick of chalk in his hand hovering an inch away from the surface of the blackboard.

"This gentleman is being paid to teach you. He doesn't have the luxury of walking out on you. He'll stay and finish your training. I, however, am leaving."

With that said, I strode out of the building, across the

north end of the village, and deep into the maize fields. Then I cried. Loud, angry tears they were, too. Like a child who hasn't got their way and the only way of expressing their disappointment is by the volume of their tantrum.

As I wandered the field, I bashed my fists against the small reedy tree branches crossing the path. I relived the scenario over and over in my mind, except this time saying all the clever, controlled, and utterly cutting phrases I had had the time to craft in the interim. Instead of looking at me with bewilderment and alarm, like I had walked in the room wearing a hat on fire, they looked at me with utter mortification for being called on their bad behavior. The few heads not bowed in shame looked up at me with remorse, their eyes begging, "How can we make it up to you?"

Who knew *amabuns* were worth striking for? And why do people have to put "ama" on the beginning of practically every English word so that it can be used like local language? Ask a bread vendor for buns and he'll give you a blank stare. Change your order to "*amabuns*" and he'll smile and ask how many you want to buy, and why didn't you just say in the first place you wanted some *amabuns*? Why were you using some high falutin' *muzungu* language nobody can understand out here?

"Stupid buns ... full of ... *jealous*," I said as I kicked a rock out of the path with more force than was necessary. This has become one of my favorite catch phrases, non-sensical as it is. The story behind it actually sums up a lot about Zambian culture, but leaves as many questions as answers in my mind. It goes like this: One day, a volunteer friend was traveling and came upon a house painted with large block letters, "STUPID NEIGHBOR, FULL OF JEALOUS." The man sitting out front explained to her that he and his neighbor were feuding, and that he had written this on his house. He also said that he would be painting over it one day soon.

When my friend asked why, he motioned to the neighbor's house and said, "Ah, that old man, he died sometime last year."

I retreated through the maize fields to where I knew no one would follow me—the fields beyond the burial ground. No one goes there, not unless they have a body in tow. It is the one place I have found I can be alone, aside from the middle of the (theoretically) haunted waters of Lake Kashiba. The children don't dare follow me, and the adults, who generally have less interest in dogging my steps anyway, would think twice before going in after me. Beyond the burial ground, past one of the Chibawe's maize fields, is a place I've dubbed Eden. It's a rich, green landscape dotted with acacias. One of the most peaceful and untouched places I've seen—a place that really says "Africa." There is a small crevice there, about the size of a large hot tub, which is devoid of water but filled with small, delicate wildflowers, more than a dozen varieties. Each one is beautifully, utterly foreign to me. I often linger here on hot afternoons, but never bring a blanket to lay out for fear of crushing the little gems I come to admire. I just find a place to plant my feet safely and rest in a low crouch.

I've been crouched out here for goodness knows how long, legs half numb, knees and ankles barking. I'm no closer to leaving my hidey-hole than when I came in.

The flowers here seem to me like miniature items in a dollhouse, and in my imagination, I conjure all the uses a fairy would have for them—which flowers make the cushiest beds and pillows, and which petals are best for drinking the morning dew. Each flower, leaf, seed, root, and stone becomes the toys of my imagination. In one corner of the empty pond lies a stockpile of treasures I have found on previous visits, for I've never walked into this place without finding some small bit of natural splendor. In the pile lies the lace of a tiny,

shed snakeskin, a handful of colorful rocks, a couple enormous snail shells bleached white from the sun, a fallen bird's
nest with tiny strips of *citenge* scraps woven through it, and a
patch of dried grass gone to seed with each pod rattling on
the end of the stalk like a tiny maraca.

I find my imagination is much the same as it was when I
was a young girl, the same things holding fascination for me.
In some ways, I just haven't grown up. Perhaps my temper
hasn't matured much either.

But wasn't that why I was sent out here to this remote
village—because I was more mature and considered capable
of handling the stress of this isolated post? Though I'm
another year older than when I began, I think my temper
may be more explosive than ever.

My birthday, roughly marking my first year of service in
Chikuni village, coincided with the first day of the training. I
really should have taken the time off to visit other volunteers,
or at least be in town and have a chance to talk to my family
on the phone. I should be taking in a movie, eating an ice
cream cone, drinking a beer, laughing with friends, anything
other than this—but this was when we were able to reserve
the meeting hall and hire a trainer, so the date stuck. Clearly,
I have been harboring some resentment about this.

I am in a grown-up world, and I can't throw a fit like a
child. I can't hide in my little playhouse with my toys and
hope that my problems will go away. My heart sinks as I
realize I need to stop hiding and go face the music. I can't
cloister myself away because my life is not acting the way I
want it to.

I've tried to control this training, mapped it out with
charts and timelines and daily agendas and menus and shopping lists, and now I'm sitting here whining because it didn't
all turn out as planned. The world isn't playing fair. Well, so
what? When has the world ever been fair?

The worst of all the things that I didn't plan on, the most unfair thing of all, finally brings itself to the forefront of my mind with heart-wrenching clarity. Tears sting my eyes again. Mr. Chisembe helped me plan this event, but he is not here to help me see it through. He was buried yesterday. I wasn't able to attend because I was here leading the training. My friend, my first mentor, the architect of every business plan put into motion since I arrived here, is gone.

The death, as it turns out, was quick and would be shocking, honestly, had I not known he had AIDS. I just thought I would have more time with him. I've got another year to live here, to see all our plans through to completion.

I know what I need to do. I have to suck it up and go back to the meeting. Maybe not today, but I'll come and work with them tomorrow at the well-improvement site, assuming anyone has stayed to complete their training. I'll go, not because I want to, or because I think they deserve a second chance, but because I don't want to dishonor Mr. Chisembe's memory and all the hard work he put into this training before he passed.

I stretch out my stiff legs and begin the slow journey home, all the while constructing phrases in Lamba to convey my grief. I yelled at them in English, but I will apologize in local language as best I can.

Swedish Tickler

Bana Ruby groans, unties her *citenge* sling and pulls the child away from her body. She is soaked. In a world without diapers, this is a mother's lot. I used to wonder why women here always seemed to smell like pee. I don't wonder anymore. She passes the child to me, lifts the tub of fritters off her head, and places it on the ground. She says she'll meet me at the market; she's going home to change. I strip off the bit of wet *citenge* swaddled around the child and drape her naked form on my back. I loosen my own *citenge* from my waist and slide it around her body, making sure her rump is covered but her legs are free, and tie the ends around my body, knotting it at the shoulder. Balancing the tub of fritters on my head, I walk across the overgrown football pitch to the lane where market vendors are camped in front of the school grounds.

"There she is! Hey, Christine!" I hear a voice ring out.

"Hey, we found her!" Another voice calls.

I look at the far end of the field and see my new friends from Mpongwe trotting over to me, waving their arms above their head, as if I could possibly miss them in this empty field.

I laugh as they approach—first because I'm touched by their enthusiasm, second because this is the exact opposite of the scenario when we first met.

A couple months ago, news had reached me that two white doctors from Sweden had arrived in Mpongwe to volunteer at the hospital. During my next visit to the boma, it was only a matter of minutes before I spotted them. Two tall, pale figures glowing like beacons in the distance. I bolted after them. Not knowing their names, I yelled, "Muzungus! Muzungus! Hey, muzuuunguuus! Wait up!"

They stopped in their tracks and waited for me to draw near. As I did, I noticed they were not just any two muzungus. They were the GQ models of all *muzungu* men I have ever seen in my life, which is saying a lot since muzungus have begun to look terribly ugly to me, like something that just crawled out from under a rock. I have become so unused to pale flesh and Caucasian features, I find white people quite off-putting on the rare occasions I see one.

Once I reached them, I found myself unable to speak. I swallowed a few times, looking back and forth at their beautiful faces, before I could think of something—anything—to say. I bought myself some time by fanning my face to indicate I was out of breath, but really, I was just stunned and embarrassed. I couldn't think for the life of me why I thought it was imperative that I run after a couple of strangers screaming at them to wait up for me.

I finally managed to introduce myself, and they did the same. Sven (blond and blue-eyed with a strong build) and Albrikt (a long, tall drink of water with dark hair and eyes) are medical professionals here to study bilharzia. They've come on a sort of Doctors Without Borders type of program run by their country to gather data for their research and to provide medical assistance at the local hospital in exchange for room and board. I've been dying for company—any kind of company—from ex-pats that I could relate to. Now I feel as if I've won the lottery—hot, Swedish, supermodel-looking doctors with hearts of gold.

Okay, so they had girlfriends. But that put me at ease, relieving any pressure I might have put upon myself to try and impress and woo one of these adorable strangers. I could just sit back and enjoy the view, and what could be better than that?

After that first awkward meeting, we've become thick as thieves. I've made so many excursions to Mpongwe to visit with them that the owner of the guesthouse has kept the room adjoining theirs vacant for me. We spend our evenings feasting, singing songs, and telling stories by the fire. One of our favorite pastimes has become "fortuneteller" in which we spin wild yarns about each other's futures using an ordinary deck of cards. This generally happens after a few beers, when we feel our powers of prognostication to be particularly potent. The fortuneteller's job, besides trying to dream up hysterical scenarios, mostly consists of assuring the client between fits of laughter, "Listen, I'm not making this up. The cards don't lie."

"Hello, gents." I call back to them. "And to what do I owe the pleasure?"

This time it's their eyes that appear starstruck, their speech that is stumbling. Seeing me here wrapped in *citenge*, rather than my city clothes as they are used to, a baby slung around my back, carrying a preposterously large tub on my head, they are the ones in awe. I slide my passenger around to my hip so they can see her beautiful face.

"I'd like you to meet Christine. She's my neighbor's daughter. I named her after myself. Obviously."

"Leaving your mark, I see," jokes Sven.

"Well, they asked me to name her, and I didn't want to bust my brain trying to think up something good."

"You said you lived in St. Anthony's, but when we asked for you at the mission, they said you didn't live there," he says.

I try to imagine what the nuns cloistered in that convent thought when these two fine male specimens came calling. If it were me, I might have considered renouncing my vows.

"I work at the clinic at the mission, but I don't live there. No, I'm a Peace Corps volunteer. I don't get to live in anything nearly that nice. I've got a mud hut back that way about a kilometer into the bush."

"You live in a mud hut? And you have somehow failed to mention this the whole time we've known each other? Can we see it?"

Their expressions of excitement and disbelief could not have been more profound if I had claimed I lived in the Taj Mahal or on the surface of the moon.

"You'll have to wait until I deliver these fritters to the market and pass Christine back off to her mother." I hold up the pee soaked *citenge*. "She went home to change."

"That's okay, we still have to go and collect urine samples from the school children. We won't be finished until later this afternoon."

"I'd lend you a hand," I say, "but I think I've had enough of urine sampling this morning. Why don't you come by for lunch when you're done? Just start walking that way and ask anyone where I live. They'll point you in the right direction."

When I reach home, I make a fire and begin boiling water for *nshima*. I figure I might as well give them the full bush experience and feed them a traditional meal. I pick sweet potato leaves from the garden and fry them with onions and tomatoes. I boil a few eggs, then roast a pan full of dried groundnuts. I salt them and add a small splash of water to the pan the way I've been taught. It sizzles and evaporates in a flash leaving the nuts with a nice, even, salty crust. I am scooping the *nshima* out of the pot into individual portions with a small, wet bowl as my guests approach. I greet them and invite them to sit in the *nsaka*. They watch as each steaming scoop of *nshima* lands on the serving platter, gels, and sets within seconds, a starchy film forming on its outside so it will be easy to pull apart from the other portions. I am gratified to see that I've gotten the correct consistency; I've been practicing my *nshima* skills for months. I figure that even if my *nshima* isn't as good as the local women who have been making it all their lives, these guys wouldn't know the difference anyway. This is as close to the real deal as they are ever likely to get.

As the men watch me, I remember something I've seen in my Peace Corps Volunteer Leader's kitchen tacked to the fridge. It reads: *TWOG's: Acronym for 'Third World Groupies' used by White Zimbabweans in reference to foreigners who travel to underdeveloped countries and consciously sink to the lowest level of society.* Scrawled in red marker underneath reads: *THIS MEANS YOU.*

This makes me laugh so hard every time I see it that I have often thought about photocopying it and posting it in my hut.

I don't think I'm a *TWOG*, though. I didn't pitch my life in a developed country with the romantic notion that living here would be better or more authentic in some way. I came to do a job and to experience this different way of living. To a white African, however, the lifestyle I've chosen must seem absurd.

Living in the African bush is not a glamorous life, but it is in its own way romantic. I mean here I am swaddled in dusty yards of *citenge* fabric, perfumed by the faint scent of baby pee which refuses to quit, and these guys are looking at me like they can't believe their luck that they know me. In their minds, I must look like the real deal: the volunteer who has gone native.

I know that I haven't, nor ever will "go native." I also don't feel wholly American anymore. This has become my home. But I know my time here is fleeting and I am an outsider. I'll never be anything other than a *muzungu*, no matter how long I live out here in the bush.

We get to chatting about life and work, and soon the men loosen up. I ask them lots of questions about bilharzia, though I know quite a bit from my health education classes. It's just that men like to talk about their work, and I like to hear them say that particular word in their lovely accent. The way they say it sounds so exotic and downright sexy, I almost want to go out and get myself a case of *beal-HAH-zye-ah* just so I could hear them diagnose me with it.

The reality of having parasitic larvae up your urethra, however, is about as un-sexy as it gets.

I remind Sven of the last time we had lunch together, and we relay the tale to Albrikt. I had arrived at the hospital just as a woman was beginning to go into labor. Sven told me I could scrub in and assist him with the birth, but it would likely be a while. We walked back to the guesthouse and set out a picnic lunch in the garden. We dined on sliced cheese and cold meat, fruit, marmite sandwiches, and biscuits. We drank glasses of mango juice, icy cold from the refrigerator. He had no idea that this meal would have cost me a week's wages; he apologized for what he considered to be a meager feast more than once.

We ate quickly and walked back to the hospital. Though we had been gone less than an hour, the mother had already delivered the child, and it was being weighed and measured. I was disappointed at having missed the chance to assist.

"Every time I go to lunch, I swear, that is what happens," he says.

"That happened to me last week, too," says Albrikt. "You can't turn your back on them for a moment. And they're so quiet. Not a peep out of them. The birth can happen when you are there in the room doing something else and you don't even know until you turn around and see her holding the child."

After we've eaten, I call to the children who have taken up residence in the mango trees all around the yard like a flock of overgrown, curious birds. I pass out my stack of *citenge* for dancing, and we put on a show for our guests. Admiration glows in their eyes as they watch me talk to the children in local language, sing songs, and perform traditional dances with them. They look about the same way I did when I visited a village for the first time and watched Jana speak and dance and cook in her village. I wanted nothing more than to be like her, and now it seems I am. I don't know when it happened, and I might have missed this realization altogether had I not seen myself through my visitors' eyes just now.

When it's time to part, I escort them back to their vehicle at the mission. As we are saying our goodbyes, an old woman rushes out of the church in order to shake hands with the Swedes before they depart. My friends climb into their Land Rover and head up the dirt road. The old woman stands with me and watches their retreat.

"He loves you more," she says.

"Who?" I ask, thinking, one of these *Swedes* loves me?

"God does," she says.

I stare at her in response. What on earth is she saying?

"He loves the white people more. You whites, you are

better than us. That's why when God came down to earth, he came as a white man."

She motions her hand back toward the church at the mission. Inside hangs one of those disturbingly realistic life-size replicas of the crucifixion. The tortured and bloodied form of Jesus is, by the artist's rendering, snowy white.

"You are closer to God than we are. We Blacks, we are not as you are. You, you are my God."

I feel a sadness that is beyond tears.

"Don't say that. We are not gods nor are we any closer to God than you are. He loves all his children. We are all equal in his eyes," I say, but it's obvious that my words are falling upon deaf ears.

She reaches up her hand as if to cradle my face, but shies away at the last moment leaving her hand hovering a few inches away from my cheek.

"You are my God," she says again.

What can I possibly say to this? I've got nothing. Nowhere in the Peace Corps handbook was there a section on what to do when people claim that *you are their god*. No way do I have the intellectual or theological chops to even touch a discussion like this. My stomach sours. I'd been feeling so tickled that my *muzungu* friends had come to visit and lavish their attention on me. Now I feel gutted. I reach out and hold her hand for a few beats, then turn and leave for home without a word.

Ain't No Sunshine

Hopping off the bed of the oxcart, I feel a sharp tug on the rear of my *citenge* and hear the popping of threads. I twist to inspect the damage, sucking through my teeth in the "tsk tsk" way that the Zambians do whenever something goes awry. The driver of the oxen makes the same noises of concern, then begins the "sorry, sorry, sorry" mantra called for in this situation. It took me awhile to get used to this sympathetic phrase when I first came to this country. It struck my ear oddly, like overt martyrdom. As if the onlooker who watched you stub your toe or drop an egg on the ground or plow your bicycle into a tree somehow wanted to take the blame for your own feeble coordination. But here "sorry" is used in a way to indicate regret for another's misfortune, and the more times you say it, the sorrier you can appear to be on their behalf.

I see that it's only a small tear in the fabric, nothing I

can't mend in a jiffy. I interrupt his litany of sorriness to assure him that it's no bother and to ask his help in loading my back, arms, and head with the multitude of Christmas packages I've received from town. I thank him for the lift and head down the road to my village as he urges his team on toward the markets near the mission.

It's been seven full days of travel to return from the shores of Namibia. The three coaches, two minibuses, and one taxi along thousands of kilometers of tarmac were the easy legs to negotiate; it was the last fifteen clicks from the Mpatamato junction that concerned me most. Not only is it not serviced by public transport, but during the rainy season (which we are smack in the middle of) it often becomes impassable for days at a time. I start down the wide dirt path that leads to the western end of our catchment area, where it butts against the shores of the Kafue River. The second village down this road is Chikuni village, my home. Only half a kilometer to go.

I weave through the maze of puddles on the road, careful to follow in the tread marks of bicycles that have successfully negotiated this path since the last rain. The Kaunda children see me struggling up the road with my parcels and rush to relieve me of them for the last few yards. Hope, Caleb, and little Maureen with my namesake strapped to her back. I offer a finger to Christine, which she immediately grasps in her chubby hand and endeavors to jam into her mouth, fist and all. We are talking on top of each other, rapid-fire, news of home, news of my travel. All the while, I am surprised by how good it feels to be speaking Lamba again, and how this village feels more like home than anywhere else on the planet right now. I'm in the home stretch of my service now, and thoughts of returning to America, to highways and cell phones and nine-to-five jobs, seem more than a little intimidating.

We turn on the path to Chikuni village at the grove of mango trees and are greeted with the sight of a very pregnant Moglie trotting over to greet us. As her tummy sways from side to side, I try to guess the size of the next litter. I cluck my tongue loudly for her—this is our version of the dinner bell—and she answers with an emphatic melody of purrs and mews.

The yard smells much like the vineyards of the California wine country at the time of the crush. The heavy, sweet tang of fermenting fruit hangs like a warm fuzzy blanket in the air. The air seems to fizz in the nostrils, a buzz of alcohol on every inhale, and you swear you could get drunk by simply breathing. Dozens of mangoes have gone to rot around the base of the trees. I make a mental note to haul this load over to Mr. Kabeya's pigs in the morning.

Caleb tugs my sleeve and asks for my plastic bags while Maureen fishes around in my pockets for sweets, but older sister Hope shushes them both. I've been gone for a few weeks to spend Christmas and New Year's with other volunteers. She and I have a lot of village gossip to catch up on.

Hope babbles on, her banter punctuated by wild hand gestures and facial expressions to emphasize the newsworthiness of her reports. She tells me how little Christine had suffered a bout of malaria but has since recovered. A swarm of *impashi* swept through the village, but not to worry, paraffin was sprinkled around my hut, so they didn't get in. I feel a bit disappointed at this, not that I wanted to be potentially eaten alive by an invasion of carnivorous fire ants, but from what I hear, they scour every bit of edible material, every crumb, every flake of termite track, even the wastes of their fellow army members, as they swarm through. There are no human means of cleaning that prove half as thorough as a voracious swarm of millions of mandibles.

She goes on to tell me that Bashi Mpundu has run away

with another woman in Luapula Province and has left his pregnant wife Bana Mpundu, their twins, and little Icoola behind. They have all moved to her mother's farm on the eastern banks of the Kafue River. My mind reels at this news. No more drunken fighting and blaring rumba music at all hours of the night? No more crying children outside my door? Could this be true? I am torn between feeling outrage at Bashi Mpundu's betrayal and relieved at his departure. I am only half listening to Hope's report of local events after the dropping of this bomb. I hear her mention my friend Mirabel. I smile and nod in her direction at the mention of my best friend's name. She must have stopped by to visit. She's probably wanting copies of those pictures I took of her and the baby before I went on vacation. Good thing I had them developed in Luanshya on my way here.

Hope grabs a hold of my arm as I lean forward to put my key in the lock.

"Umfweni, Ba Christine. Ba Mirabel bafwa."

She searches my face, waiting to see if I have understood her. All the children have gone silent. *Bafwa?* This isn't a term I use regularly. My mind goes into translation mode. I imagine my set of flash cards, crudely cut from blue poster paper, riffling in front of me until I find the right one for the root verb: *ukufwa.* In my mind's eye, the card turns over with excruciating slowness, like a film playing at the wrong speed. The back of the flash card reads "to be dead." No, that can't be right. My mind translates the phrase again only to reach the same horrifying conclusion.

I slide my finger from little Christine's slobbery fist and grab the doorjamb. My fingernails dig into the grooves of the weathered lumber, and the earth stands still. Suddenly, the aroma of the fermenting mangoes no longer strikes me as pleasant; it smells sickening. The whole place smells like rot and death, and I feel a wave of nausea roll through me.

"*Shani?*" I ask, my voice barely above a whisper.

I shudder at the sound of my own voice. This word for "how" is often used in substitution for the entire phrase, "How are you?" Friends and little children sing it out to you all day long. "*Shani? Shani?*" It's a blithe shorthand and using it to inquire after the death of my best friend seems a gross misuse of the word.

Hope hands it to me short and sweet, in language I can understand. She had a headache. She was taken to the hospital. Three days later she died.

"Sorry, sorry," she says in a quiet voice and rounds up the children to leave me in peace. I put the key in the lock and unbolt the door, but continue to stand at the threshold for a long while. When I am finally able to move again, I dump my packages inside, close the door, and crawl straight into bed. It's not even close to bedtime. I don't care.

It's not until the following day that I glean more details from neighbors and my friends at the clinic. The headaches became seizures. Tests for cerebral malaria were performed but came back negative. The end came quick. Perhaps it was a brain aneurism. A tumor. Meningitis. The hand of God. No one could say. Only one thing is clear: at the age of twenty-three, Mirabel Muntanga, mother of three-month-old baby Esther, has been called to God. And during the last hours of her life, she feared her demise.

"She was scared, that one," Bana Martha tells me conspiratorially when I arrive at the clinic. "She was crying out to God. 'Please, God, don't take my life. Let me live. Let me live for my baby.' There was too much crying with that one."

Bana Martha has always been kind to me, even exceedingly so. If I happen to visit her during a time when she's shelling groundnuts or roasting maize, she always splits the pile and insists I take the more generous portion home with me, leaving her and her nine children with the meager leftovers. Her sharing this bit of news, however, seems outrageously uncharitable. It seems indecent to be telling stories of someone who has passed, saying that she did not face the end with dignity. No one wants to hear that someone they loved did not die well. I nod, unsmiling, and walk away from her.

More days pass. I work, I sleep, I eat. My mind remains in a numb fog. I continue to push all thoughts involving my dear friend from my mind. But one morning, I wake to a memory of her. We were doing the slow African walk along the St. Anthony's road in front of the school. She was escorting me to the clinic. We were holding hands and talking in low voices. She had just confided in me about her pregnancy. "I'm scared," she said. "I'm so scared." At the time I laughed indulgently, patting her hand like a child and told her all the things that friends are supposed to say. "It's going to be okay. Of course it's going to be okay. Don't worry. You don't need to be scared." In truth, I was scared for her. Unmarried. More than one potential father. No one willing to stand by her and help her raise her child. *Everything is going to be okay.* The words are even more pointless now than they were then.

This memory, this chink in the fortress of numbness I have built around my mind, plays itself over and over until the wall breaks. The torrent of undesirable reality crashes through. Grief finally finds its purchase, and the tears flow. It is time for me to pay my respects.

With hardly an upward glance, I make the pilgrimage to her final resting place. I've known for days which burial ground she rests in. I just haven't been able to make myself go there. In truth, I've considered avoiding it entirely for the rest of my days here in Africa. As the graves come into view, my heart sinks. There are rows upon rows of mounded earth. Some are old, some are new, but none have headstones. A handful of the graves have an old enamelware plate or bowl half buried at the head of the mound. A poor marker for a poor family. I'm not sure what I expected to find, certainly not a neon sign pointing to her pile of earth flashing *THIS IS IT*, but I was thinking it would be somehow obvious when I arrived where to find her. I wander through the mounds searching for the one that looks the most recent. There are at least three that look to be dug within the last two weeks when Mirabel's funeral, her *icililo,* took place.

After several minutes of indecision, I wander out to the path on the far side of the burial grounds. I meet two children on their way to school, a girl about twelve with her young brother in tow. I recognize them as children from a village I have been working with to repair a broken water pump. The poverty of their village is evident in the children's school uniforms: the clothes are comprised almost more of patches than original cloth. I ask them to show me which grave belongs to Mirabel. The young brother takes his elder sister's hand and crushes it in a death grip. Their eyes widen like saucers at the mention of their deceased teacher, the thought of walking into the burial ground entirely too much to ask. The young boy tugs on his sister's hand as I ask again. The girl offers her apologies, claiming they have to rush to school, and the two of them take off at a run.

I watch their retreating figures with exasperation. It doesn't really surprise me that they won't go into the burial grounds. No one does unless they are there to bury someone. The fear of ghosts, of hauntings, of witchcraft, is just too great. But it would only take five steps in that direction and a point of the finger to help me out. Would it really have killed them to take five steps? In a fit of childishness, or maybe Italian-ness, I shoot the hand signal of the evil eye down the now empty path. See how they like that juju.

I wait on the path for the next pedestrian, one with perhaps a bit less superstition, but the minutes stretch in to what feels like hours, and no one arrives.

I decide to find help. My friends Bana and Bashi Grace, who live on the far side of the school grounds, worked with Ba Mirabel and would surely know which grave belonged to her. I march through the path carved out by the commuting children through the un-slashed football pitch, wary of the multiple booby traps of tied grass.

I am lucky to find Bana Grace at home, and she agrees to show me the place where they laid Mirabel to rest. We walk in companionable silence back to the graveyard. There is nothing to say. She wanders in and out of the mounds, looking for the right place. She points to a mound in the center of the burial grounds.

"Here," she says.

This grave, I explain to her, is much too old. Look how it is sunken and covered with grass. She agrees. She walks to a different area of the graveyard.

"It's this one then," she says. The grave looks even older than her last choice.

I am a hair's breadth away from flying into a rage. How could someone who saw their friend buried only two weeks before have no idea of the grave's location? I show her what I feel to be the contenders, the three most recently dug mounds of earth, and after some deliberation we come to the conclusion that the freshest looking mound, the one with the chipped green bowl as a headstone, must be the one I am looking for.

I'm angry at her for being of so little use to me. Angry at the children too scared to help me. Angry at myself for not being here when she died. Angry that I did not have a chance to weep with the other women. Angry that there is no way of knowing if I'm even at the right gravesite now. I stand silent at the grave, my eyes watering, my hands clenched in tight fists. Bana Grace, mistaking my mood for grief, silently slips away without a word. As she does so, fat drops of rain begin to pelt the earth. The sky rumbles. My anger wells up even more as I realize my lack of foresight: no umbrella, no rain jacket, not even a decent pair of shoes.

I sink to my knees and chant the words of the wailing women at an *icililo*. Words I've heard before but never used myself. I don't want to say a few last words or read a quote from the bible or say a prayer. I just want to mourn. I want the grief to pour out of me until I am empty.

"Mayo, mayo, mayo. Cabipa, mayo." Oh, mother, what a tragedy has befallen. I untuck the top of my *citenge* and loosen the knot at the end to reveal a small handful of cosmo seeds. I plant the seeds one by one into the mound of earth covering her body. Each small sharp seed presses into the pad of my thumb like a dull needle. I concentrate on the sensation like a meditation as I continue keening. *"Awe, mayo, mayo, mayo."*

All the while I hear the soundtrack of her voice on the day she told me she was pregnant. "I'm scared, Christine. I'm so scared." Her voice trembling with a kind of nervous laughter. She often laughed when she talked and nearly always had a smile on her face, an amicable gap-toothed grin like her mother's. Each time my mind plays the memory of her voice, her smile, her laughter, the sadness grips me tighter.

The seeds are all gone but I continue to pat the damp mound of her grave as if I were consoling it. *You don't have to be scared anymore, my friend. The concerns of the world are behind you now. Let us who are in the world do the worrying.* As to how she will be remembered, who knows. Soon, these flowers, the ones from the muzungu's garden, will bloom over her body, and she'll will be remembered, if for nothing else, as my dear friend. Or perhaps no one will remember that the flowers came from the muzungu's garden. Let them think it's a blessing or freak of nature or just plain witchcraft. Let them say anything they want about it. Their superstitions and judgments and fears can't touch her now.

The rain has become heavier, the air a steely grey charged with electricity. Time to head for shelter. I slide off my flip-flops, a regrettable choice of footwear, but there's nothing for it now. If you don't wear the rubber *jombo* boots, the only way to go is bare. Any other shoes get sucked off into the mud. And so, with flimsy *pata-pata* in hand, I make the tearful journey back home, carefully picking my way round the puddles and the piles of shit on the trail. No one likes to walk back into the tall, wet grass to do their business this time of year. I sing a low chant under my breath as I travel, walking away from my friend, away from the graveyard I know I will never visit again.

"Mayo, mayo, mayo, capiba mayo."

❦ 24 ❦

One Last One for the Road

No tears. That's the deal I made with myself and I intend to keep it. Susanna, the volunteer that lived here before me who I have never been able to live up to, the local language guru, the traditional dance prodigy, had one mark against her. She bawled when she left the village.

"That one, she cried too much when she left. I told her, you must not cry. Why all this crying? But she would not stop. It was very bad," is what my neighbors said.

At the time I felt it was very insulting to her, the "too much" crying. But now I realize that it is only the equivalent of how they would express this in local language, *sana*, meaning "a lot," or "very much." My friend Bana Luke uses this expression a lot but mispronounces it. "Too muck," she says. This particular phrase is something I love to hear her say, so I never correct her.

"Bana Luke," I asked her one day, "do you want to marry again?"

"No," she said, looking at me like I had asked if she enjoyed eating live snakes. "Too muck fighting, fighting." Her hands then became makeshift Punch and Judy puppets as she proceeded to act out the horrors of domestic squabbling and violence. Then she turned the tables on me.

"Your boyfriend. He write letters. He make you too muck happy."

"You think I am too happy about it?" I asked, knowing what she meant but feeling the sting of criticism in her words, nonetheless.

"Yes, too muck."

"Perhaps you're right."

What do I really know about this guy anyway? I want him to be for real. I don't think I could bear it otherwise. If I come home and he changes his mind about me, what will I do then? This is the only plan I have. Go home, fall in love, get hitched, start a family. I've been oscillating between wanting to go home and wanting to stay here for another term of service, but recently I feel my heartstrings being tugged towards California with increasing urgency. I don't want to be alone anymore. I also don't want to be the *muzungu* anymore. I don't want to be special or different or remarkable in any way. Jane Doe, housewife, mother of 2.2 kids, with a house and a dog and someone to hold me at night.

A lifetime of wanting my life to be remarkable, wanting an adventure, wanting to go to Africa, has led me here. And what have I discovered? Well, since recovering from my third, utterly-crippling bout of malaria, I discover that I would rather be at home in the States, doing nothing more exciting than taking my kids to their soccer matches, sitting on the sidelines with the other moms and swapping casserole recipes.

So, home then.

What I've decided to do is just go numb and keep all emotion in check. I've got a lot of goodbyes to get through, and I know that if I let myself really think about what is going on, let myself get emotional with anyone in my rounds of farewell, I won't be able to continue on and see everyone.

I leave my friends Abby and Ava to start packing up the car while I say my goodbyes. I walk out to the Health Center, which is about the farthest point from my hut that would encompass my greater village area, and stop at each house along the way to say farewell. First the nurses and staff at the clinic, then the sisters at the convent, the father at the mission, the shopkeepers and government extension workers along the main drag of St. Anthony's proper, then hut to hut until I reach my place again.

I pick up little gifts along the way like hard candy sweeties and a cob of roasted maize, which is handy on a journey really, because it's nourishment that packs easily. Then you are left with the cob, which is Zambian toilet paper, also handy on a journey. I'll never forget the time I went into the powder room at a dance club and found a corn cob in the corner of the stall. So many questions remain unanswered to this day, and I am not sure I want to know the answers. Was this placed there by the management for traditionalists? Was this for communal use (for it did appear quite used) or was it left by someone who brought it in case of emergency? I can't help but think that of all the little convenient things you might slip into an evening bag or the back pocket of your jeans for your evening out on the town, a corn cob seems an unlikely, if not ungainly, choice.

Some neighbors anticipating my visit have written letters. I thought they would be well wishes and thank yous, maybe a post box address for keeping in touch. But most say things like "please leave me your bicycle" and "give me a good remembrance." This is the term used for "souvenir."

When I stop by to see my friend Mr. Muyani, a government agricultural agent, he hands me a proposal for acquiring resources to help fund his research on Lake Kashiba. The end of the letter reads:

I have put the request over to you becoz 1) I believe as of now you understand the feeble financial position of my country Zambia to expect government funding for this project and 2) the potential you have as an individual and that you are hailing from an industrialized and super power country where I assume mobilizing resources could not be an economic hazard if project deemed viable. Curiously awaiting your OPEN consideration to my request.

"Ok," I say to him in farewell, "I shall keep my mind open to this request, as instructed. If I ever find someone who is in a position to give you money to study the lake, I will be sure to put this proposal in their hands."

I slip the letter back into the envelope. It is addressed: Miss Christine Herbert, Peace Cop, St. Anthony. That's me, enforcing peace wherever I go: the Peace Cop. On my way back to my superpower country, I'll just drop this letter back in the post with instructions to forward it to the Hall of Justice, c/o the Super Friends, Attn: Aquaman.

I'm really going to miss this guy. He's in the increasingly rare category of senior citizens in Zambia who grew up during its colonial period and, consequently, had a thoroughly British education. He is by far the best English speaker in the village. I've often come over for a visit just so I could talk with someone who understood what the heck I was saying. He always looks as if he's just stepped out of the fifties. From his black and chrome frame spectacles to his shiny but well-worn penny loafers, the man's a living time capsule.

This letter is a great remembrance from him. As far as

remembrances go, I have given many, but have received very few. That is to be expected, of course, since the villagers don't have much to give. Bana Luke gave me one of her best *citenge*, washed and folded neatly, and offered with many apologies that it wasn't new. I really had to try not to cry with that offering.

My favorite remembrance came from my friend Elizabeth. She went to Mpongwe and bought me a new blouse. It's a very sheer turquoise t-shirt in a crinkly, stretchy fabric. Really cheap and third-world-y looking. She said the reason she bought it for me is that I looked *exactly* like the woman on the tag. I studied my supposed doppelganger dangling from the sleeve. Bountiful waves of jet-black hair spilled over her shoulders to curve artfully around her DD, gravity-defying hooters (clearly visible through the sheer fabric), her deep olive complexion glowing like a St. Tropez ad, her sultry brown eyes beckoning with a "come hither" gaze under layers of mascara and meticulously waxed eyebrows, her pouty lips slicked with mirror-shine red gloss. Gee, I had no idea I looked *exactly* like an Italian porn star.

My remembrances have been more or less standard fare. The kids got all sorts of toys and clothes and things, mostly given to me by my missionary friends and some of the visiting Rotary Club members I met through them. One of the Rotarians had brought bags of goodies to give away: combs, barrettes, pens, hand mirrors, and the like. She realized later that she wasn't in a position to go out to the bush and distribute these things in any meaningful way, so she asked if I'd take them off of her hands.

For my last Health Center meeting, I gave each member a pen, pencil, comb and then had my picture taken with each of them. I've been here long enough to know that this is a remembrance prized above all others. As good as these gifts were, I think the whole thing may have been overshadowed by the fact that I also provided a truckload of meat for the after-meeting meal. This was truly an obscene amount of meat, more than most of these people have seen in their lives. This was a total fluke thing that happened the night before our meeting. Meat pretty much fell from the sky.

I had visitors the day before the meeting, and they invited a group of muzungus from town who arrived fully armed for a *braii*, their coolers full of steaks, sausages, pork chops, marinated chicken, cheese, buns, crisps, beer, and soda. They felt so guilty about my living conditions that they gave me as much meat as I could fit in my Styrofoam cooler and packed it with ice. Hence, the feast that will forever go down in the history of Health Center meetings. We usually count ourselves lucky to get a bit of dried fish with our lump of *nshima*. Last month we only had pumpkin leaves to eat.

I have mixed feelings about the whole thing. It probably just reinforced the mindset of many people who think that white people are infinitely rich, and if you just wait around for a handout, you might get one. On the other hand, it was a great send-off. I do love barbecue, and it was great fun to share my windfall with all the local volunteers who have given so much of their time and energy to work with me.

I walk past the home of Bana Ruby and Bashi Ruby without stopping. They are not there. They are still at the hospital with Caleb whose legs have become paralyzed. What we feared was polio has been diagnosed by the doctors as something much worse: sickle cell anemia. He will not live long. Even if he were to receive blood transfusions from his family members, which is out of the question since they are Jehovah's Witnesses, that would only delay the inevitable. Little Caleb. A few months ago, he was as carefree and full of life as any other boy, always stopping by to dance or ask for plastic bags to make a ball or beg for sweets. Now he's on his deathbed, only ten years old. I've left the family a few sacks of clothing, books, and toys in the care of the grandparents. They've been such good friends to me; it feels wrong to take off without so much as a handshake. Even little Christine, my namesake, is there at the hospital with them. I wonder if I'll ever see her again.

As I reach Bana Martha's place I find Josiah, the carpenter in charge of the woodshop class I helped build and furnish thanks to a grant from a Rotary club. The man looks up at me glassy-eyed. He's stinking drunk. Even though I know he did this because he is distraught at my leaving, I yell at him mercilessly. I tell him he needs to set a good example for the youth at the carpentry school, that I have only allowed him to lead the project because he was one of the only men who did *not* drink and that if he continued with such behavior, the donors would take back the money they invested in the school and he would be out of a job. Sobriety is mandatory. We had an agreement, and he has broken it. Though he grovels and begs my forgiveness, I remain unmoved. I tell him he can shape up or ship out, his choice.

I storm back to my place, saying curt goodbyes to the rest of my neighbors on the way. Josiah trails behind me like a kicked puppy. This poor guy. He's had a lot of hard times. When I came to town it was like the gravy train rolled in. Over the last year, I've clothed him, shoed him (we both agreed a carpenter must have shoes—he's been barefoot since I've known him) given him a home (the rear room of the carpentry school) and a career—basically a whole new life and a reason for living. Now I'm going and he thinks his world is over.

Last week he shared a dream he had about me. He was in a great deal of distress. He said in the dream I was boarding a train to America. As I stepped on the train, he cried out to me to take him too. He begged for me to marry him. The Christine in the dream—a heartless vixen to the core—simply turned away from him, laughing, and boarded the train. When he told me this story, I chuckled. Not in a mean way, just in an "oh no, that's a shame" way. This made him all the more distraught.

"Just like that," he said, his voice quavering, "you laughed at me just like that."

Ava and Abby have already loaded my bags in the Land Rover by the time I reach home. We perform a last sweep through the house and prepare to leave for the long journey to Central Province. The girls use the inside bathroom for one last pit stop before we hit the road, and I head out to the pit latrine. As I near it, a snake slithers by the entrance. Great. One last snake to kill. I reach for my snake beating stick, but the termites have decimated it to pulp and it crumbles in my grip. Cursing Murphy's Law, I dash back to the house and grab one of the long sticks that comprise my dish rack. When I reach the latrine, the snake is off and running again, its head already darting around the rear corner. I whack the back end of it until it stops writhing. Then I whack a few more times to make sure it's good and dead. I enter the latrine, finish my business in peace, then pick up the battered snake body on the end of my stick and make toward the rubbish pit. I meet Bana Francisco on the path.

"*Nacipya nsoka mu cimbusu*," I say. *I have just killed a snake in the potty*.

She takes a good look at the pathetic corpse hanging from the end of my stick.

"Spitting cobra," she says with certainty. "Very bad. *Awe, mwandi*. You are too lucky, Ba Chri." She shakes her head in disbelief.

I know she is alluding to our friend Mr. Kabeya who wasn't so lucky. He went temporarily insane with agony and terror when a spitting cobra sprayed venom in his eyes a couple of weeks ago. His family lives three huts down. I hope

I just killed the culprit; they never did find the snake after that.

"The children are wanting to escort you to the Land Rover," she says.

I chuck the snake into the pit and plop the stick back onto the dish rack. My friend Patti is sitting in the *nsaka* with Bana Luke and the drunk carpenter Josiah. My farewell committee. Actually, Patti has insisted that she escort me as far as Luanshya, which basically means I'm giving her a free ride there. It's totally against Peace Corps policy; we are not a taxi service. But Abby said she'd bend the rules to accommodate one person.

The children in my village are sitting in a circle near the Land Rover, each face wearing a longer expression than the next, all eyes on the ground. No tears, but a real show of sadness from everyone. Still wearing my armor of numbness, I put on my best sad smile and give them each the Christian handshake, as it allows me to grasp their hands three times instead of only once.

"*Mushale bwino, muane*," I say to each of them. *Remain here well, my respected friend*. I shake hands with Bashi Francisco and embrace Bana Francisco for a long time.

"Goodbye, Father. Goodbye, Mother. I will never forget you," I say.

Having said the final goodbyes, we pile into the Land Rover and start off down the bumpy dirt road to Mpongwe. Bana Luke and Josiah trot alongside the vehicle until we pick up enough speed to outpace them. I can see them out of the corner of my eye, but can't let myself look at them directly. My heart is breaking.

After an hour on the road, I realize—I didn't say goodbye to the cat! What a stupid *muzungu* thing to think of. My eyes begin to fill with tears, but I dash them away angrily, mortified that my friend Patti might report back to everyone that I bawled over my beloved Moglie. Ava said she became a sobbing hysterical mess in front of her villagers when she had to say goodbye to her cat ... perhaps it is better this way. I was able to leave the village with some semblance of dignity. Who knew I had it in me?

The Final Countdown

I f there is an amount of pizza needed to re-Americanize a person after an extended stay out of the country, I think I've met my quota. Three slices ago.

Two weeks of eating out in the capital city have been a complete free-for-all. If I am not in a debrief meeting or at the medical office getting shot with every parasite obliterating concoction known to man, I am at the strip malls and fast food joints in Lusaka eating the very best attempts at American junk food this country has to offer. Pale imitations of true U.S. greasy spoon glory, sure, but I'm not choosy. I've got four more days here before flying home. I am praying my appetite doesn't exceed the limits of my waistband. My per diem covers food expenses, not a new wardrobe.

I'm not alone. Peace Corps volunteers are here in droves, descending on the beer halls like locusts. The atmosphere is not exactly celebratory, however. If anything, it feels more like a wake. We are all eating our feelings, filling in the corners with booze. We are melancholy, nervous about what lies ahead, but also excited about finishing our service and going home. We are taking comfort in each other in ways that we never could have in the beginning. Back then, we gathered together to drink and smoke and shoot the breeze to bond, to impress, to try and make connections. Now we do it to bear witness to one another, hold each other in our shared bewilderment.

Some are taking refuge in a brief fling. I've noticed them, sitting at two-tops, hands grasping at each other with a feverish intensity. Some are hanging in the small tight-knit cliques they had formed when we began our training. Others, like me, are drifting from group to group, wandering off alone when the need for solitude strikes.

I've been in a solitary type of mood since a group of us came out to get our hair done this morning. After years of bucket baths and do-it-yourself hair trims, having a professional wash, cut, and blow dry felt like absolute hedonism. I forked over the cash, trying very hard to think about how cheap the service is by American standards, not about how I could buy food for a month with it if I were still back in my village. I feel a slow pull to return to who I was before coming to Africa. The fluffed and buffed health spa employee. I wonder if I am kidding myself thinking that I could possibly return to that kind of life after all I've seen and lived through these past couple of years.

The longer I spend in the capital spoiling myself, the farther away I feel from my village persona. This is probably a good thing. In our last group debrief meeting, as we talked about our concerns around re-entering American society, I talked about the disconnect I feel around my current identity with the life I am expected to jump back into when I return home.

"It took me a long time to find my place here. People would call out to me 'Ba Chri!' and I would be surprised that they were speaking to me. Calling out to me like we were old friends, even if we had never met. I would think who is this Ba Chri person? But little by little, I figured it out. I figured out what it was to be different, to be known, to be on everyone's radar. I figured out the routine of the volunteer. Not just how to do the job, but how to grow food and form alliances and show humility—often on my knees—and get by, day by day. I did this until I wasn't just getting by, I was thriving. I figured out stuff I didn't even want to know. Like how to set a steel rat trap without breaking your damn fingers and how to cook caterpillars and how to target the best vehicles for hitchhiking. It took me a long time to figure out how to be Ba Chri. But I've got her number now, you know? I know exactly who Ba Chri is," I said, tapping my chest. "The thing is, I don't know who Christine is anymore."

Everyone was quiet for a long time. Eventually, my friend Josh piped up.

"Well, that was deep."

My reply was a slow, incredibly ladylike, obscene hand gesture. Everyone roared with laughter and, tension broken, we went back to the business at hand.

My current business accomplished—eating pizza until my stomach waves the proverbial white flag and begs for mercy— I push aside my plate and break out my small notebook. I've become the unofficial chronicler among my closest girlfriends here. It started back at the provincial house where we gathered to carpool to the capital for our COS (close of service) program. Ava and Katrina and Abby and I sat around the living room, sprawled out on the odd collection of chairs and loveseats and twin mattresses set up as day beds. With notebook in hand, I began collecting our favorite moments, everything that made us laugh or astounded us, things that would probably never find their way into casual conversation once we return to the States. Each of us are desperate to save our experiences for posterity. Even if it just remains scribbled inside my little notebook, jammed with pictures and business cards and addresses of random Zambians wanting penfriends, at least it has been recorded.

I flip through the pages, tracing my fingers over the treasure trove of memories. A list of truly spit-take worthy names like Vaseline, Wireless, Useless, and Grievous Times. Odd terms of food-related endearments, like "I love you like I love chicken" and "I love you like I love tea." All of the outrageous fat compliments we've received, like "you look like a truck pulling a trailer" and "you could never go up in a spaceship because you are so fat the ship would just crash back down to earth." I can't help but guffaw aloud at that one. I cover my face and try to stifle my outburst, my shoulders shaking in silent laughter.

"What's so funny over here?" I hear Ava ask, as she clunks her pint down on the tabletop. "Care to share with the rest of the class?"

I keep laughing, just slide the notebook over to her and point to where I left off.

"Oh, the spaceship thing! Ha! That's definitely one for the books as far as pick-ups go." She laughs and slumps down opposite me at the table. "I couldn't possibly hope to hear a come-on like that in the States. Wait ... *would* I hope to hear something like that again? I think I'm kinda gonna miss people complimenting me on how fat I am." Her mouth twists in a wry smile. "Is that sick?"

"Speaking of fat—" I slide the remainder of the pizza over to her. "Please save me from myself. I'm begging you."

She sighs in mock resignation. "If I must."

"You must. Also, can I just say for the record? Damn you, and your glorious, sun-kissed, glossy locks of hair. Do you know how frustrated my hairdresser was seeing my hair go from flat to even flatter the more she blow-dried it? She was completely demoralized. I think she's going to hang up her hairdryer for good."

"Don't hate me because I am so gorgeous," she says with a moue and a hair flip.

"That's not exactly how the shampoo commercial goes, but you know what, I'll give you points for that anyway. It had sincerity. The sass was really coming through. And the plea to *not* hate you just stoked the fires of my resentment so hot that my heart forged a little hate monkey." I hold up an imaginary knife. "With a switchblade."

She blinks, shoves the last bit of crust in her mouth with a lopsided grin.

"I'll cut you," I whisper, deadpan.

"Freak." She giggles, wipes the pizza grease from her mouth with the back of her hand.

"Seriously, though, I want you to know that I do hate you forever. No matter what." I nudge her knee under the table.

"I hate you more."

"I hate you times infinity."

"Well, shit, I guess you win." She chuckles and takes another slice of pizza. "You'll keep in touch, right? We're not just going to drift apart and never see each other again, are we?"

"Not a chance."

Katrina sidles up to the table with a beer in hand and two colorful *citenge* bags slung across her torso like bandoliers.

"What's happening over here?" she asks.

"Not much, just talking about how much we absolutely hate each other's guts. Forever and ever."

"Awww, sweet. Not that it's a contest or anything, but I

hate you guys with the heat of a thousand blazing suns." She chuckles, clicking each of our glasses in a toast. "You got room for one more at this table?"

"You bet," says Ava.

"Looks like you hit the motherlode at the craft market," I note.

"Well, I figure it might be my last chance to haggle over chubby little hippopotamus sculptures, so I wanted to make the most of it." She pulls one out for us to admire. "I mean look at those rolls, will ya? This guy is a chunker." She gives it a boop on the nose and tucks it back into her bags. "I wasn't sure what to get everyone back home, so I decided on hippos for everyone."

"Fair." I shrug. "I mean who doesn't need a hippo?"

"Right? My thoughts exactly." She takes a swig of beer. "This up for grabs?"

"Please." I slide the pizza over her way.

"I came out with the PCVL of Central Province. We've got room in the Land Rover if you want to head back with us. Save you a taxi ride."

"Cool beans!" Ava fist-pumps the air.

We drink and talk smack and drink some more. Other volunteers visit our table while they make the rounds. We've got our American a-hole charm cranked to eleven. If we stop pretending this is a last-call, what-happens-in-Vegas-stays-in-Vegas booty call from the universe, we'll face the hard reality of our lives being completely uprooted. Again. We'll have to face our fears. We'll have to face our families and friends and all their expectations. We're all playing for time, and we know it.

Eventually, the PCVL comes to our table and tells us to load up. It's our big day and we can't be late. We knock back the last of our drinks and haul ass to the Land Rover.

Today is the day to ring out our service. And really, they

want us to ring out G.I. Jane-style when she washes out of Navy SEAL training. But this isn't a surrender, this isn't a ring of failure to continue, but a victory ring. It signifies a successful completion of service. This is a Peace Corps rite of passage. The last one I will undertake.

Returning to the Peace Corps compound, we pull up to the guard gates and wait for them to complete a bomb check under the vehicle using mirrors on long poles. Once the guards do a complete circuit and we get the all clear, we slowly roll into the gravel parking lot of the compound. We dismount from the Land Rover and crunch our way across the gravel flat-footed to avoid getting stones in our sandals.

"Oh, God. They're gathering already," says Ava. She motions to the courtyard. Groups of twos and threes are huddled together, trying to get all their faces in a photo shot held at arm's length. "I'm not ready for this."

"Me neither," says Katrina. "But we're all beauty parlor fresh, so we've got that going for us. We might go out crying, but our hair is going to look fabulous."

"This is the last time we are all going to be together, isn't it?" I say.

I look around at the group. Some faces are as familiar to me as my own, the ones I have relied on for company at every group gathering since we set foot in this country. Some faces I have seen only a few times since our training days. The volunteers sent to other provinces. The fish farming volunteers. The radio and media education volunteers. Each of these faces—every single one—holds a precious cache of memories for me. An inside joke we couldn't stop laughing at. An unexpected, white-hot slow dance at a nightclub. Singing "The Gambler" and "American Pie" and countless other songs on the long road trips from province to province. A stolen kiss at a New Year's Eve beach party. Smoking strawberry shisha at a hookah lounge in Zanzibar. Playing endless rounds of cribbage in a cramped train car clattering across the Tanzanian grasslands. Braiding each other's hair and spilling our guts about crushes and conquests. Cooking the biggest pot of mac and cheese in the world at a provincial meeting and eating it straight out of the pot, taking turns feeding each other with the serving spoon. Dancing like beasts at a rave in the Namibian desert. Walking through a million rainbows in the spray of Victoria Falls, soaked to the bone and laughing our heads off.

How do I say goodbye to these people? These beautiful adventurers. These curious and courageous souls.

For that, I think, is what lies at the core of the best volunteers. A deep curiosity—about absolutely everything—and the courage to dive in and learn more, even at the expense of our own comfort. Always willing to shatter our paradigms, to tumble from the apex of Maslow's "hierarchy of needs" and find ourselves at the base of the pyramid, over and over again.

The disparities in the world are no longer abstract constructs for us. We've shed our default settings over and over again, embraced every new experience, asked questions, put our hands to task. Our days have been flowing in an endless cycle of teaching and learning, not trying to assert our rightness or mastery of anything, just sharing our methods, our ideas. *This is how my mother taught me. This is what we use. You prepare it like this. You wear it like this. Hold it this way. Am I doing this right? No? Show me again.*

Our curiosity enabled each of us to try again and again in the face of failure. Every one of us faced incredible challenges, the odds stacked against us at every turn. We've been feared, envied, loved, hero-worshipped, mocked. We came here to try and bring about a positive change in the communities we served, but every one of us knows that the communities served us and changed us, too. We've been fed by our neighbors, sung praises with them in their houses of worship, helped them sow their fields and bring in harvests, held their sleeping children during long church services or minibus rides or nights of telling stories around the fire.

I know there isn't a single person here who is not trying their hardest to push down their feelings, staving off the heartbreak of what we have lost now that our service has ended. No one will be able to stand in front of that bell and ring out their service with anything resembling pride or a clear conscience if they are being assailed by their memories of what they are walking away from—the babes we swaddled in our *citenge*, the countless hands we held on long escorts along dirt roads, the children we danced with on Youth Day at the school grounds, the community elders we shared *nshima* with after a neighborhood health committee meeting. It's the very reason we are all swagger. We are nothing but snark and back slaps and arm punches because we are hurting. We can't let ourselves think about what and who we are leaving behind or it will break us.

We enter the compound and drop off our bags in one of the lounge areas. There is a small group huddling in the corner, inking each other with a pen and safety pin, old-school prison tattoo style.

"You next? I think I got the hang of this now," says Carla.

I pretend to think it over. "Mmmm, nope."

"C'mon. Limited edition. Badasses only. I'm not offering this to everyone, you know."

I lean over to admire the little "PC" inscribed on the web of Jeremy's hand between his thumb and forefinger. The skin is puffy and angry and about one step away from sepsis.

"Hard pass."

"Okay, but I've gotta tell you, I'm feeling pretty O.G. over here. You don't get in on this now and you'll regret it for the rest of your life."

"That's a risk I'm willing to take, but I appreciate the offer."

I head down the hall to the washroom just as my friend Ben emerges from the men's.

"Hey, Ben. How'd it go?"

He holds up an unopened stool sample kit. "It didn't."

"Oh, man. Sorry. Better luck next time, yeah?" I give him two thumbs up, and back my way into the ladies' room.

One of the medical requirements is that we submit three separate, parasite-free stool samples in order to prove we are not taking home any intestinal hitchhikers. Depending on the person, this can take days or weeks. Ben hasn't been able to collect a single sample and is really beginning to sweat it. If things don't get a move on, so to speak, he may need to delay his flight home. Me, I'm only one deuce away.

I freshen up in the mirror, give my cheeks a pinch, straighten up my flyway hair, make sure there's nothing in my teeth. I'm not keen on makeup just yet, after going years without. This is about as camera-ready as I get.

I hear an insistent clanging of the bell out in the court-yard. They are calling us together. Time to do this thing.

It occurs to me how very American this ritual is: banging a gong to assert a personal victory. The rites of passage I have been privy to in this country—marriage ceremonies, funerals, and such—were always community-oriented, with rituals that conveyed respect and humility. Usually a fair amount of walking around on our knees, too.

I feel like ringing that bell is a silly, hollow victory. I don't want to end my service, and I don't want to "toot my own horn" about it. I am going to miss drawing water and making fire each day. These simple things grounded me, engaged me fully in the business of living. My daily routine was, in every sense, lifegiving. What will make me feel that way when I return to the States?

I make my way into the courtyard, gently high fiving my way through the crowd of volunteers as I go. Once we are all there, the Country Director gives a long-winded congratulatory speech. It is meant to be inspirational. I don't hear it at all. I keep looking at the bell, which turns out to be not a bell at all, but an old tire rim.

The only thing that comes through from the speech is this: everyone is ringing that bell. No one gets a pass. We don't leave until it's done.

One by one we make our way up to the platform. Mercifully, we aren't being called up by name. Only prompted by a gentle, "Who's ready to go next?" A few are eager, ready to give the bell a loud toll, followed up with an endzone victory dance. Some step forward weeping, then turn back around with, "Nope. Not ready yet."

I wait a long time. I wait until I know I can do this without crying. I wait until I feel that I can accept what this ritual is meant to convey and that I deserve to participate in it. This moment is for me. I step up to the platform, take the stick in my hand. I want to say something to the group, something powerful or memorable. Something witty to break the tension. I've got nothing. This bell is going to have to say it for me. I tighten my grip on the stick, close my eyes.

I suddenly feel like a kid again at my own birthday party. I remember how my mom would string up a piñata from the oak tree in the middle of our backyard and line us up, smallest kid to largest, to have our go at breaking the papier-mâché beast and spill its candy guts. She'd blindfold us, spin us around a few times, put the broom handle in our hands and let us take three good whacks before handing it off to the next child.

Three good whacks, I think. *Then let the other kids have a go.*

"I'm going for three!' I exclaim. "Count it off with me!"

We all call out, "One, two, three!" as I hammer on the old

tire rim. I throw my hands up and whoop to the delight and cheers of my friends.

"Show off," mumbles Ben.

"C'mon now, be honest for once." I wink and stride by him without a backward glance. "You loved it."

❧ 26 ❧

Goodbye is a Sadness Word

A bubble of air gurgles along my ear's Eustachian tube, rudely awakening me as we descend into Heathrow Airport. I slide off the earphones I'd been using to watch movies (and apparently nodding off on) and put my tray table and seat back in the upright position as I am instructed.

Like many volunteers, I have opted to take cash in the amount equal to the plane ticket home the Peace Corps would have allotted me. By booking my own passage and taking multiple flight legs at odd hours including an overnight stop in London, I've saved myself nearly a thousand dollars. Money easily earned, I figure, for the small amount of extra time I'll be en route. And what's the inconvenience, really? I've spent more than two years in a mud hut; my idea of what's uncomfortable or inconvenient has shifted more than a little. I plan on finding a nice spot of floor or a row of chairs without armrests to curl up on until my morning flight. The place has electricity, running water, a real roof overhead—I'm good.

Also, truth be told, I am not all that eager to reach American soil. The thought of returning to my old life is still rather daunting. I don't mind having a few extra hours to get my head around the idea that this is finally happening. My Peace Corps service—the biggest adventure of my life—has come to a close.

It's late when we land, and the empty airport hallways echo with the clatter of our wheeled carry-ons as we disembark. I wander until I find a place with some comfy lounge chairs set up for people like me—people who either can't afford a night at a hotel or who can't be bothered to go through customs and re-enter security the next day. There is a couple setting up camp in the corner, stowing their luggage between two of the chairs and settling under borrowed airline lap blankets and miniature pillows. I give them a wide berth and settle into a space surrounded by a bank of empty chairs.

My body is exhausted, but my mind won't come to a rest. I'm buzzing with a mess of conflicting emotions. I feel grief at losing the life I have been living as a volunteer. All my work, my friends, my home—gone. Anything that gave my life real meaning has been stripped away. I am on the threshold of starting a new kind of existence, and that incites both excitement and fear. Somewhere among all of this turmoil, I feel relief also. I feel so proud to have accomplished this thing, coming through it alive and in one piece (I did promise my sister that I wouldn't die, so I feel good about delivering on that one). I just can't believe that it's really over. I felt so strongly, ever since I was a little girl, that I should go to Africa. And now that I have, I wonder what has it all been for?

I'm not coming home with much of anything except a

suitcase full of *citenge*, bangles of ox horn, small wooden carvings, and strands of waist beads—almost all of which I intend to give as gifts. I am coming away with my memories, my experiences. That's all I can be certain of because I'm not sure what impact I've had on the people I came to help. But living in Africa has done something to me, something profound, something that I hope will bear good fruit one day. I've experienced changes on many levels of my human identity: my sense of self as an individual and in a community, my concept of personal space and ownership, and what my capacity for mental, emotional, and physical endurance truly is.

I can point to specific accomplishments I have had a hand in. By partnering with Rotary Clubs, both in Zambia and America, I've been able to establish a carpentry school for youth in my village, and secure funding to establish ten new boreholes for safe drinking water—the first being drilled just as I was leaving. My Water and Sanitation group built four VIP latrines (ventilated, improved pit latrines) at community schools and renovated two wells. By securing training for local counterparts, the community now boasts a fish farming co-op and twelve other cooperatives run exclusively by women. My networking connections helped secure an entire classroom full of toys and materials for a new preschool in Mpongwe. And—not a concrete object, but just as important —I've provided training for hundreds of villagers in health-related fields. That's the empirical data from my final report, but when I think about a legacy—some lasting impact—I hope something else has been left behind. I know as well as anyone how easily businesses and material things tend to crumble out in the bush.

I hope, more than anything, that I've left a positive impression on the children. I tutored them, gave work to their parents so they'd have money for school, and took every opportunity to play, dance, and be an ear for them. I am glad that the young girls in my village could see a woman accomplishing things that may have seemed impossible before. They witnessed me—a woman who can barely cook *nshima* or carry water on her head properly—become a leader in a community, sit on chairs the same height as men, and even live independently. I don't know what seeds I may have planted in the minds of these girls, but if there is a legacy I have left behind, that's where it resides.

The little things I never wrote home about, the things that can't be found on any report, may be the only truly noteworthy things I actually did. Many times, I felt moved to be generous with someone—usually strangers I would never see again. A pair of shoes I left on the doorstep of someone who had none. Paying transport for passengers who were ill and were headed for the hospital, pressing a few kwacha notes in their hand for the medicine they would surely need but likely could not afford once they got there. Small newspaper packets of dough fritters I tucked by the sleeping forms of beggars on the side of the road.

To the people I knew and loved best, I gave them my time and attention, and in turn, they opened their lives to me. If my neighbors needed to go to meetings at church or were traveling late, their children would become my own. A couple of nights a week, I could count on hearing the gentle tap of a child's hand on the front door heralding the commencement of another evening of card games, coloring, and storytelling by candlelight. Most of my time with neighbors was spent working with them in some fashion: shucking groundnuts, winnowing grain, or pounding maize into meal. Somehow, I always came home with more than my equal share of the spoils, though I protested they had a family to feed, and I didn't. That was how things worked. Everyone shares everything.

There was an odd period of adjustment to this mindset when we first arrived. We just didn't get it. It wasn't about generosity or stinginess; it was something outside of our cultural experience. We had always thought of ourselves as individuals, whereas the people we were about to live among had the idea that they exist as part of a community.

I remember during our first group meeting, after being off on our own for three months, a volunteer shared a story. A man asked him if he could have some money. The volunteer said, "Sure, you give me some money first, then maybe I'll give you some one day." The man immediately took out his small wad of money and offered it to the volunteer. There was a lot of bargaining and backtracking involved in order to convince the man to keep his money. Three other volunteers said the same thing happened to them, except two of them ended up taking the money because they couldn't get the villager to take it back.

We were entering uncharted territory where neighbors buy and sell goods to each other to support their existence, where the welfare of the whole is considered above the needs of the one, and where no material possession is too valuable or personal to share, trade, or give away. The need to have basic human needs met is so dire that only the present is considered. The knowledge that money is owed in one's favor or that sheer providence may intervene holds more promise and is more conceivable than the thought of scrimping and saving so that future needs can be met. This is how life is lived outside of bank accounts.

There's a saying in Swahili they use in the neighboring Congo that seems to illustrate this point exactly: *eat cake today*. That's the mentality that has been difficult to make sense of. The suffering is so great here in this part of the world, starvation, disease, and death so close at hand, that when a windfall occurs, it is taken and enjoyed for the blessing it is. And you can always ask someone to give you something, no matter what it is, because they may just say yes. Then you would have that money, or bicycle, or helicopter, and wouldn't that be grand?

Though I came to recognize it, I couldn't always reconcile this in my mind, this "eat cake today" mentality. For example, when a baby was determined to be too underweight at a clinic, the mother was allotted a bag of HEPS (High Energy Protein Supplement) to be made into porridge to help the child thrive. The supplement is mainly mealie meal enriched with soy flour, sugar, and oil. Each time HEPS would be given to a mother, the same scene would unfold. All the children would rush the mother and she would open the bag for them to take handfuls. The kids would dip their tongues into their own precious portion of sweet, fatty powder and wander the grounds in a blissful haze. You'd think it was laced with heroin or something the way the kids took to it. In the spirit of "eat cake today," the mother, instead of looking at the HEPS as a means to saving the life of her failing child, would take the opportunity to give a gift to all the children. As many times as I witnessed this, I couldn't reconcile this with my own ideas of right and wrong. Perhaps I am too selfish, or just too individualistic, but I would not give out sweets to all the kids in the neighborhood if it meant I could not provide nourishment to my own child who might be on the brink of death.

Now that I am about to re-enter American society, I wonder what remnants of this community mindset I'll be bringing back with me, what ideas have been planted and taken root in my mind. I hope something will remain, and that I won't instantly revert to the "give me some money first, and then maybe I'll give you some" mentality. Because what conclusions can be drawn from this kind of behavior? That it is acceptable to say things you don't mean to illustrate your point? That obnoxious and cutting retorts and flip, witty repartee is more of a staple in American culture's communication than an honest exchange of ideas? As I've traveled abroad, I've tried my best to avoid being the "ugly American." I wonder how well I will accomplish this in my own country when I've got nothing to prove.

It's become chilly in the airport. I wish I had appropriated some blankets from the plane the way that couple in the corner had. I bring out a couple of *citenge* from my bag and begin bundling up. As I do so, a young black woman approaches me and asks if she can have the adjoining chair so she can sleep next to me. The place is all but empty and I think how funny, how very *Zambian*, that she asks to share my sleeping space. I invite her immediately. Though her English seems to be spoken with an American accent, I ask her where she is from. She is Canadian, she says, but is originally from Zambia. She had traveled back to Zambia for the funeral of her uncle and was on her way back home. I don't know if she recognized me from the plane, which we surely must have been sharing, or she just saw my *citenge* and felt at home with me, but I am glad of the company.

She wraps herself in her own *citenge* and we speak of our lives in Zambia and North America in a mixture of Bemba and Nyanja and English, gossiping like young girls at a sleepover until late into the night. It feels like the perfect transition from the African world to the Western world. This serendipitous meeting does not feel coincidental at all but arranged by fate, or perhaps borne by my sheer need for something like this to happen. One final guardian angel of my Peace Corps service sent to see me safely home. I had been sitting here feeling lost, wondering how I can possibly transition from one world to the next, and then this girl comes along, as if by design, to help me bridge the gap. Her presence gives me such comfort, such a feeling of being looked after by the forces great and small in this world that I begin to let go of my worries.

Eventually, in the wee hours of the morning, our chatter dies out and we say goodnight. She rolls over with her back to me, and we lie wrapped in our respective *citenge* like spooning lovers, just a foot apart on separate chairs. She dozes off and I watch the slow rise and fall of her breath as she sleeps. I am an insomniac at the best of times, but I know the oddness of the environment and the excitement of my travel will most likely keep me from sleeping at all. I envy her.

I reach down into my purse and quietly remove the stack of letters within. I've brought all my love letters, too precious to lose or even be separated from for a few days of travel. I have been in the habit of reading one before I go to bed, letting the words like gentle and loving hands tuck me in at night. But instead of opening one of those envelopes, I take out a note that was pressed into my hand by a young girl as I left the village.

Dear Christin,

It's my chanse to write you. That school is a key to sucess and I promise you from my deep down of my heart that I will never disappoint you please pay for me for all the year please help me never no where yo go apart from you I lay on you. You are such a kind person whom I have never s. The only bad thing is paining me is that you are leaving.

Goodbye is a sadness word.

Remember me wherever you will be.

I pen off

Memory

She didn't know this, but before I left, I gave her mother all the money I could spare. I did this for all my dearest friends and neighbors so they could pay their children's school fees, feeling that if this was the one thing I could do, one small thing that could change lives for the better, then all of my hardships have been worth it.

I lie awake thinking about all the friends I have left behind, wondering if I will ever see them again. I feel my heart breaking in the knowledge that I probably will not. I'll be holding their memories in my heart and hope that they will remember me fondly too. A conversation I had with my counterpart Mr. Chisala right before I left the village has been replaying itself over and over in my mind.

"You are going to go back to America and you are going to write a book about us," he said.

"I am?" Clearly, the man had seen me hunched in my nsaka, penning letters, proposals, and various reports and misinterpreted this as a passion for writing, rather than the agonizing hours of internal self-flagellation that they were. For me, writing has always gone hand in hand with debilitating perfectionism. A poorly turned phrase can haunt me for years. If a djinn came down to earth and told me I could have anything I wanted—world peace, the cure for cancer, *anything*—and all I had to do was either write a novel or eat dirt, I'd tell them to hand me a spoon. No contest.

"Yes, you are," he said with certainty, as if he'd read it in that morning's paper and he was just passing along a well-established fact. "You will write about this place. How we are suffering and the way things are. You will write about all these people, your friends. You will even write about me!"

"We'll see about that," I said, dubious but tickled by his enthusiasm on the subject.

"You will see. One day, you will see that I am right about this thing," he said, pinning me under the weight of his gaze. "You will write a book about all of this one day. This I know. You will write a book about us."

THANK YOU

Thank you for reading *The Color of the Elephant: Memoir of a Muzungu*
Please consider leaving a review so that other readers can find this title.

OTHER GENZ MEMOIRS

Nurse Papa
By David Metzger

Suitcase of Dreams
By Hazell C. McKenzie

I Went, I Saw, I Shared
Pam Canington

The Lies I Told Myself
Emma Foster

100 Days Sober
M.E. Culbreth

Made in USA - Kendallville, IN
13028_9781952919763
02.24.2022 1408